Scott's Forgotten Surgeon

Dr Reginald Koettlitz, Polar Explorer

Aubrey A. Jones

Whittles Publishing

This book is dedicated to the late Miss Ulrica Koettlitz, niece of Dr Reginald Koettlitz, who had the foresight to retain and protect his diaries, journals and other artefacts when others did not possess such splendid judgement.

Published by
Whittles Publishing Ltd.,
Dunbeath,
Caithness, KW6 6EG,
Scotland, UK

www.whittlespublishing.com

© 2011 Aubrey A. Jones

Reprinted 2013, 2014

ISBN 978-184995-038-1

Printed and bound in England by
4edge Ltd, Hockley, Essex.

CONTENTS

INTRODUCTION

The history of early Antarctic exploration is not a continuous narrative. As typically presented, it is essentially a collection of vignettes, each centred on a particular expedition separated from every other by the passage of years or decades, with coherency provided only by their common destination. These vignettes could also be said, collectively, to comprise a kind of Theatre of the Heroic Age – an unreal stage, situated in the mind's eye, on which the well-known stories of polar triumph and tragedy continue to be enacted for each new generation.

Because they usually wrote the official accounts – in effect, the scripts – expedition commanders are usually the ones remembered best. Indeed, by playing the leads in what amounted to their own productions, they are always in the spotlight. But as in any other theatrical presentation, a player's character is exposed not only by what he does, but how he interacts with others in supporting roles, on or off stage. In some expeditions these latter roles grew large, so that the players who assumed them are now remembered nearly as well as the expedition leaders – one thinks of Cherry-Garrard or Dr Wilson, for example. However, for the majority of participants, all that destiny has provided for them is a listing on the yellowing playbill of a ship's company, or a brief notice in the boss's book of his exploits. They are, in short, forgotten men – unless, of course, someone comes along later, to write a new part for a figure formerly in the background, giving him flesh, motivation and interest. Gus Jones has done precisely this for Reginald Koettlitz, chief surgeon and botanist on Scott's first expedition (known formally as the National Antarctic Expedition (NAE), but commonly referred to as the *Discovery* expedition after the vessel that took them to The Bottom).

Even for those deeply immersed in Antarctic history, Koettlitz is a shadowy figure; he is only occasionally mentioned by Scott in his book *The Voyage of the Discovery*, or in the works of other participants who wrote up their recollections of the expedition in later years. Yet he was actually among the most experienced participants in the enterprise, certainly more so than its chief, whose major occupation before being appointed to head the NAE was the care and use of torpedoes on Royal Navy vessels. Before signing on with Scott, Koettlitz had already had an extensive exploring career in the Arctic, Amazon and Africa, where he learnt how to take care of himself in many different, and sometimes very dangerous, circumstances. Among Koettlitz's recognised strengths was an unusual capacity for withstanding travel in harsh conditions, to which he had accustomed himself while participating in Frederick Jackson's expedition in Franz Josef Land in 1894–1896. At least in the early part of the *Discovery* expedition, Scott recognised Koettlitz's value in this regard and sent him on two exploring trips to the Western Mountains that were on the surface quite successful. Sadly, his strengths as a traveller were not coupled with the kind of sagacity and common touch needed in a leader. The fact is that Koettlitz did not know how to handle himself among those not of his class or intellectual standing: he was humourless, fault-finding, remote, even somewhat passive-aggressive in his interactions with his companions, who quickly decided he was either to be avoided or derided. He was proudly aware of his competencies, as a physician, polar explorer and naturalist-scientist, but fell into a funk when any of these was challenged, however playfully. The loutish Thomas Hodgson, also a doctor and also interested in scientific matters as the expedition's biologist (and thus a competitor), became Koettlitz's particular bête noir. But it didn't stop there: he does not seem to have gotten along with anyone for very long, and it must have been a long and very lonely two and a half years for him in McMurdo Sound. As Jones shows in this first-ever biography, using surviving correspondence and other documents never previously exploited for this purpose, Koettlitz's potential as an explorer and scientist was wasted over the three years of the *Discovery* expedition, so much so that he never went exploring again.

His aloofness seems to come across in one of the few previously published images of Koettlitz taken on the expedition: he is the angular, awkward-looking figure in the famous photograph of officers and scientists standing on the quarterdeck of the *Discovery* in late July or early August of 1901, just before departure from Lyttelton (see page 131). The shot is staged but the men are loosely arrayed, with participants assuming casual-to-elegant poses as the mood – or perhaps their hoped-for roles in the future history of the expedition – struck them. Dr Koettlitz looms over everyone, especially the much shorter Scott standing to his left. He looks at you directly, coolly, perhaps even defiantly, hands jammed into his coat pockets, features locked and unsmiling. On his right the boyish-looking Barne grins widely, while Scott's gaze seeks the horizon.

Fairly or otherwise, Koettlitz's major role in popular Antarctic history comes down to us as the doctor who facilitated Scott's effort to have Shackleton invalided home. Scott, Shackleton and Dr Wilson comprised the party that made an abortive run to the pole late in the 1902/1903 season. All three were suffering from scurvy by the time they gave up and started their desperate march home. If they were already experiencing the mental symptoms of depression and irritability that attend this disease, it would scarcely be surprising if fierce disagreements arose, especially between such strong personalities as Scott and Shackleton. In any case, nothing is known for certain; it was considered poor form to let pointed words and petty conflicts seep into one's journal, especially if it were destined for publication. Yet inferences were made both at the time and later, none stranger than that made by Albert Armitage, Scott's second in command. According to the book that Armitage published many years after the *Discovery* expedition, Koettlitz was told by Scott that Shackleton would have to go back on the relief vessel *Morning*, whether he liked it or not – either as an invalid, or, if he protested, in disgrace. In the event Koettlitz pronounced him unfit for duty as an expedition officer. Much doubt has always attended Armitage's recollection; on the other hand, Armitage clearly thought that this was the kind of thing that Koettlitz would acquiesce to, at least under pressure from Scott.

For reasons that appear never to have been explained to him – or, if they were, they never registered – Koettlitz was not asked to participate in the publication of any of the *Discovery* expedition's scientific reports. Ultimately, the decision to exclude him had to have been Scott's, presumably endorsed, if not proposed in the first instance, by Dr Wilson. This was unkind; of all the miserable or demeaning things that happened to Koettlitz in Antarctica, large and small, this had to have been among the worst. His letters home – all that we have to go on, in the absence of his diaries – are filled with a sort of contained, tightly wound rage concerning his treatment. He conceived of himself, first and foremost, as a scientist; to have his role diminished to that of note-taker and instrument boy for others must have been crushing. His reaction was, however, to turn his bitterness inward rather than to confront Scott or Wilson directly.

Although in later years Koettlitz attempted to organise or sign on to new expeditions, there was now something missing; a visceral uncertainty, perhaps, had replaced his former confidence in himself. In any case, he had to make a living; he went on to have a reasonably successful medical practice in South Africa and became a pillar of his community before his premature death in 1916. In this year celebrating the centenary of the conquering of the South Pole, which will naturally focus on the accomplishments of the overexposed leaders of the British and Norwegian expeditions, it is more than fitting to have one of the unregarded figures of Antarctic history brought into the limelight of remembrance.

Ross D. E. MacPhee
American Museum of Natural History
New York NY USA

'Nil Sine Labore – Nothing without labour'

The Koettlitz family motto

DISCOVERING KOETTLITZ

O n 10 January 1916, Dr Reginald Koettlitz and his wife, Marie Louise Koettlitz, died in the small Karoo town of Cradock, Eastern Cape, South Africa. They died within two hours of each other in Cradock Hospital, he of acute dysentery and his devoted wife of heart disease.

On that day one of the eminent polar surgeons and geologists of the so-called 'heroic period' of polar exploration passed away, although this was not reflected in the press of the time. His death went virtually unreported in the United Kingdom, his place of residence until 1905, with barely a murmur from the polar and scientific establishments to which he had contributed so much.

Reginald Koettlitz died aged 55 years, a frustrated and bitter man, snubbed by his scientific contemporaries and suffocated by the effects of the English class system from which he had felt obliged to escape. This book will examine why a Fellow of the Royal Geographical Society, holder of the silver polar medal with clasp and the Royal Geographical Society medal and one of the first group of men to survive closest to the North Pole for over three years, had lived his final 11 years in partial obscurity in a semi-remote rural doctor's practice in South Africa.

Dr Reginald Koettlitz participated in four expeditions of substance: two to the polar regions, the north with the Jackson-Harmsworth Expedition to Franz Josef Land and the south with the National Antarctic Expedition, also known as the *Discovery* expedition; and two of total contrast – the Herbert Weld Blundell Expedition from Berbera in British Somaliland overland to Cairo via Southern Abyssinia and the Blue Nile in 1898, and a solo expedition aboard the vessel *Sobralense* crossing the Atlantic and venturing up the River Amazon until reaching Manaos.

He had much in common with the great Scottish polar explorer William Speirs Bruce, with whom he had spent many productive hours during the Jackson-Harmsworth Expedition. The two men became close friends and Koettlitz always regretted not accompanying Bruce on the 1902–1904 Scottish National Antarctic Expedition aboard the *Scotia*. Bruce also fell foul of the English establishment whilst planning and obtaining finance for the *Scotia* expedition.

William Speirs Bruce was the foremost Scottish polar explorer of the heroic age of polar exploration and with Reginald Koettlitz and others was at the forefront of scientific polar expeditions at the time. They shared a common view that exploration was not just for the purpose of discovering new lands and peoples for the benefit of the British Empire but that all expeditions must also include a significant scientific content; this should in fact be the main aim of such endeavours.

Bruce described Koettlitz as 'a man of great charm of character and an explorer of the best type, scientific, painstaking, cheerful, and indifferent to notoriety or reward.'[1] A fitting description.

The heroic period for the purposes of this biography will be defined as the period between 1894, the year of departure of the Jackson-Harmsworth Expedition, and 1916, the year of Koettlitz's death. The latter coincided with and followed the culmination of other significant southern polar expeditions and events, including Sir Ernest Shackleton's *Nimrod* expedition and Imperial Trans-Antarctic Expedition, together with the earlier death of Captain R. F. Scott and his companions on the Ross Ice Shelf, following Scott's failure to be the first to reach the South Pole.

Many other notable polar explorers of the time will be discussed within this biography. Some of them were interlocutors with Reginald Koettlitz – in particular, Fridtjof Nansen whom Koettlitz first met on Franz Josef Land where they discovered a shared love of geology, and with whom Koettlitz maintained a correspondence until his death. This correspondence is of great interest concerning the events of the time, in relation not only to the age of rocks and strata on Franz Josef Land but also to the subsequent events during later British expeditions to the Antarctic continent.

Reginald Koettlitz would today be regarded as a 'professional', in both his attitude to exploration and the scientific results which he thought were of the utmost importance to all expeditions. He struggled with the lackadaisical, often disorganised approach which was prevalent amongst some expedition organisers and participants of the period. Koettlitz's approach can seem closer to modern standards of exploration. Practices that may seem amateurish or even negligent now were deemed pioneering in their day, often causing Koettlitz's concerns to fall on deaf ears.

Koettlitz's attitude and approach to exploration led to many disagreements with his scientific colleagues and certain expedition leaders. At the time English polar expeditions were operated on the belief that the superiority of the English class and exclusive education system would prevail against all odds. It must be remembered that at this time the British Empire was at its height, with the First World War still some years away. This attitude was particularly apparent within the officer class of the military, including the Royal Navy. It led to several situations of near disaster and in some notable cases, to real catastrophe. The English as a people were yet to learn that their methods and traditions were not always sufficient or suitable, especially when faced with the class-blind forces of the natural world.

The contradictions of the scientific viewpoint espoused by Koettlitz and the traditions of the English establishment became insurmountable during and immediately after the National Antarctic Expedition led by Commander Robert Falcon Scott between 1901 and 1904 on board the *Discovery*. Koettlitz's experiences during that expedition changed his direction in life and led to him being buried far from the United Kingdom, in the Anglican Cemetery at Cradock, surrounded by British soldiers who had fought and died during the Boer War earlier that century.

During his life Koettlitz became an expedition surgeon, geologist and botanist of great skill. He was at the time one of the most knowledgeable expedition doctors, with the skill to prevent and treat that most dreaded expedition disease – scurvy. Scurvy had been almost eliminated from merchant and naval ships making long journeys but still afflicted polar expeditions. Such preventative skill was a crucial element in the expertise of an expedition surgeon; its importance can be judged by the fact that the disease ultimately contributed to the death of Captain Scott and his brave companions whilst returning from the South Pole.

If Dr Reginald Koettlitz had possessed a more forceful, determined mind-set that equalled his scientific and explorative capabilities his name would now likely rank alongside the great names of early polar exploration. This was not to be, however, with Koettlitz being dismissed and ignored by the establishment, as illustrated by the attitudes of the leading officers of the *Discovery*. If Koettlitz had enjoyed a relationship of mutual respect with his contemporaries, the tragic events on the Ross Ice Shelf in 1912 could perhaps have been averted.

Koettlitz forecast in a letter to Fridtjof Nansen that the approach advocated in the planning of the *Discovery* expedition by its leaders and organisers, plus their lack of polar experience, could lead to possible disaster. Koettlitz's concerns warned of the tragic events yet to unfold at the pole: 'How much better it would have been if someone had been placed in command who had had former polar experience. The final result will, I fear, be much blundering and it will be muddled through à l'Anglais.'[2]

---

1.   William Speirs Bruce archive – University of Edinburgh.
2.   Letter from Koettlitz to Fridtjof Nansen dated 8 December 1900 – Koettlitz family archives.

Acknowledgements

Firstly, I must mention the members of the Koettlitz family who have cared for the Dr Koettlitz papers and other artefacts, without which completion of this project would not have been possible.

Special thanks go also to the late A. G. E. Jones. Joe Jones had researched the life and achievements of Koettlitz for over 40 years. In addition to offering guidance and advice he gave me access to his research material regarding Koettlitz and his polar interlocutors. Following his death Miss Gwyneth Jones (his sister) continued to encourage and authorise access to material that had been placed within academic institutions and at other locations.

A. G. E. Jones introduced me to the late Don Aldridge, conservationist and author. Don, the author of *The Rescue of Captain Scott*, became my mentor and until his untimely passing provided access to all his polar-related papers. He was a constant source of advice and knowledge. I would not have completed this project without his continual guidance and inspiration.

No enquiries regarding Dr Koettlitz would be complete without a visit to Dover Museum, Kent. I am grateful to the staff in the archives section at the museum who searched diligently on my behalf. It is regrettable that the bulk of the Koettlitz collections donated to the museum had been disposed of following storm damage to the original building. Valuable assistance was also provided by Dover Library who located past issues of local newspapers carrying Koettlitz-related articles. The headmaster and staff at Dover College gave access to their Koettlitz-related file.

I would also like to thank, in particular, Heather Lane, Head Librarian at the Scott Polar Research Institute (SPRI), who immediately following her appointment provided me with unrestricted access to the A. G. E. Jones collection contained within the archives. This research at the SPRI was greatly assisted by Naomi Boneham and Lucy Martin within their respective areas of expertise.

At the Royal Geographical Society (RGS) continual assistance was provided by Julie Carrington and colleagues within the RGS library. They were most helpful to this new researcher visiting the institution. The library staff at the Royal Society provided similar support. Visiting the Wellcome Trust became a delight with the assistance of Rachel Cross and Ross Macfarlane who located Koettlitz medical material which had not been examined in modern times. I would also like to thank Polly Tucker at the Natural History Museum archives for locating and providing access to the detailed records compiled by Koettlitz whilst on the National Antarctic Expedition. At the Lloyds Register of Shipping, Emma Haxhaj confirmed the identity of the ship, *Sobralense*, in which Koettlitz travelled to the Amazon.

In Scotland, Sheila Noble in the special archives department at the University of Edinburgh provided access to the Koettlitz correspondence contained within the William Speirs Bruce papers at the university. Dr David Munro and the staff at the Royal Scottish Geographical Society

(RSGS) located the photographs of the 'Koettlitz tent' in use during the *Scotia* expedition. Papers written by Koettlitz following the Jackson-Harmsworth and Weld Blundell expeditions were located within the RSGS. Geoff Swinney at the National Museum of Scotland provided excellent advice concerning the links between Koettlitz and Speirs Bruce. Gill Poulter, curator at the Dundee Heritage Trust, the location of the *Discovery*, confirmed information contained within the Koettlitz family archives.

In Europe, South Africa, Australia and New Zealand I have received nothing but excellent co-operation from the museums, libraries and other relevant institutions. Gunnar Larsen, a retired Norwegian police officer and ex-colleague, saved me many hours of research and travel by visiting the Norwegian National Library in Oslo and confirming the correspondence contained within the Koettlitz family archives. I had previously been pointed in that direction by Roland Huntford, the polar academic and author.

At the Canterbury Museum, Christchurch, New Zealand, Jo Anne Smith and Kerry McCarthy also confirmed information kept within the family records – thereby, and with great regret, making my journey to that wonderful country no longer a priority. In Australia, Dale Chatwin at the National Library, Canberra provided similar assistance and in return I could point him in the direction of the A. G. E. Jones files at the SPRI. The office of the Mayor in Calais, France confirmed and supplied details of the Butez family, whose daughter Marie married Dr Koettlitz.

In South Africa the people and institutions of Cradock, Somerset East and Port Elizabeth provided nothing but the utmost assistance and kindness during my research visit to the area. In particular, I should mention the late Sam Bergman who for many years researched the life of Dr Koettlitz following his discovery of the Koettlitz memorial in Cradock cemetery. Duncan Ferguson, an elderly resident of Cradock, allowed me access to his private collections and escorted me on a tour of the Cradock cemetery and church. The curator of Cradock museum was most helpful, once he became fully aware of the identity of the distinguished polar explorer in a photograph above his desk. I must thank David Gower and other residents of the town who assisted in locating relevant contacts. In the beautiful town of Somerset East I thank Emile Badenhorst, the curator of the museum, who was greatly enthused by my arrival and produced the Koettlitz file held at the museum. I think I had been the first person to enquire of the great doctor in modern times. This co-operation continued following my return to UK.

In Port Elizabeth, Patricia Stapleton assisted with contacts both in South Africa and the UK in addition to providing valuable social support and advice. At the University of Witwatersrand, Dr H. F. L. Immelman confirmed the content of the Bergman papers contained in the family archive.

Following my return from South Africa Dr Sydney Cullis has provided continual support from his home in Cape Town.

I am indebted to Dr Ross MacPhee, Curator of Vertebrate Zoology at the American Museum of Natural History, New York, who kindly agreed to write the introduction to this biography despite his very extensive academic and travel schedules. He has provided valuable advice and guidance following our initial meeting in Cambridge, UK.

Finally, I dedicate this book to my wife's aunt, Miss Ulrica Koettlitz, whom I have already mentioned; to my wife, Ann Koettlitz, for her patience and support; and, in particular, to my son Simon Koettlitz Jones, an accomplished writer in his own right, to whom I am grateful for his constructive advice and professional help in editing this volume and for his continual support.

If I have omitted to thank anyone who has helped me in the course of my researches I apologise.

1

From Prussia to Dover

In the years known as the heroic age of polar exploration, class was a prevalent issue, and it had a major impact on Reginald Koettlitz during the National Antarctic Expedition of 1901–1904. In a letter to his brother Maurice, who was a general practitioner in Dover, he wrote when referring to his messmates: 'They are a very different class of man to any I have associated with before, and a class not altogether to my taste, except now and then.'[1]

If they had known of the background and origins of the Koettlitz family, their approach and attitude to Reginald Koettlitz in his position as senior surgeon and a member of the scientific team might have been very different.

Reginald Koettlitz was born on 23 December 1860 in Ostend, where his father Maurice Koettlitz was a minister of the Reformed Lutheran Church. His mother Rosetta Ann Jane Koettlitz was an English citizen who had been born in Middlesex, England in 1834. Ostend during this period, in addition to being a seaport, was a fashionable sea resort and was frequented by the wealthy citizens of both Belgium and England. It is not known where Koettlitz's parents met but it is presumed to be Ostend or Brussels, Belgium.

The Koettlitz family had travelled to Belgium via Germany from the previous family home in Königsberg, East Prussia. This was formerly the capital of Prussia, a state of great power at the beginning of the 19th century. Today this area is called Kaliningrad, a Russian enclave wedged between Poland and Lithuania.

The grandfather of the Koettlitz family, Johann Friedrich Koettlitz, was born in Tilsit, Prussia, now known as Sovetsk in the same enclave of the Russian Federation. He was a nobleman with the rank of 'Freiherr', or Baron, and the family name at the time was 'von Koettlitz'. The family history is worthy of study as the distinctive prefix 'von' was dropped following a duel with another nobleman of the Prussian court, a Colonel Putscharle, in which this favoured nobleman was killed. This led to the decline of the von Koettlitz family lands and wealth and to the eventual movement west in order to avoid further conflict with the victim's friends.

These financial problems were exacerbated by debts incurred by their step-grandfather, the first clergyman in the family. He had a liking for playing the lottery; 12 tickets at 50 thalers each being purchased and squandered annually led to further loss of the family assets. So, the substantial family wealth acquired by a barrister was thrown away in handfuls over a few years by the step-grandfather, a clergyman! A further fortune was lost to the family during the protracted occupation of Danzig by the French and the death of a Koettlitz family aunt.

This family background is worthy of further examination as Reginald Koettlitz was well aware of his family's previous position, having carried out extensive research to identify the family coat of arms in order that his sledging flag could be prepared for the *Discovery* expedition. As a result of these enquiries, made through an expert on Prussian heraldry, Reginald Koettlitz discovered that the family had been substantial landowners in the area of Gross Waldeck and the correct family name was previously von Kittlitz. The expert referred to, Colonel von Hope, was of the opinion that the family name should be returned to the original without delay. For reasons unknown this of course never occurred.

The sledging flag designed and created for the National Antarctic Expedition on board the *Discovery* was from the coat of arms of the noble von Kittlitz family. It was described in detail as 'a shield party per bend dexter, above in a field is a demi bull rampant issuant sinister, Gules, below in a field Gules three oblique bars sinister argent'.[2] A variation on this flag was ultimately approved for use on the expedition by Sir Clements Markham, who was of the opinion that the use of such flags, following the naval tradition, was of the utmost importance. The alternative flag is still retained by the present Koettlitz family.

As a result of the enquiries made by Colonel von Hope the family line was traced back to the 14th century. By the time Reginald Koettlitz's family had moved west to Belgium the tradition of being a member of the clergy was well established within the family. His father, born in Königsberg around 1816, was already an established member of the Lutheran Church before the move to Dover, Kent. This move took place shortly after Reginald's birth in Ostend on 23 December 1860. Unfortunately, all records of the Koettlitz family history in Ostend were destroyed by allied bombing during the Second World War.

Koettlitz expedition sledging flag

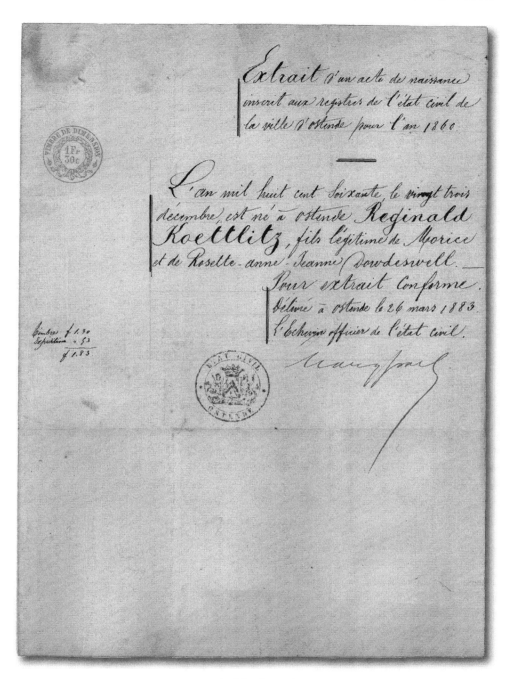

Koettlitz's birth certificate

Koettlitz family photograph – Reginald Koettlitz back row (right)

By the late 1860s the family was well established in Dover, consisting of Reginald, his brothers Maurice, Robert and Arthur and his sisters Rosetta and Elise. Their father, Maurice, still a practising minister, supported his wife Rosetta in running a boarding school at 75/76 Folkestone Road, Hougham, Dover, to supplement their income. He was described as generous to a fault, giving to any who pleaded a need. This description bears much similarity to those of Reginald Koettlitz many years and expeditions later when practising as the rural doctor and supporter of a community in South Africa. His father's compassion and social conscience had passed to the exploring surgeon and had been reinforced by his years working in the mining communities of Durham where poverty and hardship were common.

The boarding school assisted the education of the Koettlitz family and specialised in teaching foreign students from the countries of the Empire as diverse as Sri Lanka (Ceylon) and New Zealand.

With his elder brother Maurice, Reginald Koettlitz entered Dover College in the Michaelmas term of 1873. Neither brother distinguished themselves there. They studied Latin, Greek, French and German in addition to the other established subjects common to such a school in this era. This knowledge of languages was to prove most useful to Koettlitz during his expeditions in the Arctic and later when living in South Africa.

Reginald Koettlitz left Dover College in 1876 and after a brief dalliance in the world of commerce, including a trip to Canada which must have whetted his appetite for further travel, he adopted medicine as his career and in 1878 entered Guy's Hospital as a student.

His progression at Guy's was productive and successful. Many years later, Guy's students thought so highly of him as to present him with the scientific apparatus and medical equipment he needed for his voyage and duties whilst with the *Discovery* expedition. His travelling medical emergency bag is within the Koettlitz collection at Dover Museum, Kent.

Koettlitz travelling medical kit

Koettlitz travelling medical kit

Also studying medicine in London at the time was William Henry Neale, who qualified from University College in 1879. Neale later joined the *Eira* expedition as surgeon, the expedition being led by the Arctic explorer Benjamin Leigh-Smith. This expedition constructed a hut on Franz Josef Land which was later used by Koettlitz and the other members of the Jackson-Harmsworth Expedition. Neale, like Koettlitz, gained much practical information concerning the prevention of scurvy and living in such hostile territory and Koettlitz was familiar with the work of both Neale and Smith.

There is no evidence to support the view that Koettlitz actively studied the causes and treatment of scurvy whilst training at Guy's and later Edinburgh. But it is apparent that he was well read on the subject when he took up his post as surgeon/geologist with the Jackson-Harmsworth Expedition to Franz Josef Land. This subject is covered in detail later in the book. At this time the true causes of scurvy were unknown, although many theories were advocated. However, it is clear that Koettlitz was at the forefront of expedition surgeons with regards to its effective prevention.

Following his qualification at Guy's as a Member of the Royal College of Surgeons (MRCS), Koettlitz went to Edinburgh where he studied and graduated as Licentiate of the Royal College of Physicians (LRCP Edinburgh). It was while at Edinburgh that his interest in geology and the world of exploration first appeared. This was later refined in and around the mines of Durham, where he made a substantial collection of fossils from the mining deposits. His greatest geological achievement was accomplished amongst the snow and freezing temperatures of Franz Josef Land between 1894 and 1897, at times with Dr Fridtjof Nansen with whom he spent many hours walking the coastal slopes of those distant polar islands.

In November 1897 Koettlitz returned to Dover College to present a lecture about his experiences on the Jackson-Harmsworth Expedition. Regularly interrupted by loud applause, Koettlitz spoke in detail on the *Eira* expedition and the disaster of having your vessel crushed by the ice, and about having to survive in extreme polar conditions. As reported in the *Dover Telegraph*, 'The doctor, who was again loudly cheered on rising to speak, thanked the audience for the very warm reception they had given him. He had done nothing to deserve it. When at school he was one of the stupid and backward boys, but he would say for the encouragement of any present members of the school who felt they were stupid and backward that he had known many such boys become useful and indeed distinguished men (cheers). Of course they would understand he was not thinking at all of himself (laughter).'[3]

This self-deprecating humble streak within Koettlitz would hold him back in later years when a positive, more aggressive response was required in the company of other explorers.

---

1. Letter from Koettlitz to his brother in England dated 21 March 1904 – Koettlitz family archives.

2. *South Polar Times*, 1st edition – Koettlitz family archives.

3. Extract from the *Dover Telegraph*, 3 November 1897 – Dover Library.

2

A practice in Durham

Comment was made by Commander R. F. Scott when Koettlitz was appointed as senior surgeon and botanist to the National Antarctic Expedition on board *Discovery* that 'He had settled down to the quietest of country practices, where he remained for eight years, and might have remained to the present time but for a sudden impulse to volunteer his services as doctor to the Jackson-Harmsworth Expedition'.[1]

In fact, nothing could be further from the truth regarding the experience he gained whilst a general practitioner in Butterknowle, County Durham for a period of nine years. This area was at the centre of the Durham mining industry, both above and below ground. In addition to providing valuable medical experience it allowed Koettlitz to follow his passion for geology, biology and many other interests concerning the flora and fauna of the region.

Perhaps his most valuable experience was gained dealing with the miners and their families, witnessing the poverty and extreme hardship which was common in these areas at that time. This guided his values until his death in South Africa. As a result of these experiences he was able to make accurate and at times critical judgements of his travelling companions' conditions and attitudes during his later expeditions.

Compared to modern attitudes Koettlitz's socialist values would be inclined to the left. This would have placed him clearly at odds with the traditional middle-upper class Victorian and Edwardian values that were common amongst his wardroom companions on both polar expeditions. This was particularly the case during the National Antarctic Expedition on board *Discovery*, where his letters indicated he found certain attitudes of some wardroom members distasteful.

Far from being simply a doctor in a quiet country practice, Koettlitz was medical officer and public vaccinator to the Hamsterley district, the Auckland Poor Law Union (Advising GP), and surgeon to Butterknowle, Woodland and New Copley collieries, all in the area of Butterknowle, County Durham. This gave him daily access to the same mining areas where he studied geological formations, with a particular interest in coal measures and carboniferous vegetation, which formed his consuming interest in, and knowledge of, geology. He assembled a large fossil collection from the mines of Durham and immersed himself in studying all available material on the subject. As recognised by Nansen in later years, Koettlitz possessed an incredible wealth of geological knowledge for someone who had been entirely self-taught.

Koettlitz in Butterknowle surgery, County Durham

In 1891 he was also appointed Acting Surgeon to the 2nd Volunteer Battalion, Durham Light Infantry, being promoted to Senior Lieutenant in 1893 before resigning his commission in June 1894 prior to his departure for Franz Josef Land.

This combined role of general practitioner for the general public, amongst the mines where accidents were common, and honorary surgeon to the military gave him a wide and varied medical experience. By overlooking these skills the leaders of later Antarctic expeditions committed their crews to unnecessary hardships and illness. The onset of scurvy in particular could have been avoided had Koettlitz's knowledge been applied. Whether his abilities were dismissed by the senior officers or he simply lacked the confidence to espouse his point of view will be examined through the course of this book.

It was in Butterknowle that Reginald Koettlitz was initiated into the Brotherhood of Freemasons, having joined the lodge at Barnard Castle. There is no record of his participation within the Freemasons, but we must presume he was an active member. His Will stated that only Freemasons must carry him and his wife to their final resting place in Cradock, South Africa, and this was duly carried out by the Cradock and Somerset East lodges. This at least was something Koettlitz had in common with Commander Scott in the wardroom of the *Discovery*; it was not unusual for serving military officers to be Freemasons.

Despite many years serving the mining community of Durham with great success, while at the same time continually enhancing his geological knowledge and skill, Koettlitz was possessed by a desire to test himself further and put his experience to use in extreme conditions. This meant exploration, and he decided to hand over his practice to his brother and return to Dover to achieve this aim.

Koettlitz returned to Dover by touring England on a bicycle, which in the early 1890s was an achievement in itself; bicycles at that time were of a rudimentary nature and the roads of England were unpaved and similar to level farm tracks. This grand tour allowed him to continue his studies of geology and botany en-route.

Thus by 1894 he was living in the family home in Pencester Road, Dover, and looking for exploration opportunities. The Koettlitz family were by now respected citizens within the medical and religious communities of Dover. In fact, they remained stalwart followers of the Baptist Church and influential members of the medical community until the death of Dr Maurice Koettlitz in 1960. Dr Maurice Koettlitz was the nephew of Reginald Koettlitz and was for many years the custodian of the extensive collections made by Koettlitz during his time in the polar regions and Africa at Charlton House, Dover.

The Koettlitz family home, Charlton House, Dover

Formal portrait of Reginald Koettlitz

No. 7931

(A.)

NATURALIZATION ACTS, 1870.

Certificate of Naturalization to an Alien.

HOME OFFICE, LONDON.

WHEREAS *Reginald Koettlitz*

an Alien, now residing at *75 Folkestone Road. Dover, in the County of Kent.*

has presented to me, the Right Honourable *Herbert Henry Asquith* one of Her Majesty's Principal Secretaries of State, a Memorial, praying for a Certificate of Naturalization, and alleging that he is a

Subject of Belgium, having been born at Ostend ; and is the son of Maurice and Rosetta Ann Jane Koettlitz, the former being of Prussian Nationality, and the latter being an Englishwoman = of the age of Thirty three years = a Surgeon and Physician = is unmarried

and

Naturalisation certificate

and that in the period of eight years preceding his application he has resided for five years within the United Kingdom, and intends, when naturalized, to reside therein:

And whereas I have inquired into the circumstances of the case, and have received such evidence as I have deemed necessary for proving the truth of the allegations contained in such Memorial, so far as the same relate to the Memorialist:

Now, in pursuance of the authority given to me by the said Acts, I grant to the aforesaid

Reginald Koettlitz

this Certificate, and declare that he is hereby naturalized as a British Subject, and that, upon taking the Oath of Allegiance, he shall in the United Kingdom be entitled to all political and other rights, powers, and privileges, and be subject to all obligations, to which a natural-born British Subject is entitled or subject in the United Kingdom; with this qualification, that he shall not, when within the limits of the Foreign State of which he was a Subject previously to his obtaining this Certificate of Naturalization, be deemed to be a British Subject, unless he has ceased to be a Subject of that State in pursuance of the laws thereof, or in pursuance of a Treaty to that effect.

In witness whereof I have hereto subscribed my Name this 7th day of July 1894.

Oath of Allegiance.

I, *Reginald Koettlitz* of 75 Folkestone Road Dover in the County of Kent Surgeon and Physician

do swear that I will be faithful and bear true allegiance to Her Majesty Queen Victoria, Her Heirs and Successors, according to law.

So help me GOD.

(Signed) *Reginald Koettlitz*

Sworn and subscribed this 9th day of July 1894

(Signed)

before me.

H. Moss Hewitt.
A Commissioner for Oaths

Justice of the Peace
[or other official title].

13

Throughout the many years the Koettlitz family practised as doctors in Dover, they also remained stalwart supporters of the deprived and poor children of the town, in particular during the Victorian and Edwardian periods. Maurice Koettlitz Snr, Reginald Koettlitz and subsequently Maurice Koettlitz Jnr provided treatment to these deprived sections of the community. This further added to Reginald's medical experience prior to his departure on the National Antarctic Expedition in 1901.

Thus it is clear that Koettlitz had a wealth of experience and had not been confined to working in 'the quietest of rural practices'. Come the voyage of the *Discovery*, Koettlitz would be one of the most highly qualified members of the senior officers and scientific staff aboard the expedition ship.

Koettlitz had also recently become a British citizen, by following the arduous naturalisation process. With the certificate finally signed by Herbert Asquith, Secretary of State at the Home Office, all was set fair for the next chapter in Koettlitz's somewhat unorthodox medical journey.

Whilst in Dover Koettlitz noticed an advertisement by one Frederick George Jackson for suitably qualified persons to join him on an expedition to Franz Josef Land, an Arctic archipelago to the north of Russia. This expedition became known as the Jackson-Harmsworth Expedition, after Jackson himself and the expedition benefactor Alfred Harmsworth (later Lord Northcliffe), an eminent newspaper owner of the time. Reginald Koettlitz was duly appointed following a recommendation to Harmsworth from the editor of the medical journal *The Lancet*, and the expedition would prove to be the highlight of his geological career.

Given Scott's 'quietest of rural practices' comment it is worth reporting a more generous testimonial of Koettlitz provided by Alfred Harmsworth himself. Of Koettlitz's professional capabilities as an expedition surgeon Harmsworth asserted: 'The members of the expedition came back in better health than in which they had started.'[2]

---

1.   *The Voyage of the Discovery* – National Antarctic Expedition 1905.

2.   A. G. E. Jones papers – Koettlitz family archives.

3

Frederick George Jackson

Frederick George Jackson was born in 1860, the same year as Koettlitz, in the quiet country town of Alcester where his father shared the same profession as Koettlitz's father, as rector. By the time of Jackson's death in 1938 he was already a near-forgotten man – not due to any reticence or modesty on his part, but because his expedition to Franz Josef Land achieved little in comparison with later expeditions. It was not entirely through his own failings but he offended many people in his career, resulting in him having few friends in the right places.

Jackson was not a skilled writer, unlike Robert Falcon Scott, and his dull, two-volume work on the expedition entitled *A Thousand Days in the Arctic* had only limited appeal and sales. In appearance he would not have stood out in a crowd, much to his annoyance, being slightly above average in height with an unremarkable personality compared to his contemporaries Nansen, Amundsen, Shackleton and Scott.

His other drawback was a lack of scientific knowledge and academic learning. He went to Denstone College where he excelled as a sportsman, and subsequently studied for a short time at Edinburgh University, which unfortunately did not culminate in a degree. Whilst at Edinburgh he demonstrated his future Arctic credentials and capacity for tolerating icy waters, by plunging into the loch at Linlithgow to rescue a 17-year-old boy from drowning. For this he was awarded the Royal Humane Society's Bronze Medal. There followed a period when he travelled the world, including a spell on a cattle ranch in Queensland, Australia where he learnt to handle and break horses. It was here that he discovered his physical strength and made up his mind to test himself in the Arctic.

Why he chose the Arctic is not clear but he may have been influenced by other expeditions to the region. His attention may have been caught by the *Eira* expedition led by Leigh-Smith in which the ship was lost but all expedition members saved. On Jackson's return to England he made a journey to Greenland on the whaler *Erik*, and a second similar voyage followed later. He even offered his services to Fridtjof Nansen who was preparing for his voyage on the *Fram*. However, Nansen wanted all his crew to be Norwegian and Jackson possessed neither scientific nor seamanship skills. In an interesting twist they met some three years later on Franz Josef Land when Nansen was returning from his attempt on the North Pole, with Jackson claiming that he thereby saved the lives of Nansen and Johansen. With the survival skills possessed by Nansen and Johansen, who had already survived the most extreme conditions known to man, it is probable they would have returned safely to Norway using their own skill and resources.

Jackson first published his plan to take an expedition to Franz Josef Land in 1892 but could not find financial support at that time. He decided to make a journey to the Arctic regions of Russia to test his survival skills, clothing and equipment. He travelled to the Yugor Strait region with the intention of exploring the southern island of Novaya Zemlya and the Yamal Peninsula. However, the Samoyed people who were with him were not prepared to accompany him that far so he changed his plan and instead explored Waigatz Island and crossed the tundra with reindeer to Archangel.

Jackson followed this up with a crossing of the Kola Peninsula by dog sledge to Vadso, allowing him to compare the Samoyed with the Lapps in terms of the equipment and clothing used. These journeys took in excess of five months and were undertaken at both good and bad times of year. It was a very credible performance for someone with limited previous polar experience.

Returning to London in February 1894 Jackson became immersed in the preparations for his expedition to Franz Josef Land. He had shown himself to be a good organiser, and had allowed five months to complete his preparation. His equipment showed no striking omissions and the lessons he had learnt in northern Russia were incorporated into the plan. The main house was based on a timber building from Russia and constructed there, with a number of portable huts included for further storage. The clothing chosen by Jackson was based on that used by the native peoples of northern Russia, utilising natural furs and other materials which were generally found to be most satisfactory.

The expedition sledges were of the Norwegian pattern rather than the older Royal Navy style and therefore more efficient and suited to the conditions expected in Franz Josef Land. The experience gained on his recent journeys in Russia led Jackson to reject reindeer for hauling the sledges, and he was against the naval tradition of man-hauling. Instead he took hardy Russian ponies and dogs, although the dogs were never utilised to their full potential. Jackson was extremely cruel to the dogs, according to Koettlitz, and consequently he got little work from the most valuable transport animals in polar regions. Even the experience with the ponies was somewhat limited, and their shortcomings in these conditions were not thoroughly examined.

It is noteworthy that many of these proven techniques, particularly the design of clothing, were rejected on subsequent expeditions joined by Koettlitz, despite his presence and knowledge being available at the planning stage. This was due to a combination of factors – in particular, Koettlitz not being the type of man to push his case coupled with the expedition leaders being assured of their own superior but inadequate knowledge and experience.

As it transpired, Jackson had great shortcomings as a leader of a polar expedition, lacking skill in man management, but by the standards of the time his organisational abilities could not be faulted. So, by the middle of 1894 – and thanks to the financial generosity of Alfred Harmsworth – the Jackson-Harmsworth Expedition was ready to set out for Franz Josef Land.

Following this expedition Jackson saw a further opportunity for action, with the outbreak of the Boer War in South Africa. He was commissioned into the Manchester Regiment and with the rank of Captain saw action in South Africa, where his knowledge of handling horses, gained in Australia, proved invaluable. During actions in this arena he

Koettlitz in polar clothing on board the Windward

was mentioned in dispatches, and in 1905 transferred to the East Surrey Regiment with the rank of Major.

There followed action in 1914 in the First World War, at La Bassée, France, where Jackson was further decorated following battles in which he was forced to take command due to the death of senior officers within the regiment. He was later invalided back to England, where he commanded the Southwark Recruitment District for two years. In 1918 he was once again abroad in command of prisoner of war camps in Germany.

In the early 1920s he transferred his interests to exploration in Africa. He traversed the continent from east to west, visiting many countries en-route as well as the sources of the three great rivers of Africa, the Zambezi, the Nile and the Congo, and followed the length of the Congo to the sea. Jackson's interest in exploration and travel ended following his appointment as a member of the League of Nations Commission investigating slavery in Liberia. Return to England followed, with retirement on the River Thames.

Major Jackson died in 1938 at the age of 78, having led a full and very active life (in addition to his exploration, this included mass slaughter of big game in the northern polar regions and Africa). There is a memorial to him in St Paul's Cathedral, London, but by the time of his death he had become an obscure figure in polar exploration history.

4

Franz Josef Land and the Eira

Franz Josef Land is an archipelago lying east of Spitsbergen (Svalbard) and north of Novaya Zemlya, extending northward towards the North Pole. It consists of a group of glacier-covered, mountainous, volcanic islands, with the main geological formation being Jurassic basalt, much studied by Reginald Koettlitz during the three years he spent on these islands.

There is an opinion that William Baffin, the English explorer and navigator, may have sighted the archipelago in 1614. The first confirmed discovery was made by Julius Payer, a lieutenant in the Austrian army, who was a member of an expedition to the polar regions on the ship *Tegetthof* in 1872. In August 1873 the ship was 'beset' in the Arctic ice but land was seen to the northwest. Subsequent journeys made whilst the ship continued to be ice-bound led to the discovery and naming of islands and sounds including Austria Sound, Wilczek Land and many others. Maps were drawn by the expedition which were used, and the subject of much debate, by later expeditions.

Frederick Jackson's reasons for choosing Franz Josef Land as his base for exploration were practical, although he may have hoped the location would produce an opportunity for glory for him and the country. Based on information from Payer, the archipelago was normally easily accessible during the summer season. It extended to a known latitude of 83 degrees north but there were still many gaps to be filled on the map. There was an abundance of animal life to provide fresh meat for an expedition. Finally, and most importantly, it provided a starting point for an attempt on the North Pole.

Alfred Harmsworth was keen for the expedition to be a scientific one and confided to another Fellow of the Royal Geographical Society:

> As to Mr Jackson's chances of reaching the Pole, I shall say nothing. For my own part, I shall
> be entirely satisfied if he and his companions add to our knowledge of the geography and the
> fauna and flora of Franz Josef Land and the area lying immediately north of it. With 'beating
> the record' north I have very little sympathy. If Mr Jackson plants the Union Flag nearer the
> Pole than the Stars and Stripes (who head us by four miles only) I shall be glad, but if he came

back, having found the Pole but minus the work of the scientists, of which our expedition consists, I should regard the venture as a failure.[1]

A stay of between two and five years was envisaged. In its planning both Jackson and Harmsworth obtained assistance from the Royal Geographical Society, the Meteorological Office and Kew Observatory, amongst others; this included information from men with Arctic experience. As mentioned earlier, Benjamin Leigh-Smith and Dr W. H. Neale, in particular, had both spent an unintended winter there whilst sailing in the area aboard the motorised yacht *Eira*. Jackson's expedition was deliberately planned on a small scale with limited numbers. Advice concerning the prevention of scurvy was based primarily on the experiences of the *Eira* expedition and the success of Dr Neale in keeping the expedition scurvy free.

The *Eira* made two voyages to the polar regions and it followed a trend started in 1856 when Lord Dufferin began the fashion of yachting in the Arctic. Benjamin Leigh-Smith was already an experienced Arctic sailor by the time of the first *Eira* trip, which sailed from Peterhead in 1880. The steamer was built to his specification and strongly fortified for use in the polar ice. He also appointed Dr Neale, already an established and gifted physician in London, as the expedition medical officer.

Leigh-Smith landed initially in Spitsbergen then headed for Franz Josef Land. Knowledge of the archipelago was still very limited, with the northern, western and eastern parts uncharted, a state of affairs which Leigh-Smith was determined to change. In this objective the expedition was successful, and many new islands were visited and named, including 'Eira Harbour' on Bell Island. Further knowledge was gained concerning the wildlife of the region which supported Neale's opinion regarding the prevention of scurvy and the use of fresh meat to achieve this – a lesson not overlooked by Reginald Koettlitz some years later.

In September, having discovered a number of discrepancies in previous charts by Payer and others, the *Eira* headed home. It had been a most profitable season's work in the high Arctic. They had opened up new walrus hunting grounds and gathered collections of plants and animals, in the process making many scientific observations of interest.

When Leigh-Smith's paper was read at the Royal Geographical Society by Sir Clements Markham in January 1881 the importance of Eira Harbour as a new route to the North Pole was stressed.

On 14 June 1881 Leigh-Smith set sail on the second *Eira* expedition to the high Arctic. He headed for Greenland, expecting a journey lasting five months. By November the ship had not returned to Peterhead and concern was mounting. Search parties were being discussed; the Balloon Society suggested that a search by balloon should be launched. Others took the view that Leigh-Smith, an experienced Arctic yachtsman, was waiting calmly on Franz Josef Land.

Leigh-Smith was indeed waiting at Franz Josef Land but not under pleasant circumstances: the *Eira* had been crushed by the ice and sunk. On arrival in Franz Josef Land Leigh-Smith had found the ice so tight that he could not make the northern latitudes he had intended. Although they sailed and continued to map the areas not visited on the first journey Leigh-Smith was unable to even approach Eira Harbour, which was closed fast by the ice. Bear and walrus were hunted and a store house was erected on Bell Island and named Eira Lodge. The ship steamed on, and a landing was made at Cape Flora.

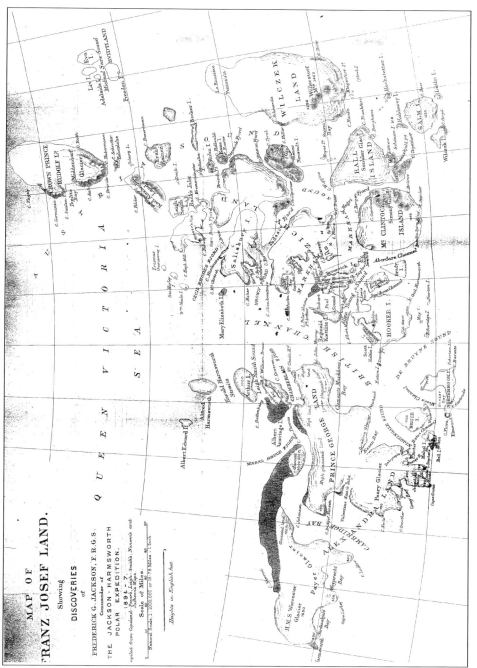

Map of Franz Josef Land – showing Reginald Koettlitz Island (centre)

It was at Cape Flora on 21 August 1881 that the *Eira* was nipped between the ice and land floe. There was little warning, and the ship went down in two hours in 11 fathoms of water. In this short time the crew were able to salvage about two months' supply of meat and a considerable supply of vegetables. In the following days the stores were taken with the ship's boats to Cape Flora, where a hut was built of stones, turf and any other material available. Journeys were also made to Eira Lodge to collect coal and other stores previously deposited there.

Once the sun had disappeared in October it was apparent they would have to over-winter at Cape Flora. They made good use of their time, improving their clothing and hunting for food. A number of the crew even looked fondly on this period, despite the severe cold and deprivation.

To avoid scurvy one item they were not deprived of was fresh meat. The meat available included walrus, polar bear and birds. A delight at Christmas was a handful of broken biscuit, which one crew member recalled as a one of the most pleasant recollections of his life.

Great credit was due to Leigh-Smith and Dr Neale for the good health of the party. Apart from bronchitis there was nothing worse than snow-blindness and frostbite, which were seen at the time as an irritation to be expected and endured in polar regions. Dr Neale's ideas on the causes of scurvy were as vague as those of other medical practitioners of the time – he believed it was brought on by anaemia for which the cure was fresh food and blood. He described his views on his return home:

> In my opinion if we had saved our salt meat from the wreck of the *Eira* we should not have been here now, and I attribute in no small measure the good health of the crew to the fact that we supported ourselves on the meat of the country, the blood of bears which we shot always being saved for food.[2]

During the winter 24 walrus and 34 bears were killed, which provided ample food for all on a daily basis. It was also noticed that the lack of the polar staple lime juice did not affect the party's health at all – another lesson subsequently absorbed by Koettlitz which would be derided in later Antarctic expeditions.

Discussing the expedition later at the Royal Geographical Society, Dr Neale summarised their daily menu:

> Our breakfast was bear and walrus, our dinner was walrus, our tea was walrus and bear for ten months, during which time we had no lime juice at all and no sick men amongst the party.[3]

During the winter Leigh-Smith also prepared the ship's boats for the journey south from Franz Josef Land once summer returned. He put stocks of fresh meat, boiled and tinned, in for the journey. Aboard the boats they were able to make hot meals daily, together with hot tea. In late June they set out. By August, after an epic journey threatened by the ice and Arctic weather, they had reached the western entrance of Matochkin Shar. Here they sighted the relief ships *William Barents* and *Hope*. The ill-fated *Eira* expedition had become a remarkable journey led by experienced polar travellers, all of whom had gained further invaluable knowledge of living and travelling in the Arctic regions.

Although Leigh-Smith continued to show an interest in polar travel and advocated

Eira Harbour as a base for further exploration in the region on his return, he did not carry out further expeditions – though he dearly wanted an Englishman to carry out such an expedition before Nansen. Ultimately, Jackson completed the mapping of the bulk of Franz Josef Land but was defeated in the quest for the pole by open water. It was left to Nansen to achieve the 'farthest north' in the 1890s, until the North Pole was conquered by the Americans. Dr Neale returned to general practice and published articles on scurvy and its prevention which Reginald Koettlitz keenly digested.

There is some credit to the theory that the appointment of Koettlitz to the National Antarctic Expedition on board *Discovery* was in part due to Sir Clements Markham's admiration of Leigh-Smith and Dr Neale and the experiences of the Franz Josef Land expeditions. He knew Koettlitz possessed the necessary knowledge, experience and capability in the prevention of scurvy and, despite his doubts concerning Koettlitz's common sense, Markham was shrewd enough to know that Koettlitz could be crucial to the success of an expedition to the Antarctic.

1.   A. G. E. Jones, Jackson-Harmsworth Expedition papers – Koettlitz family archives.

2.   Scurvy research paper by Don Aldridge – Koettlitz family archives.

3.   *Ibid.*

5

The expedition sets out

With the funding in place, primarily from Alfred Harmsworth but with notable contributions from others including the Royal Society and Misses Dawson and Lambton (who later supported other expeditions), as well as many lesser donations, the expedition was set to depart aboard the *Windward*.

The ship S.Y. *Windward*, captained by Captain Schlosshauer, had been a whaler before being obtained for the expedition and flagged to the Royal Thames Yacht Squadron. Koettlitz describes the ship as being heavily laden both above and below deck as she departed St Katherine's Dock on 11 July 1894, anchoring off Greenhithe until noon on 12 July. Prior to departure many friends and members of the societies of London had come aboard to wish the expedition bon-voyage, including Sir Clements Markham, Admirals McClintock, Ommaney and Markham plus other old polar grandees and their ladies.

In addition to the expedition members, also aboard was Mr Arthur Montefiore, the honorary secretary of the expedition and a prominent member of the Royal Geographical Society, and Herbert Ward, of Stanley's Expedition for the relief of Emin Pasha in the Sudan, who had been besieged by the Mahdi Army some years previously.

Strong head winds were encountered on leaving the Thames Estuary, causing considerable delay to arrival at their first destination of Christiansund, Norway. Koettlitz described Christiansund as a beautifully situated town with fine wooden buildings and churches. The ship did not remain long in these Norwegian waters and was soon heading north. On 22 July *Windward* crossed the Arctic Circle between the Lofoten Islands and the mainland, on the 24th passing Tromso which was still showing a large amount of snow cover and a glacier here and there. On 25 July 1894 the ship passed Hammerfest, at that time the most northerly town of substance in the world.

During the following days, the inevitable monotony of the daily routine and sea-sickness, which Dr Koettlitz suffered on all his sea journeys, was broken by the appearance of the occasional whale and schools of porpoises. Koettlitz describes them as swimming hither and thither across the bows of the ship, which he found most interesting and amusing.

On 29 July they traversed the White Sea and after some delay due to foggy conditions the *Windward* was met by the pilot ship which guided them to a berth at Solambola close to Archangel.

The ship arrived in Archangel during the evening of 31 July. The objective of calling there was to take on board ponies, the wooden house, sheds and stables which would be constructed on reaching Franz Josef Land, plus furs, coal and other equipment essential for the extended time closer to the North Pole than had been survived by any humans previously.

The officers and scientific staff of the *Windward* were enthusiastically welcomed and assisted by HM Vice-Consul Mr D. W. Wilton, who was later to join the expedition, as well as the local inhabitants, the Provincial Governor and members of the Russian Imperial Navy.

On later expeditions Koettlitz was often criticised for not being a jolly member of the party, unable to take a joke or be the subject of naval pranks which seemed humorous to others. There is certainly some truth in this, but his attitude was adversely influenced by the often amateurish approach taken by others towards polar expeditions in general, and scientific research in particular. To rebut this stereotypical image of Koettlitz it is worth transcribing in detail a letter he sent to his brother Dr Maurice Koettlitz, who was still administering to the poor and often deprived citizens of Dover.

The letter, dated 24 August 1894, was written on board the S.Y. *Windward*, the location given as 'Lat 79oN, Long 44oE'. Koettlitz indulged in the normal pleasantries and explained it would probably be another two years before he would send another letter:

I shall however mention a few points which I think would interest you most. The first thing I shall mention is our reception in Archangel, which was most enthusiastic, the Governor of the province showed us particular attention even going so far as to order the customs authorities not to molest us, so we had no bother that way. This is a most particular mark of favour and gratified Mr Jackson very much.

He also invited us to a soirée, where I tasted the best tea that I have ever tasted. I have got to like to drink my tea after the Russian manner which is with sugar and lemon without milk and drunk out of glasses, they do not make it strong. At about one o'clock in the morning we sat down to a meal. I suppose supper is the only name you could call it.

This was a very fine collection, sterlet, a fish and great delicacy, was on the menu, every kind of wine accompanied it, toasts to our honour were drunk most enthusiastically with musical honours and with cheers – the Russian cheer is Urrah, Urrah, Urrah. We returned it by toasting the Governor, and giving him musical honours and cheers L'Anglais, the Russian naval officers of the war vessel, *Vestnik* then lying in harbour who were present we also toasted. In drinking healths the Russian way is to move round the table tipping glasses with those we toast, or if it be only one to all go and tip glasses with him.

They finished up by drinking our special healths and success in a brew they call Jonka, this is composed of white and red wines with spices in the bowl, over this is stood a grating of sugar loaf, the lights are then turned down and vodka, a colourless spirit made from corn is poured on the sugar loaf and set alight. I do not know how many bottles of vodka were poured on but I should think it was kept burning for about five minutes. The flame is then put out by having a couple of bottles of champagne poured over it, glasses are then filled and passed round, and I must say the brew was very good, the Russians are devils at drinking, though I did not see anyone get drunk, but they can put it away.

The Governor soon found out that I could talk German, so he often conversed with me, he could not speak English, and gave me in charge of the surgeon of the warship *Vestnik* who comes from the Russian provinces bordering the Baltic where German is spoken, we therefore got on very well, others also talk German or a little French and I managed to get on very well with them. Mr Jackson found me very often useful to him because he talks very little Russian and I could act as his interpreter through my German.

Another incident is the drive we had the night before. Our party had hired four droskys, these vehicles are something like the Irish jaunting car, as regards the seating accommodation and manner of sitting in them, but on account of the horrible streets of the place which are paved with the roughest of cobble stones with all kinds of holes and ruts and there unfilled and uncared for, they have a special kind of arrangement to prevent the jolting being felt so much, which is that under the seats two long poles twice or three times the length of the seats are laid and those are supported by springs which connect them with the axle and wheels.

Well as I was saying, we got these four droskys and somehow they got it into their heads we wanted to race and the reckless driving and tearing through the streets at that time of night was tremendous I can tell you. I thought over and over again we were going over, but everyone seemed to be thoroughly enjoying it so I would not spoil the fun, but I have heard of the Russian driving and now I can well believe all I have heard about it.[1]

Koettlitz continues with a description of the collection of stores, reindeer meat and 30 dogs sourced at Harbarora in the Jugor straits from the local Samoyeds who had a summer settlement there (discussed further below). He finishes the letter: 'I must now conclude for I have other letters to write so goodbye and believe me to be your affectionate brother, Reginald Koettlitz.'[1]

This letter demonstrates that alongside his serious, professional side Koettlitz also had the social abilities to take part in off-duty moments. It also highlights the benefits of being a member of the political and military classes in Russia during a time when the bulk of the population lived in serfdom and suffered a life of extreme hardship. It is interesting that Koettlitz had not encountered the spirit vodka previously, despite years of medical training in London and Edinburgh and working amongst many different classes of people in England and Scotland. The letter suggests that even the military messes and wardrooms of the English military establishment had something to learn from their Russian counterparts when it came to alcoholic entertainment and social interaction.

In another letter, written following the collection of the stores, animals and other equipment from the villages of the Samoyeds, Koettlitz describes that community in some detail. This anthropological interest existed outside his normal duties as surgeon and geologist, and was one that he indulged in further in North East Africa later in his life.

Koettlitz outlines the design of the Samoyed living accommodation at their summer campsite. It was constructed by a number of poles fastened at the top and spread out in a wide circle, forming a framework. These poles were then covered in strips of birch bark, reminding him of the wigwams of the Native Americans. He was impressed with the accommodation's construction and durability in the hostile conditions of northern Russia, found even in summer. It is possible he formulated his later design of the pyramid-type tent first used on Franz Josef Land, and still used by explorers today, whilst with the Samoyed people.

He describes the Samoyeds thus: 'A flat headed, Mongolian-type people, who live principally by herding reindeer which they treat most cruelly, the reindeer also supply the meat from which they live and provide clothing and extra covering for the wigwam type structures when winter comes on. They are friendly folk, much infected with syphilis caused by frequent intercourse with all and sundry.'[1]

Jackson, who had lived amongst these people on his previous visit to the region, completed his bargaining for fresh meat and supplies by exchanging red cotton handkerchiefs and snuff, much prized by the Samoyeds. After they had bid farewell to their Russian and Samoyed friends, the *Windward* continued its track towards Franz Josef Land.

The *Windward* skirted Waigatz Island and the south island of Novaya Zemlya, and on 20 August came up against heavy ice together with a heavy fog which greatly reduced their speed. Within two days the ship had approached the main northern pack ice, in an area which they knew had been little visited previously. They pushed on using the channels and leads which opened before them or were created by the *Windward*. The temperature was hovering around 28 degrees Fahrenheit and new ice was forming fast.

On 25 August 1894 Franz Josef Land, their goal and home for the next three years, was sighted, with Bell Island and other features identified. All aboard were hoping and expecting to arrive soon at their destination, and began writing letters home in great haste. It was hoped that the ship could unload the stores, animals and accommodation quickly and return to England. However, as Dr Koettlitz wrote, they were to be grievously disappointed: though they were in sight of their destination the ice was tightly packed and impossible to penetrate. The *Windward*, under the guidance of the ice master John Crowther, continually probed, searching for a lead which would take them to land, but Crowther was continually frustrated. It even appeared as if the ship might get frozen in before land was reached. This would create a perilous situation.

The ice master had been in these regions twice before and pointed out the landmarks on the islands of Franz Josef Land, including Capes Flora, Crowther and Grant, and Bell and Mabel Islands. His knowledge came from his previous trip aboard the ill-fated *Eira* with Leigh-Smith – he was one of the shipwrecked crew who were forced to over-winter at Cape Flora in a hut made from mud and stones. A man better qualified to be their guide could not be found.

Since leaving Archangel they had been travelling in perpetual daylight, a phenomenon that proved fascinating for the freshest members of the expedition, for whom this was their first journey to the far northern regions. When the opportunity arose they took a walk on the ice, spellbound by the beauty of the shapes and colours of Arctic ice and marvelling at the beautiful shades of azure blue to green and the purest blue-white. Years later Koettlitz was to compare these colours with the Antarctic but at that time his polar travelling was only at its formative stage. He felt that such beauty had to be seen to be appreciated.

Koettlitz was intrigued by the amount of wildlife that could be seen on nearby ice floes, especially the substantial numbers of birds. Seals, fulmar petrels, kittiwakes, auks and many species of gull were commonplace. On 29 August their first polar bear paid the ship a visit but, to the regret of some, did not come close enough to be shot. It did however allow them to examine the creature's hunting habits. The following day saw the first shooting of a polar bear, an activity which became increasingly common during the winter and spring; in total nearly 60 fell to the guns of the *Windward* crew and scientific members. Polar bear meat became a crucial part of the expedition diet – Koettlitz knew it was essential to eat fresh meat to prevent scurvy. With the amount of fresh meat available, the dreaded polar explorer's disease would not present a problem as long as this policy was followed.

A polar bear shot by Koettlitz during this expedition can still be viewed in the museum at Dover, Kent, and remains in excellent condition after 113 years. For many years it had stood in his brother's surgery in Dover, much to the delight – or fear – of the local children visiting for treatment.

The Koettlitz Polar Bear, Dover Museum

The *Windward* searched south, east and west in an increasingly desperate attempt to find a way through the tightly packed ice, using precious coal reserves in the process, but without much success. As the passing of time became ever more crucial, the tight ice pack was finally broken up by a northerly gale, at last allowing access to land. It was decided that Cape Flora would be the most convenient landing place and expedition base. Eira Harbour, Bell Island and Mabel Island were still ice-bound. Speed in unloading the stores was the order of the day, and unloading commenced on 10 September.

All hands, including the expedition's scientific members Jackson, Armitage, Fisher, Dunsford, Child, Burgess, Heyward and Koettlitz, worked 16 hours on and eight hours off to take advantage of the continuing daylight. Supported by the regular crew of the *Windward* this ensured that work continued 24 hours. After a period of hectic activity work was halted by ice forming between the ship and the shore, allowing a vital rest for all. Once the ice had hardened enough, operations resumed. By this time it was becoming clear that the *Windward* was becoming trapped by the ice and would have to over-winter with the expedition's land-based team. Accordingly, the pace slackened as the ship would not be returning to England that year.

By 27 September the unloading was complete; all was ashore apart from the coal. Winter was rapidly approaching, with frequent gales occasionally impeding work. The temperature continued to fall and the birds, so noticeable previously, began to move south. The expedition was well equipped with buildings, which included five store houses, a main house for residence and stables for the ponies. The expedition's land-based members remained on board *Windward* until the interior of the Russian log house was complete and caulked both inside and out. On 17 November the expedition residents moved into their new accommodation at Cape Flora.

By now the Arctic night had set in, the sun having disappeared below the horizon on 19 October, not to appear again until the following February. Koettlitz was struck by the clearness and clarity of the stars and encouraged by the regular visits by polar bears, most of which were shot to enhance the larder. Despite the expedition's weaponry this was not always a straightforward activity, as polar bears are fearsome and aggressive. A number of Cape Flora residents had narrow escapes from the jaws of the Arctic's top predator.

Koettlitz described in detail the wonderful auroras which were a common sight during this period. The coloured streamers, zigzags and flashes of light moving rapidly in the sky fascinated him, and marvelling at the infinite variety of shapes provided much pleasure to Koettlitz and the other expedition members. Koettlitz's journal descriptions were enhanced by drawings, to remind him of their beauty many years later. Despite their beauty, however, the auroras failed to increase the overall light levels to assist camp activities.

---

1. Letter from Koettlitz to his brother in England dated 24 August 1894 – Koettlitz family archives.

6

The first winter at Cape Flora

As confirmed years later in the Antarctic by Reginald Skelton, engineer officer aboard the *Discovery*, 'Koettlitz was an experienced skier and survivor in polar conditions. Armitage is supposed to be our authority on sledging – personally I would sooner take Koettlitz's advice on the matter'.[1] These lessons and skills were learnt by Koettlitz in the harsh conditions of Franz Josef Land, experience which was regularly ignored by others on the *Discovery* expedition. Personality clashes and class prejudice often affected the judgement of certain senior members on the journey to the southern regions. The particular combination of strong personalities on an expedition would often prove critical to its success or failure.

By the end of November the Jackson-Harmsworth Expedition members were settled into the log house brought from Russia, which was named 'Elmwood' after the home in Kent of the expedition sponsor Alfred Harmsworth. The long winter night settled into a familiar routine involving meteorological, astronomical and magnetic observations, and taking regular exercise. Activities ranged from clearing the deep snow which built up around the buildings to regular skiing practice and fine-tuning the use of the Norwegian snow shoes by taking long walks in the moonlight of the Arctic winter.

Although the wooden hut was well constructed and suited to the conditions it was soon found to be too small for the number of men expected to live there for up to three years. The hut contained eight men in the first and second years and seven in the third year. From the general space within the building, three small individual interior areas measuring eight feet by five were taken for the use of Jackson, Armitage and Dr Koettlitz, with a stove in the centre. The other team members slept on mattresses on the floor and kept their personal belongings on shelves. There was only one large table for the use of all, so personal space and privacy was at a premium; walking and skiing became popular pastimes to avoid tempers flaring in such a confined space. Stores and the other equipment were kept in the outside huts.

Initially, Jackson shared the watches and duties with the other expedition members and there was a feeling of fairness amongst the residents, but as time progressed the confined space began to tell on them all. Apart from the outdoor activities recreation was limited. There was a musical box organ in the hut but when one man played it everybody had to hear it, even if the tune was not to their liking. When one man whistled, everybody had to listen, and Koettlitz mentions this in his diary entries as being at times much to his annoyance.

Whist, chess and cribbage were played in the evenings and thanks to the generosity of a number of the expedition sponsors a fine library of over 500 volumes was available for the long winter nights. Koettlitz was a voracious reader and worked his way through the majority of these books during the three years spent at Cape Flora, but the lack of privacy is apparent from his comments. Living by routine in the hut was essential but it did not always run smoothly.

A large tub of snow was kept in the hut to provide bath water, which was heated on the central stove. All the men had days assigned to them for bathing, and bad feelings were generated when one man took his bath out of turn. This delicate situation was exacerbated if the leader Jackson decided he wanted a bath when it suited him or when a late bath delayed meals. The cramped space allowed little room for drying clothes and consequently clean laundry became a rarity, adding to the odour of those present. When washing was undertaken, the wet garments were draped around the stove for drying, much to the annoyance of Jackson in particular.

Koettlitz records the way of life at Cape Flora in detail in his diary and on one aspect there was general agreement: the quality of the food was generally first class and the quantity sufficient. A typical day's menu is described:

Breakfast: Porridge, cold tinned meat, fried ham or tripe, honey with bread and butter with tea.

Luncheon: Cold tinned meat with scurvy grass (found locally) or tinned tomatoes, fried fresh bear meat with bread and butter and cheese.

Dinner: Soup, fresh meat or pony, fresh bear meat or loons (birds), potatoes, vegetables, tart and bread.[2]

Once a week, normally on Saturday, they had port wine with dinner. All meals were supposed to be at set times within the hut but they tended to vary according to the whims of the cook and Jackson himself, much to Koettlitz's annoyance. It is already apparent that Koettlitz preferred regulation and professional commitment and did not suffer easily those who did not share this attitude.

The food was carefully designed to combat the risk of contracting scurvy. It is worthwhile examining the issue of scurvy in greater detail as it blighted later expeditions to the Antarctic. This expedition remained free of scurvy for the land party over the three years spent on the archipelago. Koettlitz was clear in his methods and objectives in the prevention of scurvy and the advice and information he had gathered before the expedition set out were put to good use. It should have benefitted future polar parties.

Others[3] have written that the Jackson-Harmsworth Expedition suffered 'cases of scurvy'. This is a misrepresentation of the true situation. Before leaving England Jackson and Koettlitz had consulted the experts of the time, including Dr Almroth Wright who attributed the disease to 'an acid condition of the blood'.[4] Both Jackson and Koettlitz had studied the experiences of Leigh-Smith's stranded party and observed that they had remained scurvy free through living largely on fresh meat.

To put the record straight it is important to set out the true facts concerning this expedition. You will recall that the expedition ship, *Windward*, was beset by the ice and was over-wintering offshore. This resulted in there being in effect two parties for the first winter on Franz Josef Land, one ashore and one offshore aboard the *Windward*. When the weather allowed, Koettlitz visited the ship on a daily basis as part of his duties as expedition surgeon. His diary sets out clearly the situation on-board ship with regard to the crew's physical condition:

> On board ship the condition of the men was not so healthy, the officers being a poor lot, unable or too lazy, to keep up any discipline or enforce rules, with natural result that many of the men did not take regular exercise, did not eat fresh meat, which was far superior to any civilized viand, preferring the salt pork and beef. This they ate without my knowledge and against my direct orders, so that although I saw a regular quantity of lime juice was taken every day, scurvy made an appearance.[5]

Dr Koettlitz had kept a close watch on the crew and other expedition members since leaving England, this being his primary duty despite his keen interest in geology (as proved by the quality of his later geological papers). The health of Captain Schlosshauer seems to have been a constant source of discussion and examination. In a memorandum to Jackson on 19 October 1894 whilst the *Windward* was beset, Koettlitz writes that 'the health of Captain Schlosshauer is of concern; he seems to suffer from just about every disease going including syphilis'.[5] This captain did not return on the second voyage of the *Windward* to Franz Josef Land; that voyage was under the command of Captain Brown.

It was an unfortunate ending to the colourful career of Captain Schlosshauer. He had disagreed with Jackson at an early stage of the expedition. Jackson insisted on interfering with disciplinary matters related to the crew and on giving orders to the master. Schlosshauer, who despite his various diseases, was a man of marked physical power, an old backwoodsman from the Rocky Mountains of America accustomed to living in rough conditions and severe climates. He was said to have served with the Northern Army in the American Civil War. Schlosshauer was effectively written out of the *Windward* expedition reports and the subsequent two-volume book by Jackson.

The health of the crew aboard the *Windward* remained a constant source of concern to Koettlitz. Despite his regular checks some members of the crew declined in health. In a further memorandum to Jackson dated 15 March 1895, towards the end of the Arctic winter, Koettlitz writes about a case of scurvy on board the ship:

> Crew member Mr Moatt, aged 52 years, up to the present is the only case. The man in question is one of the two men, numbering 31 in all who have passed the winter of 1894–95 at Cape Flora and who have, persistently refused to partake of the fresh meat in the shape of bears and walrus which is obtainable in the locality. The boatswain and all others having eaten it regularly.
>
> The last named (boatswain) although not attacked with scurvy is not in first class condition. All the others are in good health.
>
> The case has occurred notwithstanding the fact that one ounce of lime juice has been regularly served out under my personal superintending every day to each man since September 23rd last.
>
> His symptoms are, a blue haemorshape patch with stiffness and pain about the left ankle with oedema of both ankles, loss of appetite, coated tongue which is large and flabby with dental notches along the edges, tenderness of teeth and gums which are bluish, swelled and spongy looking. He is also markedly anaemic and had been taking iron for the last week or

more. I have advised him to take bear's meat every day and also soup with bear's blood added. This I have every reason to hope will prove efficacious and restore him to health.

Despite Dr Koettlitz's care and advice, Moatt refused to eat the fresh meat available and his condition gradually worsened. His body was failing month by month, and by June this debilitating illness had wasted his mind and body and he died. He was buried on the plateau at the rear of the house at Cape Flora. To Koettlitz the signs were clear, and though he was no wiser than any other authority at the time as to the medical cause of scurvy he did know how to prevent the disease. His knowledge and skill in this area increased with every month spent on Franz Josef Land.

At Jackson's insistence, memorandums were always very formal, and they were always signed, 'I have the honour to be your obedient servant, Dr Reginald Koettlitz, expedition surgeon'.[5] Whilst accepting the formal means of address was common at the time, it seems a strange convention to keep among a group of men confined to a single Arctic hut, with some sleeping on the floor for up to three years. Perhaps Jackson felt it was even more important given those circumstances.

The crucial importance of fresh meat consumption in combating scurvy cannot be over-emphasised and is something Koettlitz came to appreciate during the expedition. Although he had studied all the available material prior to departure he was now implementing practical day-to-day procedures to combat the disease. This message was reinforced by William Speirs Bruce, who joined the expedition in its final year. He wrote:

Similarly Dr D W Wilton, myself and others on the *Windward* on our voyage to Franz Josef Land in 1896 were told by the late Captain Brown that we were that day eating the last of our beef from Norway and we had enjoyed it particularly when he told us that it was the first polar bear steak, recently killed by us, that we had eaten. Polar bear was always a favourite dish after that especially the psoas and iliacus muscles, or undercut.

Many of these polar animals are excellent, nutritious and health giving meat foods. All whalers have for centuries lived and worked hard and efficiently on them. Whale, bear, seal are all first rate meat-producing animals and walrus, though not so delicate in flavour and texture, is good meat and supports life admirably. These animals also have particularly dainty morsels which whalers and explorers luxuriate in. The heart of the polar bear stuffed with sage and onions is a king's dish, or newly cut out kidney of a seal, fried, especially if you can serve it with bacon is a piece de resistance. I say fried but imagine it from a silver grill instead of the galley or camp frying pan of an exploring or whaling expedition. There are many other animals – reindeer, moose, musk ox, hares with their excellently well flavoured and healthy meat products, all of the north.

No Arctic party of men has ever died of scurvy and such horrors, which has used these northern mammals as their main food supply, and all have carried through most strenuous and dangerous periods in exploration that have put their faith in the natural meat stuffs of the arctic. European whales are all as excellent.

So we may go from pole to pole, from Arctic to Antarctic and why not make use of the best meat provided by the enormous whales, approaching and exceeding 100 tons apiece.[6]

Never before or since has such an exotic and accurate description been made of the natural foodstuffs available to expeditions. Koettlitz, who became a close associate of Speirs Bruce, wholeheartedly endorsed these comments.

Despite the abundance of the life-giving food and the advice and instructions of Dr Koettlitz, Mr Moatt, known as old man Moatt, had died from scurvy. He had been in a state of almost continuous deterioration for a considerable time.

Whilst Mr Moatt suffered, the daily routine of the men on Cape Flora continued. Much of it was designed to assist and plan for the sledge journeys which were due to commence once the spring weather had returned and Franz Josef Land was once again a more hospitable location. At the forefront of Jackson's thinking was the objective of exploring and mapping the archipelago and finding a route to the North Pole.

Before any of these events Christmas and New Year were to be celebrated in some style. In this respect the expedition was no different from previous and later English-dominated polar expeditions, where good food, wine, port and champagne had to be consumed no matter what the temperature and conditions, even if the group were in a perilous position. While it can be argued that indulging in traditions is good for morale, there is nevertheless an unprofessional and amateurish streak to such behaviour, suggesting the English did not always fully appreciate the inherent danger of their circumstances. The contrast to the successful Norwegian and to a lesser extent Scottish polar expeditions could not be greater.

A quantity of reindeer meat brought from Russia had been kept frozen and, together with polar bear steaks, formed the bulk of the meat dishes. The Christmas meal commenced with real turtle soup. The main course of baked bear and reindeer venison pie was supported by tinned potatoes, green peas and French beans, with champagne and whisky to drink. After this came Christmas pudding, together with lemon and raspberry jellies, blancmanges, stewed plums and custard, followed by cheese, Brazil nuts, port wine and liqueurs.

It seems a fine feast was enjoyed by all, and Jackson, at times a surly, bad-tempered man, seemed relaxed. The usual loyal toasts were followed by songs and music accompanied by the musical box, with the celebrations going on until the early hours. New Year's Day was celebrated in a similar fashion, and a few suffered from aching heads after each occasion. Despite the scale of these celebrations, readings continued to be taken both inside and outside the hut.

Another cause for celebration was the fact that the winter seemed to be easing and the worst of the weather appeared to have passed, although the *Windward* stayed locked fast in the ice adjoining Cape Flora. They were all eagerly awaiting the return of the sun and a gradual return of daylight which would allow sledging to commence. At times the moon was bright enough to allow a game of football on the hard-packed snow. This had been tried earlier but the very low temperatures caused pain to the lungs and haemorrhaging amongst some of the men. Koettlitz stated, therefore, 'that no man cared to play up well'.[7]

Lessons were continually being learnt during this first winter living in these extreme polar conditions. Two whaleboats from the *Windward* had been brought ashore for use in an emergency by the shore-based team. These had been left close by the huts, and although they were sheltered the continual snow and ice had frozen them solid. They were covered by at least four feet of packed snow and ice. This was a prelude to identical circumstances that occurred during the National Antarctic Expedition led by Scott in 1901, when Scott ignored the advice of Armitage and Koettlitz and brought boats ashore.

The days continued to lengthen. The month of January produced huge amounts of snow requiring constant removal from the sides of the hut – at times up to ten feet deep – and winds of between force 8 and 10. The party enjoyed taking longer and longer walks, as the sky changed colour through tints of rose to orange and purple and became more brilliant to the south. At last, in February, these tints spread to the cliffs, the fine basalt and crevices encrusted with ice which Koettlitz described in great detail, continually wishing he was a better artist in order to be able to set down such a scene.

By 22 February, to the delight of all, the sun had returned. At first the days were short but day by day they lengthened and by the middle of April the midnight sun had returned to Franz Josef Land with perpetual daylight which would last until September. In October the sun would sink once again. And so the years passed by.

It was as well the sun and daylight hours had returned, because life within the hut had not been easy at times throughout the winter, with tempers flaring and the smallest issue becoming a major event. Close confinement in continual darkness tests the most pleasant and even-tempered of men. The continuing health problems on-board ship caused friction and disagreement between Jackson, Armitage and Koettlitz. At times, despite their obvious benefits, Jackson refused to allow Koettlitz to distribute vegetables to the ship, accusing the crew of being idle and lying in their bunks all day. But the main problems remained ashore.

Koettlitz wrote regularly about the bullying tactics of Jackson. On-going disputes arose over such peculiar issues as the location of London streets and boroughs. Particularly, for reasons not set down, Camden Town and Regent's Park.

On 9 January the following year Koettlitz wrote:

Slept badly last night as did three others. On rising, syringed J's ears [Jackson], did mending, no walk, after luncheon finished my ivory gull's skin and put it away. J in a nasty temper most of the day, at luncheon because of wanting to let off his spleen because of something A.B.A [Armitage] had said. He fixed on me and insulted me because I said I should be interested to see the black cap put on and sentence of death pronounced upon a criminal and also the sentence carried out. He spoke very strongly and nastily, strongly condemning such morbid fancies and having no patience with people who had them etc., etc. When J is in a bad humour he makes it so unpleasant for us that the place is little better than 'hell upon earth' and I always think I shall not stay another year here if things do not improve, or if anything wants me at home when we get news. We, I especially, are subject to continual daily insults.[7]

Whilst accepting that discussing the gallows is a strange subject for a doctor to be wishing to witness it is interesting to note that at such an early stage a senior member of the expedition was considering returning home with the relief ship. It also shows the strength of Koettlitz's character that he stayed for the full three years and achieved much in the way of geological research whilst fine-tuning the skills of an expedition surgeon.

Jackson's regular bouts of bad temper may have been caused by his continuing ill health. He suffered continually from piles (haemorrhoids), ear and throat infections, neuralgia and other ailments including frostbite, to which he seemed prone. Koettlitz was constantly providing treatments for these problems, all of which Jackson disputed, but they were obviously successful. He seemed to distrust the treatments Koettlitz advocated and was continually asking for quinine and other medicines which he then described as useless.

Koettlitz wrote: 'The fact is J knows everything medical including better than anyone else. I am of no account, he questions all mine, or any authority I quote. They are all "rot" an expressive term used by him. He is so superior in knowledge.'[7]

This tension among the party continued throughout the first winter period spent in the hut. All suffered from the leader's temper but the main victims were the dogs – he beat the dogs regularly and thought they were of no use unless they hunted bears. In fact, it seems not a day passed without some dispute between Jackson and his team members or among the other Cape Flora residents.

Dr Koettlitz was not immune to well-placed criticism. As mentioned earlier, he had been recommended to Alfred Harmsworth as surgeon and geologist by the editor of *The Lancet* and kept a meticulous journal throughout his time on Franz Josef Land, which he completed whilst on watch during the night-time periods or whilst flensing skins in one of the huts. Like the rest of the party, he was at odds with other members from time to time, but it does not seem to have struck him that he might occasionally have been genuinely at fault.

He was a serious-minded man and when a trick was played on him he rose to the bait, much to his annoyance. This attitude was a constant companion and he was to suffer similar problems during the *Discovery* expedition to the Antarctic years later. He was rather old for his years and could not bring himself to join in the jollity and fun of the other men – probably a result of his upbringing in a Lutheran family with a serious work ethic. He found younger men, in particular those from the officer class within the services, difficult to communicate with.

It was apparent that their environment and living in such close proximity was having a deleterious effect on the party, and sledging operations could not commence soon enough.

As part of his duties Koettlitz examined all the bears, other animals and birds which were caught by the party. He kept meticulous records of these creatures including their size, weight, stomach contents and many other details, no matter how small. He was later to write a paper on the polar bear. This was presented to the Royal Physical Society in Edinburgh in November 1898 by William Speirs Bruce.

The paper provides an accurate record of the number of polar bears shot by members of the expedition, the final total being 94 bears. The expedition also kept young polar bear cubs, taken when their mother was killed, as pets and objects of scientific study. Koettlitz admired their extraordinary tenacity for life, writing that they seem to suffer very little shock, even after being desperately wounded:

> The young cub shows similar tenacity of life. We kept three in the house in a warm atmosphere, with very little exercise, fed on sweet condensed milk, bear, walrus and other meat (cooked or raw), biscuit, in fact anything, and yet they throve. The youngest was once nearly dead with diarrhoea and in severe pain. A good dose of castor oil and chlorodyne soon put it right again.[8]

This behaviour and treatment of wild animals would be totally unacceptable today, but it shows the lengths to which expedition members of the period would go to increase their knowledge and enhance scientific understanding. Koettlitz understood the impact the killing of these creatures was having on the environment and food chain on the islands, but thought it possible the continual hunting of the bears was driving them from the area as opposed to decimating the overall population.

Koettlitz writes in detail of the effects of eating bear's liver. He was aware of the rumours that it had a peculiar effect on humans, but was sceptical on this point – so as an experiment a few of the team, including Koettlitz, tried it (an unwise activity considering it could have resulted in the expedition doctor being laid low or worse). They found that

> in about four or five hours after consumption a gradually increasing frontal headache, of a cumulative, congestive type, came on, which nothing would ease. Lying down makes the condition worse instead of better, one cannot sleep because of it and it gets worse for another six or eight hours, with occasional nausea and vomiting especially if a large quantity has been consumed. Altogether one is in a most miserable condition. Eventually, the symptoms gradually decrease in severity, until after twenty four hours relief is sufficient to allow sleep and eventual recovery.[9]

They discovered that eating bear's kidney occasionally caused the same symptoms but to a lesser degree. Koettlitz noted that ivory gulls and other birds also avoided the liver and kidneys, eating them only rarely, if food was scarce.

Detailed knowledge of the polar bear was gained from three years of study in their native environment. At the time it was one of the most comprehensive studies yet compiled. Koettlitz had plenty of specimens to examine as polar bears were being shot on a regular basis. As part of this research he bottled the bears' livers, and these were eventually returned to England for further examination.

The winter progressed in the same difficult manner for the residents on Cape Flora. During a period at the end of January the majority stated they would be returning home on the *Windward* when she was freed from the ice. The spring weather and the journeys inland could not come soon enough.

As a way of getting used to the climate on sledge journeys, Jackson would sometimes sleep outside on the roof of the hut. On 17 January Koettlitz, having risen at 0200 hours for his watch, found Mr Jackson going out to spend the night on the roof in his reindeer sleeping bag. Although the night was calm and fine the temperature was minus 29 degrees. At nine-thirty in the morning he was still there but had not had much sleep, having been kept awake by the dogs barking.

Those taking part in the anticipated sledge journeys had been busy during the winter months preparing and fine-tuning their clothing and equipment. The garments were made primarily from animal skins and fur, and based on the clothing worn by the Samoyed people and tested by Jackson on his previous journeys in northern Russia. Koettlitz had made face and nose masks to counter the effects of frostbite; these he considered most successful as the others seemed to suffer from frostbite on a regular basis while he did not. He had also made a most successful pair of elk skin boots with strong leather soles which proved both warmer and more durable than the finnesko-type footwear favoured by others. Another benefit of wearing this type of footwear was that it got rid of painful corns on his feet that he had developed walking the hard roads in the Butterknowle district of Durham whilst practising as the resident doctor in the area.

The team prepared fresh meat, mixed with herbs and mustard, for the forthcoming journeys, frozen in ration sizes for ease of use whilst camped. Bear meat was cut in four-pound lots, mixed with hot lard and when cooled placed in calico bags for transportation. At this time Koettlitz was also being tutored in navigation by Armitage and to a lesser extent Jackson, neither of whom were ideal teachers, but Koettlitz was persistent. In addition to their instruction he read every book that was available on the subject.

Even in this air of activity the disputes continued. On 9 February Jackson threatened to send the whole of the land party back to the ship and head for the pole on his own – on reflection not a sensible option, even for one as highly strung and physically strong as Jackson. However, despite the daily bickering and disagreements, as the end of February drew near the party commenced regular exercise in an effort to obtain a good level of fitness before the sledging season commenced.

The intense cold also appeared to bring on severe toothache with Jackson. Koettlitz was a competent dentist, having pulled teeth from crew members previously, and he now treated Jackson with morphine and replaced fillings in his tooth.

As part of the acclimatisation process they pitched their tents in the area of the hut to test their effectiveness in withstanding the wind chill and low temperatures. The wind often blew to a strength of force 10 and snow continued to fall in large quantities. It was essential to be able to erect the tent in such conditions.

During this continuing process of preparation Jackson and Armitage started using the Russian ponies in harness on short journeys to get them used to pulling light loads. They did the same with the dogs. Koettlitz and others had been working throughout the winter months on creating a suitable harness. By 1 March Koettlitz had created 18 sets of dog harness for the forthcoming journeys. All the party had widened their local explorative trips in the region of Cape Flora and their proficiency in using the ponies, dogs and ski was growing.

Preparations were gathering pace and the first depot-laying journey drew near; this was to include hay and oats for the ponies and foodstuffs for the expedition party. But the weather remained very cold and windy, with even Koettlitz being nipped by frostbite despite wearing his face mask at all times. It was planned that Jackson, Armitage and the Finn, Karl Blomkvist, would make the initial depot-laying journey. The sledges, together with the loads to be carried, were measured and weighed to obtain the correct balance. Throughout all this hectic activity Koettlitz continued to visit the ship daily to check on the health of the crew and monitor their diet and fresh food intake. It was whilst making some of the journeys to and from the ship that he suffered attacks of frostbite, but generally he and the rest of the land party remained fit and well.

Koettlitz seemed to be an able stitcher and creator of garments and other equipment for use on the sledge journeys. These included a set of snow shoes for the ponies to prevent them falling through soft snow, although early attempts did not prove a success. Amidst all the activity there were clear signs of the changing season; birds could be heard on a daily basis on the cliffs behind the house and around the ship. Polar bears were still being killed, but not on such a regular basis. Nevertheless they continually supplemented and enlarged the provisions available.

1. Skelton Diaries 10 March–30 April 1902 – sourced from Don Aldridge papers.
2. Koettlitz expedition journals retained in Koettlitz family archives.
3. Sir Clements Markham RGS – *Antarctic Obsession*, page 82.
4. Scurvy papers following Don Aldridge research – Koettlitz family archives.
5. Koettlitz expedition journals retained in Koettlitz family archives.
6. William Speirs Bruce archive – University of Edinburgh.
7. Koettlitz expedition journals retained in Koettlitz family archives.
8. Koettlitz expedition journals and paper submitted to the Royal Physical Society, Edinburgh.
9. Koettlitz expedition journals retained in Koettlitz family archives.

7

Spring sledging operations commence

O n Sunday 10 March 1895 the first sledge party, consisting of Mr Jackson, Mr Armitage and Mr Blomkvist, set out from Cape Flora. They were photographed on departure and Koettlitz called three cheers, to which the remainder of the party and crew members responded. The first sledge party was on its way to the north. It consisted of four sledges pulling about 450 lbs of provisions, with two sledges to each horse. The day was fine with good visibility. It was also 20 years to the day that Payer had commenced his own sledge journey on Franz Josef Land, heading north. The hut at Cape Flora seemed strangely peaceful with Koettlitz left in charge. The plan was to continue packing and planning for further sledge journeys whilst Jackson was away. This included the preparation and flagging of a large number of bamboo poles for marking the route and depots in difficult terrain.

It is evident that the planning, and to an extent the physical training for these sledge journeys, was thorough, carried out in a professional manner for a team with limited previous polar experience. They had read all the material that was available from previous expeditions and because of this, as well as the local knowledge gained from polar inhabitants in northern Russia, all were in confident mood to tackle the journey north.

During Jackson's absence Koettlitz had continued to visit the ship daily. It was during this period that Mr Moatt, who as mentioned ultimately died of scurvy, took a serious turn for the worse despite the best efforts and advice from the doctor.

On Saturday 16 March at around 5 p.m. the initial sledging party returned to Cape Flora. Their appearance indicated they had been through a rough time, and all three were suffering from various degrees of frostbite. Their main problem during the journey had not been the cold, ice or snow but incessant fog; this had forced them to stop for two days when visibility was reduced to almost zero. Because of this the depot had to be placed closer than intended, rather than pushing on to Cape Trieste. A sizable amount of hay, oats and human foodstuffs had been left, clearly marked by a cairn with flags atop.

The following day was spent discussing the journey and drying the furs and other clothing worn by the returning party. The day was interrupted by a fight between the dogs which resulted in one of the best dogs being killed by the rest of the pack, despite Koettlitz injecting a full syringe of whisky into the animal in an effort to stem his injuries. Jackson flew into a rage and thrashed every dog that had had a hand in the killing. Following this incident the dogs were given stronger ties and greater space put between them, but as all polar explorers know this type of dog is prone to fighting over the slightest issue.

By the 19th the sledge party had recovered strength and ski and pony trips to Bell Island and the vicinity of Cape Flora resumed. Jackson was planning the next sledge journey, which would involve the majority of the land-based party in three sledging teams. In the following days Jackson and Armitage made a number of journeys collecting polar bears that had been shot. On one of these journeys they covered a distance of 20 miles in one day with a pony and sledge – a significant achievement and one which showed their increasing skill in using the ponies and surviving in polar conditions.

As the weather improved and the snow began to clear from the rock faces in the area around Cape Flora, Koettlitz began to study and examine the rocks and the structure of the hills around them. On 23 March he wrote:

> At 12 o'clock went out with Fisher, Dunsford, Child and Burgess east to Shell Gully glacier, going up the rocks dividing Shell gully from Windy gully. These rocks are basalt but of fantastic shapes and look exactly like the rock which is quarried near Butterknowle and Middleton in Teesdale in Durham that is they fracture in very much the same way. In other places they are also in the typical columnar condition.[1]

Whilst there they also examined the possibilities of obtaining birds' eggs, both for consumption and for scientific purposes, as birds large and small seemed to be plentiful. At the same time as these geological and other scientific examinations were being carried out close to camp, preparations were continuing for the forthcoming sledge journeys to the north and to enlarge and chart the unknown areas of Franz Josef Land. This included fine-tuning the equipment to be used, pitching the tents and refining the clothing to suit each individual.

Jackson, despite his failings, was undoubtedly a good organiser and planned the trips with care and skill, certainly when compared with the sledge journeys of later Antarctic expeditions. During Scott's *Discovery* expedition the initial sledge journeys were carried out in an amateurish, 'suck and see' manner, ignoring and failing to draw upon the proven polar experience of some of the expedition members.

Koettlitz was to be used by Jackson to lead a forthcoming sledge journey. Jackson issued his sledging instructions in a very formal but concise document, which showed his experience of living and travelling in polar regions. This knowledge was passed down from the outset to Koettlitz and Armitage, both of whom were destined to become leading members of the *Discovery* expedition in 1901.

To illustrate this, it is worthwhile setting out Jackson's instructions in full, as given in Koettlitz's journal:

> On deciding where to camp, first thing to do is to look out for suitable hummock or pinnacle of ice to secure ponies to. Allow a length of 4 feet of halter rope so that it cannot get entangled in pony's hind feet.
>
> Ponies to be hobbled in addition to be secured by halter and the bell to be placed on each. Frost to be rubbed off backs of pony's by horse sheet before placing it upon each. They are then to be fed, 4lbs of oats and 3lbs of hay per day to each pony, the larger feeds to be given morning and evening.
>
> Dogs to be then secured to stake driven into snow at near distance to ponies and 1lb of meat to be given each of them per day.

Tent to be pitched within 10 yards of the animals, and entrance to be placed if possible facing ponies.

For pitching tent place plenty of snow upon snow cloth, beginning at corners so as to leave them fast and if blowing or inclined to blow, sledge to be drawn up to weather side and stays fixed to it.

All change foot gear as soon as convenient, damp socks to be removed (one pair to be worn) and placed in an inner pocket to dry. This can be done with Militzas on (underneath them). Avoid getting heated on march by taking coat off for a time if too warm, and placing it upon sledge, as, if underclothing gets damp one quickly gets chilly.

Rifle to be invariably taken into tent at night but never to be loaded until the point of being used, and after use at once unloaded.

In morning pimmies (long reindeer skin boots lined with fox or cat skin stockings and produced by the Samoyeds) and tobocks to be removed the first thing. Feed pony's at once.

In harnessing never take off hobbles till bridle is on and in unharnessing always put hobbles on before taking bridle off. Buckle hobble straps to prevent the straps getting adrift when off and then buckle them on sledge.

Before starting see that everything is tight and secure on sledge. Travel in reindeer skin finesko, with only a little hay in them.

In travelling, Heyward to walk behind my (Koettlitz's) sledge and Child behind Fisher's, both to see that nothing falls off and to direct course of sledge. In going down ice slopes always go down at right angles to the sledge.

Take care that bow of sledge does not run under ice pinnacles.

Never have tea at night but cocoa.

On no account burn all spirit out of lamp cooker. See that canteens are secure on sledge where it cannot be bruised or bent.

Keep spirit cases upright and protected from damage. Turn in at 11.30 p.m.[1]

These instructions covered in detail the essentials of survival: clothing, heating, food and the draught animals – all vital information to share when living and moving in a hostile environment with men who might be experiencing this situation for the first time. As mentioned, Jackson passed his experience and knowledge on to Koettlitz and Armitage in particular. It would transpire that this invaluable wisdom would be overlooked by later expedition leaders.

Preparations for the journeys continued, often interrupted by heavy snowfall and high winds but with the temperature continuing to rise. The weather created active movement within the ice surrounding the *Windward* and it was hoped the ship would soon be released. At the same time many birds, especially dovekies (little auks), continued to return to the islands, much to the delight of Jackson who took the opportunity to shoot many, both for the larder and to satisfy his lust for hunting. In addition, the party continued to gain in fitness by daily use of the ski and running the dogs in harness.

Between 9 and 11 April Jackson instructed Koettlitz to ready the sledges for commencement of the journeys north as soon as the weather was set fair. The rations for each man were substantial. They included, in addition to foodstuffs brought on the ship such as biscuits, tea, bacon, butter, soups, German sausage and cheese, a large quantity of fresh bear meat which had been slaughtered since their arrival on the archipelago. The lessons in the prevention of scurvy had been thoroughly absorbed by Koettlitz and the other land-based team members. Also included were sizable quantities of tobacco, an essential element on polar expeditions at the time, and another proven morale booster.

By Monday 15 April all letters home had been written by the men preparing to set off into the unknown regions of Franz Josef Land. The sledges were taken down to the ice floe in readiness for departure and all took their final baths before commencement. The following day produced a fine morning and all hands were present to cheer on the expedition members.

At 12 noon, after photographs had been taken, the team set off: Jackson with a pony pulling two sledges, Armitage again pulling two sledges, and between the two of them also carrying two sections of the aluminium boat. Koettlitz was third, pulling three sledges by pony, one of which carried a smaller Norwegian light boat. Finally came Blomkvist with a pony and two sledges, carrying the bulk of the hay and other food for the ponies. Supporting the pony drivers was Heyward, whom Koettlitz describes as 'very elated' as they were making their departure.

Despite initial problems with the ponies and two of the sledges carrying the boats, the first day's journey made nearly 20 miles, which was an outstanding achievement. After a somewhat undercooked meal the men followed Jackson's instructions as given earlier and slept well until around 5 a.m. when the dogs barking revealed a polar bear some 150 yards from the camp. The bear was promptly shot dead by Jackson, who seemed surprised to find a bear so far from open water. After a most satisfactory breakfast, the men butchered the bear and the party set off, making another 15 miles in the day's march – thought to be a record in polar travelling over a two-day period.

At each stop Koettlitz continued to make geological notes and examined the area around the camp. He was already asking in his mind – and setting down in his journal – questions concerning the origins of the rocks of the islands. They had reached the depot made by Jackson and Armitage a month previously, and discovered it had been damaged by polar bears – tins had been opened and other general vandalism caused. They were relieved to leave the boat that had been pulled by Koettlitz, which had been causing a number of sledge stability problems on the march.

The day's march on 18 April was only four miles, with most of the travelling uphill and at times in deep snow. The ponies often sank into the snow and suffered damage to their fetlocks but they managed to climb to a height of 1,300 feet, where camp was made. All enjoyed a very successful dinner of soup, bear, bacon and cocoa with roll and butter and the party slept well.

The following day, 19 April, delivered the most difficult travelling conditions so far, with treacherous snow conditions. There were crevasses on the glacier they were traversing: the ponies were spooked by these and by the tendency for them to open up due to their weight – a distinct disadvantage to the use of ponies rather than dogs for sledge hauling. It was around this time that Jackson and Armitage began to question the reliability of previous maps and bearings made by Leigh-Smith. It appeared that either Armitage's compass settings and readings were incorrect or the maps they were using were themselves faulty. Despite the difficult travelling conditions Koettlitz continued to make detailed geological notes that would later assist in his ageing of the basalt rocks in the region.

The party struggled with great difficulty down a glacier face, the ponies being under great stress and suffering damage to their legs in the process. The men were also suffering injuries due to constant falling during their efforts to control and lead the ponies through this dangerous area. Eventually they reached the glacier base and camped on the floe. The usual excellent dinner was prepared and all took a well-deserved rest. They had marked their route of descent with flags, as two sledges remained to be brought down after dinner. Jackson declared he had 'had enough of that damned infernal glacier from which we had got off cheap'.[1] But in truth it was due to their preparation and knowledge of the ponies and equipment that they had been able to traverse the glacier without serious mishap.

Koettlitz prepared mugs of hot cocoa; Jackson declared his 'the best cup of cocoa he had ever drunk in his life'[1] and added for good measure, 'Doctor, you are an angel'.[1] Praise indeed but it showed his mood swings.

Their sleep was disturbed by the arrival of a polar bear which Jackson, never one to miss an opportunity, shot at. The animal made off and the team continued with their well-earned rest. After rising, Koettlitz and one other returned to a previous depot along the floe to pick up hay and any other provisions that had not been ransacked by hungry polar bears. This involved a journey of approximately ten miles and was accomplished with two ponies without mishap. During this journey Koettlitz continued his study of the geology in the area and was beginning to form an opinion on the age of the rock strata which on his return to England was to place him at odds with current thinking on the subject.

In discussions with Jackson and Armitage on Koettlitz's return, all three were convinced that the map produced by Leigh-Smith had a number of inaccuracies and that they were currently on Hooker Island at a point greater than that achieved by the Leigh-Smith party.

Koettlitz was beginning to suffer from blisters to his feet, which he blamed on failure to wash all the soap from his socks. He also suffered severe cracking to his lips and fingers, which was eased somewhat by the regular use of Hazeline cream.

On Sunday 21 April they moved on a mile and placed another depot in a spot which would be more secure from polar bear attack. The Monday produced heavy snow showers and poor visibility, but this did not restrict their speed of travel. They stopped for a luncheon of cheese, biscuits and warming tea, and afterwards continued to press along Markham Sound until the stop for dinner. The day's travelling, in dismal conditions, still amounted to 16 miles, a good day's march under any circumstances.

Following dinner Koettlitz went to Jackson's tent for his instructions. Koettlitz and Heyward were to return to Cape Flora whilst Jackson pushed on with Armitage. Jackson's instructions included detailed orders regarding the work to be accomplished at Cape Flora. A letter was to be sent to Mr Harmsworth and letters from Armitage were to go to his family in England. Koettlitz mentions that back in his tent he had to give Heyward 'a good talking to for insubordination and impertinence'.[1] He was being very unhygienic in the tent in his personal habits. This demonstrates once again Koettlitz's impatience with others who did not reach his own high professional standards.

Extremely bad weather, with heavy snow, strong winds and low temperatures, delayed Koettlitz's departure for Cape Flora. This gave him time to reflect on travelling in the high Arctic, including the benefits and drawbacks of different clothing types. He admired the clothing produced by the Samoyeds – this generally kept them warm and windproof but after a long day's march it tended to make them sweat, and then froze if great care was not taken in changing clothing whilst in the tent.

All the team members lost at least one tooth on the sledge journeys as a result of biting on frozen biscuits. The importance of removing all facial hair prior to departure was explained:

frost froze on beards and moustaches and prevented the opening of the mouth for food or drink. As facial hair grew on the march it was necessary to dip the beard or moustache around the mouth into the soup or hot drink in order to thaw the whiskers to allow the mouth to open. This became a ritual before all meals and doing it without spilling any of the precious hot liquid took a while to master.

Koettlitz explained in detail the difficulty of preparing food in such low temperatures, with most items having to be chopped by hatchet prior to cooking. This highlighted the importance of carrying sufficient cooking oil, without which preparing hot food would be an impossibility, leading to inevitable death.

The importance of possessing adequate quantities of cooking oil when travelling in polar regions, or access to blubber from wild animals in emergencies, cannot be emphasised enough. It is imperative to be able to quench 'Arctic thirst', caused by loss of body liquids due to extreme sweating during the exertion of the march. Koettlitz describes these issues of polar marches and their resolutions, in detail– once again, knowledge that was often ignored or overlooked in subsequent expeditions to the Antarctic.

By Thursday 25 April the weather abated allowing Dr Koettlitz and Heyward to commence their return journey to Cape Flora, leaving Jackson and his companions to push on to the north. They set out at 4 p.m.; sledging operations were normally carried out during the polar night which provided better conditions for both ponies and men, with sleep being taken in what is ordinarily considered the daylight hours. The two men made good progress through deep snow and awkward conditions and pitched camp at 4.30 a.m., a good day's march under such conditions.

At 12 noon on Friday 26 April they rose to a calm but slightly misty day, with a temperature of minus 8 degrees. They set off at 2 p.m. and made good progress, picking up their outward tracks between Eaton and Hooker Islands and eventually locating the previously laid depot, where they halted for lunch for one hour. Having collected various items including spare ski they covered a good distance further, then set up camp at about 12.30 a.m. and prepared dinner, which consisted of lentil soup, bear mince and bacon, cocoa, roll and butter. Both men turned in at 4.30 a.m., with the temperature reading minus 17 degrees.

Bad weather again delayed their push for the warmth and safety of Elmwood but by 9 p.m. Koettlitz and Heyward were underway, moving slowly through considerable snow drifts. There were strong winds and visibility was poor. The ponies found it hard going and at times floundered up to their bellies in the snow; often they had to be unharnessed in order to remove them from the deep snow or when they had broken the ice surface and fallen into water. This was hugely tiring and by 6 a.m. they had set up camp. They had great difficulty getting the tent up in an increasingly fierce wind which eventually rose to gale force. The men were very grateful for the practice they'd had in pitching the tent in such conditions.

Although the gale was still blowing when they rose at 7 p.m. Koettlitz was determined to push on to Cape Flora. Despite very strong winds and foggy conditions Koettlitz advanced by compass bearing and eventually made out the faint lines of a plateau which they believed to be Camp Point and safety. They moved on through knee-deep snow with much difficulty but by 2 a.m. had arrived at Camp Point, where they stopped for hot tea and cheese and biscuits. Somewhat rejuvenated by the hot drink and with the weather clearing Koettlitz pressed on, eventually making out Windward Island and the western end of Cape Flora. After another short stop for refreshment they arrived at Elmwood at about 1 p.m., after 15 hours on the march. Although both men and ponies were tired, the successful completion of such distances under difficult conditions demonstrated their level of fitness, expertise and resilience together with the nutritional value of their supplies. They had been spotted by the crew at Elmwood, who came out to cheer them in and assist them on the final slopes to camp.

The following 48 hours were spent resting, drying clothes and recovering from the journey, much fortified by a glass or two of whisky and substantial meals. By Tuesday Dr Koettlitz was resuming his duties as expedition surgeon and checking on the health of both the ship's crew and the shore party. There was also another sledge journey to plan and prepare: setting out for Hooker Island as soon as possible. The same procedures were put in place with regard to the equipment, clothing, supplies and animals, and by Saturday 4 May the party was ready to set out.

Many substantial sledge journeys covering great distances were made by Koettlitz and other members of the Jackson-Harmsworth Expedition. I do not intend to cover these in the same detail as this first journey made by Koettlitz. I have described this in some detail to show the professional planning that went into these trips and the manner in which they were accomplished without serious mishap or any sign of scurvy or associated illnesses.

Koettlitz wrote after a number of sledge journeys had been completed by Jackson and the other expedition members:

> The results of the sledge journeys were on the whole very startling, for they transformed the land, which had now for over twenty years been thought a continent – and it had been believed because of the reports brought home by Julius Payer – into a broken mass of small islands, it specially startled us also, because it gave us the first inkling of what we later found to be the case, namely, of the impossibility of our making Franz Josef Land – because of these changed conditions – the base from which a journey could be made, with any hope of success, with the object of getting to the pole.[1]

In short, Franz Josef Land did not provide a land bridge to the North Pole which at the time of setting out was the prize most wanted by Frederick Jackson and would have sealed his place in polar history.

In the following two weeks Koettlitz led two more sledge journeys under fairly extreme weather conditions. The first used a pony as the means of hauling and the second trip was by means of dog power. Koettlitz describes clearly the benefit of utilising dogs as the preferred means of sledge hauling, particularly in poor weather conditions and when the snow and ice underfoot are slushy with a tendency to give way. The ponies continually fell through the snow and ice surface into the water below, at times up to their bellies. The dogs moved across the surface under similar conditions with ease and at a greater speed. Despite little previous experience in driving dogs Koettlitz soon mastered the technique and made a successful journey to Camp Point to recover geological specimens and other equipment. He recorded the great benefit of being able to ride upon the sledge when conditions allowed whilst Child his partner led on ski when required. He even found time to record the welcome they received at Camp Point from a group of snow buntings with their 'sweet little voices', singing from a nearby hummock. It was a song similar to a robin or lark at home and for a short moment there were thoughts of England and family in Dover.

Koettlitz found Child, the botanist, a far more knowledgeable and agreeable travelling companion than Heyward. He regarded Heyward as lazy and insubordinate, and felt he needed constant supervision in his work and correcting of his attitude and manners. At times Koettlitz would cuff Heyward around the ears for being rude or insubordinate, not only to Koettlitz but also to others in the group.

This reflects clearly the purposeful and serious side of Koettlitz's whole demeanour on this and the other expeditions of which he was a member. Some might see this as a sign of insecurity or even weakness as a human being. But Koettlitz set a certain professional standard which he expected others to reach – both leaders and other colleagues of his polar and African adventures – and unfortunately this was not always possible. As will be seen, this attitude did not sit well with others on the subsequent *Discovery* expedition to the south.

Both Child and Koettlitz found time whilst at Camp Point to carry out geological and botanical examinations of the area. By Saturday 25 May, examinations complete, they loaded the sledge and set out for Elmwood. Despite difficulties with unstable ice the return journey was achieved in good time and they reached Cape Flora by 12 noon on the Sunday. After a good meal and some rest, by late afternoon Dr Koettlitz was on the *Windward* carrying out examinations of the crew, a fine example of his commitment to his profession and the welfare of the men on board. They expected and hoped the ship would break free from the ice at any time and all those who were remaining on the islands were busily engaged writing letters home and packing specimens to be taken on board for carriage to England. The snow buntings around Cape Flora were in full song, which reminded Koettlitz again of the song of the robin, lark and yellow hammer at home. He thought them the most pretty of song birds. In fact, the area of rocks and cliffs surrounding Cape Flora was alive with thousands of different species of bird.

Although the weather remained changeable, during the clear periods Jackson continued to hunt on a large scale. He hunted not only for polar bears and many birds which added to the larder, but also for species and specimens for examination and return to England. Jackson seemed happy when hunting and when writing his letters to send with the *Windward*. However, he continued to make verbal attacks on other members of the group, including Koettlitz. One of these centred on a prolonged debate as to the correct pronunciation and spelling of 'coup-de-grace'. It is remarkable that such trivia had the ability to undermine the expedition at crucial moments. Such behaviour led Koettlitz to describe Jackson as bad tempered, erratic, self-opinionated, overbearing and selfish. Often Koettlitz would walk away when Jackson was looking for a companion for an evening walk.

As June progressed the weather continued to improve, and the thaw was evident on the ponds and ice around Cape Flora. Koettlitz continued to make his daily visits to the ship to check on the health of the crew and Mr Moatt in particular, but on Monday 17 June 1895 he found Moatt dead in his bunk. To the last he had refused to take Koettlitz's advice about diet to combat his scurvy and finally the disease beat him. As mentioned earlier he was buried on the hill behind Elmwood at Cape Flora the following day. Dr Koettlitz read the funeral service, which was attended by nearly all hands and the shore party. They managed to dig three feet into the semi-frozen soil; Koettlitz mentioned that Moatt's body would freeze solid and be preserved for perhaps hundreds of years.

Jackson was getting noticeably agitated with the delay in the ship breaking free from the ice and as a result all suffered from his often abusive tongue. But he continued shooting anything that moved within his gun sights, including four arctic terns which were dispatched purely for practice.

By the end of June the ice was moving with the swell and blasting with explosive around the ship was also beginning to have an effect. The wrist of a crewman was broken when a section of driftwood used in the blasting process flew through the air at great speed, striking him on the forearm.

Koettlitz was about to set off for a stay at Cape Gertrude to carry out geological examinations in the area and on 1 July he visited the *Windward* for the last time, expecting her to be gone by the time of his return. He left for Cape Gertrude with Child and Fisher, making a dedicated scientific group, at 11.50 p.m. Using Indian snow shoes they made good progress, despite the risk of falling through the ice and snow into the water below. Arriving in time for dinner at 6.30 a.m. they pitched camp and slept until around 2 p.m. Around Cape Gertrude was much driftwood and six whale skeletons and Fisher quickly found a new plant for this latitude, *Saxifraga stellaris*, which he described as a 'surprise packet'.[1]

Cape Gertrude was within sight of Cape Flora and they noticed during a clear spell that the ship had steam up. On Wednesday 3 July when the weather cleared they saw the *Windward* had broken free from its ice trap and departed.

During the following days Koettlitz spent much time examining the sand, shale and sandstone strata around Cape Gertrude; this was after all the main objective of the visit. After the intensive physical activity Koettlitz took a bath in one of the pools which had formed as a result of melting snow and ice. As part of his continuing scientific research he even made a note of the water and air temperatures, 37 degrees Fahrenheit for the water, and 45 degrees for the air. Cold-water baths were a common practice in the Koettlitz family, a practice fine-tuned in the snows and ice-pools of Franz Josef Land and continued until the death of Dr Maurice Koettlitz in 1960.

For several days Koettlitz and his assistants continued to 'geologise' and 'botanise' on and around Cape Gertrude. One particular scene caught his attention which he instructed Child to photograph. Near their camp was a large boulder measuring about 10 × 10 × 7 feet in total, 15 feet above sea level, and with five large boulders on top of it together with seven smaller ones. He estimated that the largest would weigh in excess of one ton. Koettlitz assessed that these huge boulders had been deposited by movement of ice when the beach was under the sea, being dropped into their present positions when the ice melted, remarking: 'Another proof if more were needed as to these being raised beaches.'[1] In addition, the party continued to collect specimens for later examination. After a week it was time to return to Cape Flora, with the sledges laden with rock and other specimens. Koettlitz's views on the formation and age of Franz Josef Land were further developing.

---

1. Koettlitz expedition journals retained in Koettlitz family archives.

8

Russian roulette and heading west

The day after returning from Cape Gertrude, Monday 8 July 1895, Koettlitz describes another example of Jackson's extraordinary behaviour possibly brought about by boredom and his continuing bad health. During dinner, Jackson jokingly asked Koettlitz, if he was 20 paces away, how many shots with a rocket pistol would it take before he succumbed? Apparently he had been taking pot shots at the chained dogs in recent days, much to their distress. Koettlitz, thinking he was joking, said a dozen. So, after dinner Jackson called Koettlitz out and instructed him to stand against a rock. He looked around to see if the others had followed him to witness the fun; all but Fisher had stayed in the hut. Koettlitz was still thinking this was some kind of prank until Jackson fired at him from a distance of 35 paces. Koettlitz moved back, attempting to dodge the shots as best as he could, thinking this was the most dangerous kind of fun that Jackson could initiate. One shot grazed the side of his hip, scorching his trousers. The other members never came out to witness the 'fun', deciding these actions simply confirmed Jackson as mad. Despite this behaviour, planning continued for the next trip that was to set out from Cape Flora.

This next major journey was to be undertaken in the whale boat *Mary Harmsworth*, named after the wife of the expedition sponsor, and it nearly led to the death of the expedition leaders. Many days were spent in final preparation, while Jackson continued to fire the rocket pistol at the dogs to appease his thirst for amusement, on one occasion setting a dog on fire. A very strange form of fun.

On Wednesday 10 July the boat was taken down to the shore and launched and the stores and equipment required for the journey were loaded. By the following day the boat was fully laden and with a crew composed of Jackson, Armitage, Burgess, Fisher, Blomkvist and Child, was ready for departure. Koettlitz, left in charge of the expedition base with Heyward to assist him, cheered them off. They soon lost sight of the *Mary Harmsworth* with the canvas boat in tow. The boat was eventually spotted through the telescope from the top of the hut roof the following day when it had reached Bell Island.

Koettlitz's relief from being used for target practice was not to last long. On Monday 15 July Heyward thought he could see the whaleboat approaching from the direction of Bell Island, sailing at some speed. Within the hour it had come alongside the floe ice at Cape Flora. It transpired that Burgess had been involved in a very heated argument with Jackson over the shooting of a polar bear. Jackson threatened to dismiss him whereupon Burgess resigned and had been sent back to Cape Flora pending his return to England which would be some months later. Jackson instructed Dr Koettlitz to join the sailing expedition in Burgess's place. Needless to say Koettlitz leapt at the opportunity for further exploration, thereby taking part in a journey that was to discover and map unknown areas of Franz Josef Land.

The following day the boat with Koettlitz on board set off to re-join Jackson and his team who were waiting for them near Cape Grant. When they arrived Koettlitz wasted no time in carrying out geological studies in the area surrounding the camp. The others added to the growing larder by shooting a number of seabirds and a polar bear. Roped together with Fisher, Koettlitz climbed the extensive glacier rising from Cape Grant, with no large crevasses being encountered. Koettlitz was delighted with his geologising but was somewhat surprised on their return to find that Jackson wanted to head for Cape Crowther without delay. The *Mary Harmsworth* was made ready and after a journey undertaken in a heavy swell they landed at 3 a.m. on the northern shore of the Cape. When he arose at around 1 p.m. Koettlitz immediately set about examining the slopes around the area. He made extensive notes and sketches of the geological formation of Cape Crowther, being impressed by the massive basaltic columns rising to 50 feet in height which in places formed a sea wall for the raised beach on which they camped.

On Monday 22 July, they made ready to leave for Cape Neale and at 6 p.m. pushed off and headed out once more into the wilds of the Arctic sea. Koettlitz was moved by the wonderful sight of Cape Crowther as they pulled away and described it in detail:

> Cape Crowther is a splendid extended headland with rocks more or less columnar looking in many places to all the world like Norman architecture, buttress columns, notches looking like saints where complete pedestals abound![1]

With the exception of one hour's sailing they rowed all the way to Cape Neale, arriving at around midnight. After they had pitched camp and had dinner, Jackson called everyone to his tent where he proposed a toast to Dr Neale of the *Eira* expedition which they drank in port wine, followed by cigars all round. It was pointed out that Koettlitz had been the first to jump ashore at Cape Neale, previously uncharted territory; this was felt appropriate as they both came from the same profession. The following day Koettlitz continued to examine the geology of the Cape whilst others killed birds and other animals, both for food and for return to England as specimens for further study.

Fisher located many plants rare to both Franz Josef Land and other polar regions. The area was viewed as being rich in botanical and geological observations. Whilst out with Koettlitz, Jackson spoke of the joys of the explorer, 'that it exceeded that of any other'.[1] He added that the next discovered land would not be other people's land but Jackson's land. Koettlitz agreed without hesitation, thinking that it certainly is exhilarating to feel oneself to be the first to set foot on a new land as he had at Cape Neale. During this stroll Koettlitz collected beautiful flints, quartz and other rock specimens as well as flowers and plants for return to the botanist Fisher. It was a day with a wonderful parhelion, or mock sun, caused by the mist that hung in the area, which lasted for many hours. At times it waxed brightly then waned with parts looking prismatic. Koettlitz was drawn to sketch such a grand sight.

On Wednesday 24 July, Armitage, Child and Blomkvist returned to Cape Grant to collect further supplies as Jackson intended to push on as far as possible on account of the open water available. Koettlitz, with Jackson and Fisher, decided to ascend the summit of Cape Neale for further geological and botanical research. This resulted in what Koettlitz described as a 'day of discovery'.[1] As they climbed, the mist lifted, allowing clear views between Cape Neale and Cape Ludlow. Even Cape Lofley could be seen by the naked eye, and the shoreline by use of the telescope.

As the weather continued to clear beyond Cape Lofley they could see two rocky headlands. Leigh-Smith had seen no further than Cape Lofley. Therefore they were looking at new land, with a high glacier dome clearly visible through the telescope. All three were excited by this new discovery and it reinforced Jackson's determination to push on. They built a cairn with a 'Jack' (Union Flag) upon it and placed a record of their discovery. Koettlitz also discovered many fine flints and bones and a very weathered seal skull on top of the Cape, which indicated to him a much raised sea level at a not very distant geological date. Otherwise how could they have got there? They were the first humans to their knowledge to have stood on this spot. All returned to their camp at the base of the Cape, with Jackson so buoyed by their discovery that he assisted with preparation of dinner.

On Saturday 27 July the *Mary Harmsworth*, heavily laden, returned from Cape Grant. It took all hands to haul the boat up the shore. Armitage and his companions, after a substantial meal, turned in to catch up on much-needed sleep following their journey. In the meantime Koettlitz retraced his steps to the summit of Cape Neale to continue his examination of the terrain. Whilst there he found rounded pieces of petrified wood as if worn by water, together with further seal bones and stones rounded by the action of ice and water. He was convinced that at some time in the past this area had been at or below sea level. There was no other 'locomotive agency' that could have placed these bones, wood and rounded stones at this location.

---

1.   Koettlitz expedition journals retained in Koettlitz family archives.

9

Death nears the Mary Harmsworth

The following day Koettlitz recorded his mother's birthday in his diary before the *Mary Harmsworth* was made ready to push on northwards into the unexplored regions of Franz Josef Land.

Although the glass was falling and the wind rising they made good progress, soon passing Cape Ludlow. They were heading for Cape Lofley when the weather worsened, with a rising swell. The intention had been to pitch camp on new land past Cape Lofley but the changing conditions made this impossible. The wind had risen to gale force and the prospects of finding a landing place looked bleak. To the relief of all, Armitage took over the tiller from Jackson. He turned the boat and they decided to run with the wind and attempt a landing back at Cape Neale or Crowther. However, the swell was so great this proved impossible and the boat was in danger of taking in too much water.

Fisher wrote at this point: 'The gale caught us up all too soon and compelled us to hove too. We then had a fearful time in snow, hail, rain, and wind with tremendous breakers.'[1] This was a prelude to a terrifying three days which could have led to the deaths of all aboard the *Mary Harmsworth*. It was only the seamanship of Armitage and the fitness and fortitude of the others that saved them.

To keep the whaleboat afloat continual baling was required. They all took turns at this, apart from Armitage whose skill was required to steer and manage the boat. They lashed two oars to the ice anchor in an effort to stabilise and control the craft but, after some 24 hours of the men struggling with them, these were swept away by a large lump of floating ice. They then lost the deep sea anchor and the boat was in extreme danger of being swamped as their attempts to bail it out were being overwhelmed.

The tremendous seas soaked their militza outer garments and underclothing, the freezing, water-logged materials weighing heavily on the exhausted crew. Their reindeer boots and stockings were so drenched they slipped off their legs into the water in which the men sat up to their knees whilst baling for their lives. Koettlitz was sure they would never reach land again and that they were destined to perish at sea. He was plagued by continual seasickness which soiled his already drenched clothing. By the third day they were completely exhausted by the continual efforts to survive and to keep the sea at bay. They had only eaten a small amount of biscuit, cheese and a nip of port although Jackson and Child had eaten a raw bird each on a break from bailing duties.

They had not seen land for over two days when the wind began to moderate and they spotted through the mist either Cape Grant or Crowther, which Armitage calculated as about

40 miles distant. Armitage decided to risk putting up limited sail and the *Mary Harmsworth* leapt into action and sped through the water towards the distant shoreline. After about four hours of speedy sailing, continual baling and great tension the boat grounded back on the shore of Cape Grant from where they had set out several days earlier. The relieved men fell out of the boat into the freezing water, unable to stand due to the weight of their clothing and utter exhaustion. So weakened were they by their experience they were unable to pull the boat up the beach until she was fully unloaded. After this had been done it was port wine all round, which had been such a life saver during those dreadful three days at the mercy of the sea.

They managed to get the tents up and prepare a meal from the sodden provisions, eaten mainly cold. It was essential to get their clothing dry before the effects of the freezing wet weather took their toll. Armitage appeared to be suffering the most. His efforts to keep everyone alive and the boat seaworthy had taken him to a point of utter exhaustion and fainting. He looked very sick, but improved after the others managed to get some clothing dry for him; they hung the clothes in the strong wind whilst Armitage remained inside the tent with the little warmth it provided.

With the use of a winch they managed to haul the boat further up the beach, where they toasted their survival, in port, to:

> The *Mary Harmsworth*, the boat and the lady whose name she bears coupled with that of Mr Armitage whose seamanship alone had pulled them through.[2]

The navigation, seamanship skill and knowledge of Armitage had saved them all. It was this incident more than any other that led Alfred Harmsworth to insist that Armitage be a leading member of the *Discovery* Antarctic expedition led by Commander R. F. Scott in 1901–1904.

With their lives spared they attempted to get some sleep in the wet and foul-smelling clothes in which they had survived this horrendous sea journey.

The wretched weather continued, with rain, hail and wind. They were unable to properly dry their clothes and had to move the camp further from the shore due to the huge seas still pounding the beach. In addition to the difficulties suffered by the human cargo on the *Mary Harmsworth*, one of the dogs, Nimrod, was now in a sorry state. He had not eaten for the entire journey and was now terrified of going near the sea. In addition there were seven live glaucous gulls, which were being taken to Cape Flora for further scientific examination. They were kept in a box, the lid of which was held down by a large boulder used for ballast. Not surprisingly they were found dead on arrival at Cape Grant. Two other gulls had been eaten raw by Jackson and Child during the journey.

In the days that followed they continued to dry the clothing and regain their strength for the next leg of the journey to Cape Flora, where they looked forward to the relative luxury compared with their recent experiences. Koettlitz made the most of the opportunity to carry out further geological research of the area, in particular of an adjacent glacier and ice pebbles which were strewn in huge numbers on the shoreline following contact with ice and sea water. In true Koettlitz fashion, no time must be wasted.

On Monday 5 August, as their strength recovered, Jackson called Dr Koettlitz to his tent for luncheon. Jackson often slept and ate alone, not an uncommon practice amongst English expedition leaders of the time.

Jackson was concerned and asked if they were all eating scurvy grass, which was common on the islands, and then directed most emphatically that Koettlitz saw to it that it was eaten every day, together with fresh meat. Koettlitz recorded:

> Of course I have known, so has Fisher, the importance of eating the vegetable food obtainable and have neglected no opportunity of partaking thereof, so also the fresh meat. What however strikes us all is the sudden conversion of Mr Jackson to the value of vegetables, especially such a humble one as this, for until recently he pooh-poohed their importance, saying that fresh meat was all that was necessary. The scurvy on board the ship (*Windward*) has however to my mind opened his eyes to the fact that scurvy is not such a simple disease as he has always held it to be. That is, that its causes are far more intricate than he at first supposed.[3]

Although not known at the time, scurvy grass contains high levels of vitamin C in its leaves, so Jackson and Koettlitz's insistence on its consumption was appropriate. It was an ideal supplement to the fresh meat diet already being followed by the expedition members.

These comments highlight two interesting points: firstly, that Jackson took no part in the preparation of the food he ate every day, and secondly that Koettlitz was an expert in the field of preventing scurvy on polar explorations. He understood the food they ate should be fresh meat and vegetables when available. Of crucial importance was the freshness of the food – one must live off the land not from tins or other preserved foodstuffs.

This is not to say tinned or preserved supplies were not used to supplement fresh food. Koettlitz was well aware of this on the National Antarctic Expedition with Scott on the *Discovery*. It displays clearly how his expertise was disregarded on that expedition, risking danger for the sledging parties. The errors made on the second Scott-led expedition to the Antarctic mirrored those made on the previous *Discovery* expedition, when the views of experienced polar explorers were ignored. This particularly applies to the prevention of scurvy on polar expeditions, in which Koettlitz was the expert.

By Tuesday 6 August, despite their recent near-death experience, they were ready to launch the *Mary Harmsworth* and continue the journey, with Jackson keen to explore further and reach the amended objective of Cape Stephen.

Whilst en-route a large section broke off from a glacier, creating a huge swell that threatened their boat despite the fact they were sailing over one mile offshore. At first they were unable to land at Cape Stephen so landed instead at Potentilla Rock, named after the first potentilla found by Fisher on the archipelago. Koettlitz was excited by the rock formations here and discovered lignite in thin layers near the beach. The records he kept throughout the expedition were meticulous, containing sketches, maps and detailed descriptions made at regular intervals. They include a record of Koettlitz finding a spider in his tent similar to the English house spider, which was collected in a jar for later research.

The boat required repair following damage caused by continual hauling over rock-strewn beaches. This completed, on Thursday they continued sailing for Cape Stephen, which was reached without further incident. Cape Stephen proved rich in both plant and bird life and the raised sandstone beaches created further excitement for Koettlitz who spent as much time as possible geologising. They erected cairns at the top of the Cape and on the highest raised beach. After two days of research at Cape Stephen they again set sail, heading for Eira Harbour, although they were hampered by floating ice lumps. By 4.30 a.m. they had landed and pitched camp, prepared dinner and turned in.

On rising at around 4 p.m. on Sunday 11 August, they spotted ducks and seabirds in nearby pools. Jackson and Armitage bagged a number of red-throated divers and arctic terns, which meant further skinning duties for Koettlitz whose skills as a surgeon made him the most accomplished member of the expedition at such activities. Koettlitz visited Eira House, the hut built by Leigh-Smith and his crew whilst stranded on these islands. The timber was in perfect condition, as though just erected. There was much-needed coal outside and Koettlitz removed one lump as a memento of his visit. The interior, also in perfect condition, had portraits of Leigh-Smith and Neale on the walls, as well as food and beer containers and a record of their stay in 1892.

Once Jackson and Armitage had returned from a short visit to Mabel Island, the party once again boarded the *Mary Harmsworth*, with Leigh-Smith's small boat in tow containing Nimrod, the dog that gave warning of approaching bears, as its sole occupant. With a combination of sail and rowing they reached Cape Flora at 7.30 a.m. on Tuesday 13 August – and not a moment too soon. The sea off Cape Flora was full of icebergs and beginning to ice up in places. It took all of Armitage's skill to ease them to the shore, where the boat was beached for the final time. To celebrate their safe return, Jackson proposed once again a toast in port wine, 'to the *Mary Harmsworth* and the lady whose name she bears',[4] which Armitage followed with a the toast, 'peace to her bones',[5] presumably referring to Lady Harmsworth. Armitage thought the boat was 'done' and would not be fit for further exploration. During the journey all had lost weight, Koettlitz only 4 lbs but Child a debilitating 15 lbs.

Koettlitz took great pleasure in removing his clothes, which had not been taken off for over a month, taking a cold bath and sleeping undressed. The following days were spent preparing and labelling the birds and other specimens brought back from the journey. These included buntings, glaucous gulls, ivory gulls, kittiwakes, arctic terns, eider ducks, brent geese, red-throated divers, loons, dovekies (auks) and skuas.

In the meantime, Jackson decided the winter larder needed replenishing and spent the next four hours shooting. He killed 148 loons, meaning there would be no shortage of fresh meat in the coming winter. In total over 1,000 loons were shot for the larder and hung around the outside of the house roof where they froze. These provided an alternative to bear meat and one generally considered much tastier fare. Koettlitz also started collecting the scurvy grass that grew in great quantities in the area to freeze for use in the winter. This would act as a fresh vegetable to supplement the fresh meat they ate in large amounts.

The rest of August was spent increasing the larder and flensing the skins of polar bears and walrus. It was agreed by the land party that sightings of bears and walrus would not be reported to Jackson in future because of his enthusiasm to hunt and kill these animals. Each time he did, it resulted in a mass of work for the rest of the expedition members – flensing the skins, cleaning walrus heads and other filthy, unpleasant jobs associated with preserving these creatures. This particularly affected Dr Koettlitz who, when applying for the post of expedition surgeon, had expressed a willingness to help with zoological examination, and as a result was given the bulk of the work in this field. This led to his geological work having to be neglected, much to his annoyance.

to keep her too close to wind to do any good, after a long pull
Bell island was sighted & pulled for. seemed however never
getting nearer we were making for the spit upon which
Leigh Smith's house is situated, (by the way last march
when J. & A. eledged there they did not see any trace of
the house so that the news will be carried home that
it has been blown down, now however that the snow is
gone it has been found,) by mistaking the position
Mr J. made the journey much longer, no doubt the place
is a puzzling one to find especially when the light is
bad, & weather misty at last the position was made
but ice face was found all round the point preventing
our landing so we pulled round into Eira harbour
where at last a small portion of beach was found
free of ice (floe had been here when the boat party
last visited the island which was before B's own?
resignation, & before I joined the boating party)
(? the action of floe ice in formation of raised beaches)
Arrived at 4.30 am, unloaded, got camps up, upon
boulder strewn beach, many having to be removed, dinner
& turned in by 7 am.
Sunday 11th Aug: 1895

Up at 4 pm. misty and saw ? casting after breakfast
as geese or ducks were thought to be swimming about in
pools not far away, J. and A. took guns & went to
shoot them, J. shot the two which turned out to be Divers
? Red throated diver., in skinning them noticed the
extraordinary projection upwards upon femur of the
tuberosity of the tibia causing very limited movement
at knee joint, patella would be incorporated in this
development, had to help carry a section of
canvas boat up to pond to get one of the birds
which was in the water a. had in mean while
shot an arctic tern –
Then went up to Eira house, which looked as tho' just
erected, timber like new,
coal outside, chips
of wood, shing tik
lying about, for nails
of Neale & Smith, & the
inside, program of dance &
of Eira's crew there,
empty Bass bottles, &
inside, as well as the containing ? letter, & record of L Smith
which was sent here when he left C. Flora in 1882. Last

Koettlitz journal pages showing a drawing of Eira House and its location

away, a piece of coal & much chalk found lying outside.
Very little weathered, also piece of st'n ... & ... potchai
small ... boat left there & which C. who told
to make certain "repairs on" to take with ... to ...
B.C. & I while J. A. ... & F. were away at Mabel Island
carried it across spit to where we were camped.
Before lunch I left Eira house & went for a walk
by myself to try and get to the main rocks 2 or 3 miles
away, all this part being long stretches of
raised beaches, & in walking in that direction
found that I must have got on grounded floe
much covered in part with heaps of sand and
stones, with cracks full of water in every
direction, I at last got into a labyrinth of cracks
impassable & the wind getting very cold, & blowing
strongly, while my feet got sore thro' walking in
the nearly worn out sea boots which had nails
sticking thro' I turned back not however without
a most instructive lesson in how a grounded floe
may play an important part in helping to form
a raised beach, & associating perhaps for the ice
many feet thick, formed in layers under a
mass of stones, & soil, of which one of the best
examples I have seen is at wild gully
meiris channel end in a land slip there, and
in other places, such as under the higher beach of
C. Stephen —

noticed here as I had also before
at meiris channel end of
windy gully small plants
of poppy growing among
the rounded boulders of
the raised beach, and cannot
under the circumstances
conceive as to how these plants
could get here unless by seed,
this F. maintains is not the case
but that they spread by the roots
how they could to these situations
and in such isolated plants
in that way I cannot understand
therefore I am inclined to think though
it has not been proved possible
that yet on animal particle seeds
are now another produced which originate these plants situated under these
peculiar conditions —

Instead of going to Mabel island to which excursion I was invited at
its suggestion (most kindly) & which I declined owing to the cold wind
footsoil now, & the fact that I thought they were going to cross Eira harbour

Sketch of the port as far as I could
judge of Bell Island & Eira harbour

Rgt
Grounded
Floe
Eira Harbour
Shoal
apu.than
... lane
& boats
Stone
...

1. Koettlitz expedition journals retained in Koettlitz family archives.
2. Frederick G. Jackson – *1000 Days in the Arctic*, and Koettlitz expedition journals.
3. Koettlitz expedition journals retained in Koettlitz family archives.
4. Frederick G. Jackson – *1000 Days in the Arctic*.
5. *Ibid.*

10

The second winter at Cape Flora

As August slipped into September snow began to fall at regular intervals and the temperature dipped below freezing point. The larder continued to be filled with birds, bears and scurvy grass but with the major sledge and boat journeys behind them the old niggles in the house re-appeared. The long Arctic nights would soon be upon them and it seemed that a long, at times unpleasant, winter was ahead.

It didn't take long for tempers to explode. On Thursday 5 September Jackson ordered Burgess, who had resigned from the expedition some weeks earlier, to get his boots on and help pick scurvy grass. Burgess answered that as he was no longer a member of the expedition Jackson could not issue him orders. At this, Jackson flew into a rage and with many an expletive knocked Burgess to the ground. Both of them fell through the doorway fighting, a scene witnessed by Armitage and Fisher. Burgess managed to leave the hut and was relaying the story of the assault to Dr Koettlitz, who was outside picking scurvy grass, when Jackson and the other expedition members arrived, and a meeting of all parties was convened on the spot.

The assembled party debated Burgess's fate. Jackson was of the opinion that he should be given a 'good thrashing' for insubordination but as he was no longer a member of the expedition this was not possible. The conclusion reached was a classic compromise. Burgess would now be supervised by Koettlitz as regards his exercise and health, as Jackson did not want another case of scurvy in the group. All directions by Jackson would be relayed via Koettlitz. Peace was restored, although Jackson simmered for almost a week following the assault. He also ordered Koettlitz to lock up the tobacco supply to prevent Burgess accessing it without authority.

Saturday 7 September saw the first anniversary of their arrival in Franz Josef Land and the landing the following day on Cape Flora. As a way of celebrating, Jackson shot four walrus, which were towed ashore by boat, a pastime much disliked by the rest of the party. At dinner that evening port wine was passed around as all present toasted their first year on the islands. The year had seen substantial achievements in both boat and sledge journeys, although insufficient scientific research had been accomplished in the view of Koettlitz. But overall the results had been considerable, despite a good deal of bad feeling between the members of the party. The expedition looked headed for success, in spite of the unstable management and poor leadership skills displayed by Jackson.

The winter of 1895 and into 1896 was spent in a similar fashion to the previous one, although the temperature at times fell to record lows, often between 40 and 46 degrees below zero. These temperatures made it impossible to work outside and the party were grateful that the larder had been well stocked before the onset of severe weather. Armitage alone appears to have skinned over 1,000 loons in addition to other birds, polar bears and walrus. Scurvy was not to be feared this winter.

The lack of travel opportunities led to the re-emergence of the bickering and at times personal abuse that plagued the first winter on Franz Josef Land. Jackson's leadership methods led to constant disputes which ended up with Koettlitz escaping for many hours to the outer sheds, skinning and preparing specimens for return to England for further study. Koettlitz's diary records these disputes in great detail, and it is clear that the atmosphere in the hut was frequently dire. The most minor of disputes led to major rows and long periods of silence between members of the group. And it was not just the human members of the expedition who were suffering – with a lack of exercise and an inappropriate feeding regime the dogs were also in a wretched condition. They fought amongst each other, often leading to death and injury, and on Jackson's insistence – and despite Koettlitz's protestations – were fed solely on a diet of meat without the biscuit of the previous winter, thus did not receive a balanced diet.

Although gulls and other birds were disappearing south, hunting continued apace. On Monday 30 September Jackson and Armitage pursued polar bears in their pyjamas, halting only when they reached open water. They failed to kill the bears and instead took a number of seals on return to the hut. As a result of pursuing these animals in such attire Jackson's haemorrhoids worsened and gave him great discomfort, requiring treatment from the doctor. It's not wise to pursue polar bears in winter dressed only in pyjamas, with inflamed haemorrhoids.

As October progressed and the temperature dropped, the ice continued to form in the bay. Outbursts from Jackson and disputes within the group became less frequent. Skinning of birds and other animals continued. In addition large quantities of driftwood, presumably originating in northern Europe, were collected to supplement the dwindling coal stocks, with supplies washing up on the shores of the otherwise barren Franz Josef Land.

By the last week of October snow was falling on a daily basis and the light was dimming with the onset of winter. The bonus, of course, was the return of the wonderful auroras in the northern sky. Tuesday 22 October brought the finest aurora Koettlitz had ever seen, with brilliant zigzag streamers and fantastic cloud-like formations. The group often took walks whilst gazing at the incredible displays set in the sky before them, though twilight all too rapidly was spent.

November saw the return of the winter night watches and the routine continued much as before. Some of the group objected to the night watch but Koettlitz was content with the 2 a.m. to 4 a.m. period as it allowed him a time of peace and reflection during which he could read and update his journal. A 24-hour watch was essential for the safety of the group and the assorted animals within their care.

Towards the end of the month a heated debate between Jackson and Dr Koettlitz arose concerning the causes of scurvy. Jackson stated that the salt pork that was being eaten by some members of the crew of the *Windward* was a possible cause, and claimed that Koettlitz should have identified this and introduced a more rigid regime to combat the disease. Koettlitz, standing his ground for once, firmly insisted that the causes were as yet unknown but that the cure and preventative measure was undoubtedly fresh meat and vegetables daily.

He also clearly stated that responsibility for the ship's provisions was not within his remit and that he did his utmost to ensure the crew ate fresh bear and bird meat. Koettlitz's argument was sound and after three days of back-and-forth Jackson said he had heard enough of scurvy and did not wish to discuss the subject again.

Dinner was often followed by a glass or two of port wine. Thoughts turned to the sledging season of 1896 and what might be achieved in the push to the north. In anticipation, the young pups born since their arrival were being introduced to the harness so they would be prepared for early sledging operations. Koettlitz's team of eight dogs were soon pulling sledges up to 500 lbs in weight.

Early December saw an increase in the number of polar bears visiting the area around Cape Flora. Most of them were shot, and on examination many of the females were found to be pregnant. This convinced Koettlitz that the pregnant female polar bear only hibernates when the cubs are nearly due or newborn. In addition, one day saw the deaths of four large walrus that had strayed too close to shore. In fact, the hunting of bears and walrus became almost as much a part of the daily regime as the syringing of Jackson's ears, a task which was a morning ritual for the surgeon. At times this was accompanied by a dose of arsenic which served to dull the pain.

In addition, preparations were being made for celebrating Christmas, and in particular for the luncheon. The main course this year was to be goose. Individual menu cards were being drawn by the multi-skilled doctor.

Monday 23 December was Koettlitz's birthday. As he performed the daily syringe of Jackson's ears it was apparent that Jackson was in a reflective mood. Commenting on the recent arguments within the group Jackson said, 'I wish I could get rid of my expedition during the winter, they are all so depressed,'[1] and asked Koettlitz if he had noticed. When answered in the negative Jackson continued, 'Your observation doctor is not good, damn their depression. Men should not come out here if they are going to be depressed.'[1] Jackson failed to recognise that he was frequently the cause of such depression.

After the daily syringe Koettlitz spent the rest of the day sledging with his dogs in fine weather and enjoying an excellent dinner with port wine – a 'delightful birthday'.[1]

Christmas Day was a relaxed affair and dinner was taken late, at 9.15 p.m. In addition to the individual menus, Fisher had drawn an elaborate main menu written in Latin. The goose was supported by large quantities of wine, champagne and port, and Jackson offered his fine cigars. A multitude of toasts were made, commencing with the Queen, Mr and Mrs Harmsworth and proceeding to many others in descending order. Singing and conversation continued until 2.30 a.m. when, after taking digestion pills belonging to Armitage, the party turned in. All slept in on the 26th; Jackson did not rise until around 3 p.m. It was a relaxed day, although Koettlitz had to draw a tooth for Heyward who was in some pain.

Koettlitz and Armitage kept busy with their respective duties during this period. Armitage in particular was occupied with meteorological observations which had to be taken every two hours then recorded on his daily record charts. Koettlitz was disappointed with the amount of bird and walrus skinning he had to do, which restricted his geological activities. Although he had offered to assist Jackson with the skinning he seemed to have subsequently inherited the entire job.

He also recorded the changes in weather in this second winter, noting that by Christmas there had been much less snowfall and ice formation offshore. The temperature also varied continually, and affected Jackson's ears, which required enhanced syringing from the doctor. The second winter was leading to early irritability amongst the Cape Flora residents. Koettlitz complained of not being able to sleep well so he took 15 grams of sulphonal one evening after a long read and enjoyed a pleasant pipe, which seemed to have the desired effect.

Tuesday 31 December, New Year's Eve, produced a fine, moonlit day but cold, with temperatures down to minus 36 degrees. All agreed that acclimatisation had improved their resistance to both the cold and frostbite attack. Although they all now wore face masks when outside, incidence of frostbite was considerably down on the previous winter.

By early evening Jackson had roused himself from his daily gloom and proposed making a punch to celebrate the New Year. Having found a recipe in their cookbook Fisher then brewed two very decent bowls containing a mixture of sugar, lemon, allspice, mixed spice, sherry, whisky and water which was described as most favourable. They all enjoyed as convivial a time as possible under the circumstances, and once again there were many toasts. The only dispute was over the astounding assertion by Armitage that malaria and similar fevers in the West Indies and West Africa were caused by a cold wind. Koettlitz took a totally different view and regarded this opinion as absolute rubbish. With this comment 1896 was welcomed in on Franz Josef Land. In fact, New Year's Day was a fairly subdued affair when compared with previous celebrations, although they did manage to celebrate until 3 a.m.

January proved an uneventful month although the disputes over duties and other minor matters continued. A number of polar bears were shot to supplement the rations, which led to much flensing of the skins for Dr Koettlitz, at times in freezing conditions in the outer shed. Koettlitz kept detailed records of the bears' size, weight, health condition, stomach contents and many other details. During the month the temperature often fell to minus 40 degrees, and winds rose to hurricane force 11. The men all took exercise as often as the weather allowed and there were regular spectacular auroras.

All seemed to suffer from lack of sleep and this became the subject of some discussion. Koettlitz believed it was because they all ate too late in the evening – this led to a sluggish liver and intestines, which caused indigestion and stomach pain, further aggravated by the long winter darkness. Jackson thought this was 'absolute rot',[1] a term he often used, but could not offer an alternative explanation.

There was also another heated debate between Jackson, Armitage and Koettlitz concerning the causes of scurvy. Jackson described lime juice as 'rot muck'[1] and said it was no use whatsoever – there was of course some truth in this. He asserted again that the cause of scurvy was salted meat and that a small amount of fresh meat was not enough. Armitage chipped in with the fact that the Board of Trade considered that tinned meat was fresh meat and it was not legally necessary to provide lime juice. Koettlitz added that it was well known that salt meat did not prevent scurvy and that some even thought it caused it. At this Koettlitz recalls Jackson exploding and demanding to know, 'Why the heck had I not said so at the beginning of last winter and he would have stopped it being issued as part of the rations on the *Windward*'.[1] Koettlitz countered that salt meat was only issued twice a week and that it was a regularly changing diet, including fresh meat and vegetables on a daily basis, with exercise, fresh air and plenty of artificial light during the winter months, that kept scurvy at bay. All these things were in short supply on board the *Windward*.

The question of fresh air was later raised on board the *Discovery*, when the question of opening the vents, when and who should open them, became a topic of heated debate along with the question of a daily consumption of fresh meat.

---

1. Koettlitz expedition journals retained in Koettlitz family archives.

11

Jackson heads north once more

The beginning of February saw thoughts turn to the next sledging season which would commence when the weather allowed and the sun returned. The men were already exercising the dogs and improving harnesses and personal clothing. Before any journeys could be started, improvements were needed in the condition of some of the dogs. A combination of dog fights and polar bear attacks had injured several of them and some were in a serious condition. It was another duty of Koettlitz to carry out veterinary care of the animals, which he did with some success. This included major surgical operations in efforts to save both dogs and ponies.

By mid-February the dogs were being run on a daily basis, carrying loads between 200 and 600 lbs. The weight gradually increased as the month progressed. Jackson was preparing the supplies for an anticipated sledging commencement in March. He planned to make use of the remaining ponies in addition to the dogs. Unfortunately, the internal disputes and disagreements between Jackson and the other team members continued, often over the most minor of issues – but the causes and treatments of scurvy would often be the catalyst.

By the end of the month the weather had improved dramatically, with sunshine temperatures approaching 20 degrees Fahrenheit, but with regular snow showers at night when the temperature fell to minus 20 degrees. The improvement in the weather meant the return of the thousands of birds which spend the summer on Franz Josef Land, prompting great excitement from Jackson at the prospect of the resumption of the shooting season. Friday 28 February produced a total eclipse of the moon which Koettlitz recorded in his journal with an accompanying sketch.[1]

Polar bears returned in substantial numbers and almost every day saw a bear hunt in some form, with many continuing to be killed. On Thursday 5 March Jackson, when being told there was a bear on the floe, rose from his bed, grabbed his rifle, once again pursued the animal dressed only in his pyjamas and, supported by Armitage, actually brought the beast down.

By the end of the following week the sledges were loaded and ready for the season to commence. The only remaining obstruction was the weather, with virtually nil visibility and very heavy snow, forcing the anticipated commencement of the journey north to be delayed.

Jackson was busy writing letters to be returned home in case of accident. He also wrote a letter to Koettlitz instructing him to take charge of the expedition in his absence. This is set out in full below, and shows the formal nature of expeditions of the time.

Elmwood, Cape Flora, March 16th 1896.

Dr R Koettlitz, Esq: M.R.C.S. Etc:

During my absence you will take sole charge of the expedition and its affairs at Elmwood and will be solely responsible.

I look to you to see that things are carried on here as before and that such work as I shall specify in particular, and other that may be for the wellbeing of the expedition be carried out.

I expect every member of the party to obey you, to support you in all things, and to carry out your instructions: this I have little doubt they most willingly will do.

(Signed) Frederick G Jackson

Commanding the Jackson-Harmsworth Polar Expedition.

The specified work is the following:

Household work as usual

Heyward to clean up kitchen, pantry, lobby etc.

Dogs to be fed. Pups to be carefully looked after and Gladwys to be fed and kept in house

No 2 house to be cleaned out and straightened up, all belonging to No 2 to be returned

No 4 house to be cleared out of snow if weather is decent

Child to collect all tools, dry & oil them, & put in box in No 1

He is to put hooks round in No 1 or 2 to hang all pony harness on, before which the harness is to be brought into house to dry. He is to load up cartridges. To teach me (Koettlitz) soldering and glue mixing.

Fisher to see that his botanical specimens are dry etc. and they are then to be soldered up.

To go through stable store and collect specimens and to put them into No 2. Passages to stable store, dog house and No 4 berthon to be kept clear.

No firearms to be touched by anybody without my (Koettlitz's) instruction.

It is obvious that there was to be no idleness whilst Jackson was away.

On Tuesday 17 March Jackson, Armitage and Blomkvist, with one pony and 16 dogs pulling 2,300 lbs of stores between them, made a start, but the barometer fell dramatically and after making only a few miles they were forced to return to Elmwood. This suited Armitage as he felt a broken tooth, which the competent doctor stopped that evening. The following day another start was made and, supported by Koettlitz, slow progress was made towards Windward Island. It was immediately apparent that the pony in particular was not fit and had suffered from a lack of exercise during the winter months. Koettlitz mentioned on his return journey to the hut that he did not expect them to be away more than two weeks due to the poor condition of the animals and Jackson being flushed and overweight.

The following days at Cape Flora were largely spent carrying out the tasks set by Jackson. On the Friday, hearing the shout of 'bear, bear' from outside, Koettlitz grabbed his Martini-Henry rifle and got within 24 feet of a huge male polar bear close to the hut. With two shots he killed the bear outright – his first bear kill without the supervision and interference of Jackson. This specimen now stands proudly in Dover Museum, Kent, looking a little worn but otherwise in fine condition. In fact, polar bears were making an almost daily appearance and a number were shot to supplement the larder and for scientific examination.

The base at Cape Flora seemed to be a hive of activity and, without the leader Jackson, free from disputes and the usual tense atmosphere. However, on Thursday 26 March this situation took a turn for the worse. Child and Fisher were having a fairly heated discussion about Child's dirty clothing and other bad habits, which came to a head over the minor issue of who had spilt some ink. Child would not let the issue drop so Koettlitz felt obliged to ask him to be quiet, first in a friendly manner but then more forcefully in his position as leader. Child refused to back down or shut up, despite numerous requests from Koettlitz. His journal states:

> My interference as a friend had no effect on Child, so at last I had to order him to stop. He then included me in his remarks in fact denied my right of authority to interfere, so after warning him that I should make him if he did not desist and it having no effect upon him, I hit him a right-hander on the upper jaw, which shut him up for a moment while he held his cheek and nursed it. He then said something more and I again warned him to stop and he would not so I gave him another which did shut him up.[1]

This rather extreme manner of resolving a dispute seemed to work as after dinner they all went for a walk together, although Child seemed 'rather glum'.[1] It obviously didn't upset Koettlitz too much as he describes the beautiful sunset in detail. The only lasting effect of this incident was Child's inability to eat hot pudding due to a swollen mouth – although he did mention to Heyward that he intended to get even with Koettlitz one day.

In the period Jackson and his travelling companions were away the daily routine was much as before, with Jackson's instructions being carried out in detail. Time was still found to shoot four polar bears, one of which managed to kill a dog called 'Tommy Rot', named after Jackson's favourite saying. Koettlitz, as always, examined all the bears in detail, and kept the penises of the males as trophies.

They all spent much time skiing and sledging, and this activity would be followed by fresh bear steaks which were greatly appreciated by all. The atmosphere was generally congenial following the altercation of 26 March. Every day thousands of migrating birds passed over, heading north, including loons, burgomaster gulls, kittiwakes and mollies. Koettlitz thought this indicated there was open water to the north, which might impede the sledging party.

On Monday 13 April 1896 Heyward woke Koettlitz at 5 a.m. saying, 'They have returned, I can see them on the pond'.[1] Initially, Koettlitz thought it was another bear; he dressed, and then spotted Jackson and his companions heading towards the huts. Jackson shook hands with Koettlitz and confirmed they had indeed been stopped by open water to the northeast, which involved substantial diversions from their planned route of return. They had returned safely, however, including all the dogs bar one, Carlo having died on the march. There was also an addition to the collection of animals – a baby polar bear had been carried home on the sledge. It was apparent that Armitage and Jackson had had a number of major rows, culminating in Armitage telling the leader a 'few home truths'.[1]

Jackson and Koettlitz talked for three hours about the journey and how things had been at Cape Flora. It was clear that much new ground had been explored and the map of Franz Josef Land greatly enhanced. Jackson seemed most disappointed to hear that the doctor had not fallen out with Burgess who had earlier resigned from the expedition following a heated dispute with Jackson.

Normal behaviour resumed the following day when Jackson ruined a number of photographic plates and negatives he was developing. Flying into a terrible rage, he threw the equipment onto the floor, with much abusive and insulting language. Jackson was sure Burgess had tampered with the liquid; this prompted Armitage to ask Koettlitz if 'Jackson was not suffering from insanity?'[1]

On 22 April Koettlitz noted in his diary that it was their regular daily diet that in his opinion kept them all fit and free from scurvy. Despite being well into their second year on Franz Josef Land, this regular daily menu continued to provide good health, fitness and stamina. It is set out below:

Breakfast – Porridge, honey, bread and butter, tinned cold meat for anyone that liked it, fried ham or tripe with tea.

Luncheon – Cold tinned meat, bears meat or brains, scurvy grass for each man, tinned tomatoes, cheese and bread (with lime juice on the table) and tea.

Dinner – Soup, fresh joint or fried polar bear or pony, fried or stewed loon, potatoes and vegetables, pudding or tart of different types, bread and cheese with port wine.[1]

There was no official supper but biscuits and cheese were available for those who desired them.

In the 21st century this would be described as 'a balanced diet', although fresh fruit should ideally be added. This was only available on special occasions, from their now limited supply of preserved fruit.

It is clear that it was Koettlitz and Jackson's insistence that this daily food allowance be adhered to that kept all the expedition members in such good health. This positioned Dr Koettlitz as an expert in the field of scurvy prevention and guaranteed the fitness of expedition members in the severe polar environment.

In fact, the only physical ailment that had grown worse during and following the last sledge journey was Jackson's haemorrhoids, which were bothering him a good deal. Koettlitz prescribed him some Hazeline cream, salts and rhubarb pills to be taken three times a day. It seems that rhubarb pills were effective in easing many ailments; Koettlitz often prescribed them for various stomach and other minor conditions. Rhubarb leaves and oils had been used for the treatment of indigestion and other stomach conditions since the ancient Chinese dynasties.

Jackson later asked Koettlitz if he could 'Just have them snipped off?'[1] Koettlitz was not keen to carry out this operation on the leader of the expedition and said he was low on chloroform and did not have the necessary instruments. He also explained it was a little more than just snipping them off and he felt he should preserve the instruments and chloroform for any emergencies that might arise. Koettlitz was also keen to resume his geologising now the ground was clearing and did not want the distraction of minding a patient following surgery and the likely fall-out if it did not go to plan.

Early May brought fine spells of weather and much relief to Dr Koettlitz. He was able to make regular trips to Cape Gertrude and the surrounding area to collect geological specimens he had stored there before winter had set in. He mostly travelled alone or with one or two companions, using up to three sledges pulled by the dogs. He spent many hours examining the composition of the hills, gullies and beaches, which reinforced his opinion that some of the previous papers on the geology of the region were incorrect. These geologising trips also provided the opportunity to escape Jackson and the continuing difficult atmosphere at Cape Flora. Jackson was impatient for the *Windward* to arrive, so that he could send back to England those he thought disruptive. He did not think for one moment that he might be the cause of their disruption.

As the month progressed the weather was variable but the number of birds continued to increase, with snow buntings in abundance. Polar bears continued to be shot, resulting in Koettlitz being engaged for many hours in the flensing and detailed examination of the animals. Although at times repetitive this activity provided the information which led to his subsequent paper presented to the Royal Geographical Society. Walrus also occasionally came within shooting distance of Cape Flora but at their peril. The end of the month brought ever increasing numbers of migrating birds including eider duck and turnstone, all of which came before the sights of Jackson's guns.

The party kept a regular watch for the return of the *Windward* from the roof of the hut. With the calm weather they even managed to play a few games of cricket on packed but fast-melting snow. On Saturday 23 May the sporting activities took a more serious turn, however. Child and Heyward had argued at breakfast and harangued each other with foul language, culminating in Child challenging Heyward to a fight. At 4 p.m., when Jackson and Armitage had gone out to shoot birds, they 'had it out' on the frozen pond using boxing gloves. Koettlitz describes it as a most absurd sight, although Child did 'draw the claret'[1] from Heyward's nose. Child said he preferred using gloves so as not to cause Heyward unnecessary damage.

There were so many disputes going on between the Cape Flora residents that they managed to overlook the Queen's birthday on 24 May, which added to Jackson's frustration and temper. The situation was everyone's fault 'bar his own'.

---

1.   Koettlitz expedition journals retained in Koettlitz family archives.

12

An historic moment

June 1896 proved to be the most dramatic and, some might say, most significant month of the expedition. It started with a typical dispute between Jackson and Armitage which lasted the greater part of Thursday 4 June, which culminated in Armitage informing Jackson that if it hadn't been for him saving the *Windward* on the outward trip and saving Jackson's life during the small boat journey aboard the *Mary Harmsworth*, he would not be alive today. This resulted in the ultimate outburst from the leader – with clenched fists he described Armitage as a 'damned lurcher'[1] (a phrase he often used), a damned cad, a damned bounder etc., etc. The *Windward* could not return soon enough.

On 24 June 1893 an expedition led by the eminent Norwegian scholar and explorer Dr Fridtjof Nansen, with 13 companions, had set out from Christiansund aboard a purpose-built ship named the *Fram*. Their intention was to travel north, become beset in the polar ice and drift across the polar regions as close as possible to the North Pole. This was a scientific expedition but if the opportunity arose to make the North Pole that opportunity would be taken. It was to become one of the most epic journeys in polar history.

The ship was designed to survive in the polar ice; the crew were all experienced seamen and possessed the skill to survive in extreme polar conditions. This was just as well, as the *Fram* was to drift in the polar ice for almost three years before breaking free into open water and returning to Norway, with all hands and with notable scientific achievements and observations.

Once the *Fram* had proved her worth in conditions that would have crushed other ships, Fridtjof Nansen decided to set out and explore areas to the north, away from the drift of the *Fram*. He was confident that Captain Sverdrup would get the ship home. It could not be in better hands.

He chose as his travelling companion Lieutenant F. H. Johansen, an experienced skier and a man used to travelling and surviving in the severe northern climate. They left the ship on 14 March 1895 with three sledges, two light boats, provisions for 100 days and 28 dogs. They carried enough food for the dogs to last about 30 days, the plan being to feed the dogs to the remaining animals until they had been expended.

During the following year both men survived a journey of the most extreme hardship. Only their skills in polar survival – skills learnt in their native Norway and on previous polar expeditions, including living off the land once their provisions were exhausted – guaranteed their arrival on Franz Josef Land in June 1896.[2]

By August of the previous year they had been reduced to the last two dogs, which Nansen described as 'Their two most faithful companions'.[3] However, it was decided they had to be shot. Being unable to shoot their own dogs it was agreed they would shoot each other's. This was duly carried out and was described as the hardest work they had to do during the whole expedition.

The two men pressed on. They had previously decided to head for Spitzbergen, but by the end of August, making slow progress due to the weather and travelling conditions, Nansen decided they had better start making preparations for the forthcoming winter. This included shooting up to 15 polar bears for food and many walrus for food and heating; the blubber of the walrus was used for both fuel and oil. A small hut was constructed from stones, earth and moss, covered with stretched walrus hides. It had low walls and, as stated by Nansen at a subsequent presentation to the Manchester Geographical Society, 'It was tolerably comfortable inside and the heat from the walrus oil lamps kept the temperature at about freezing point'.[4]

At Christmas they dreamed of what might be happening at home in Norway. By way of celebration they both turned their shirts inside out, which meant their grease-soaked clothes didn't stick to their bodies quite so much. With the approaching spring they made preparations to resume their journey and by the middle of May were ready to strike out once more for safety and a return to civilisation. Nansen was not sure of their exact location but knew they had over-wintered on Franz Josef Land. They moved south on open water, often attracting the unwanted company of aggressive walrus.

By 12 June they were in a position to move westwards along the south coast and head across open sea to Spitzbergen. In the evening Nansen decided to stop at the ice edge to stretch their legs and take some food; they had been sitting in their kayaks all day long. They stepped ashore to reconnoitre their position when Johansen called out, 'the kayaks are drifting out to sea' – a most perilous situation. Nansen made a life-or-death decision to strip off most of his clothing and swim in the freezing Arctic Ocean to recover the kayaks. Johansen later described this as the worst moment of his life, but eventually Nansen, with extreme effort, strength and luck, made it to the boats. After many failed attempts, and despite severe cramp and frozen limbs, he managed to climb aboard the small craft. Eventually he paddled towards the ice edge where Johansen was waiting to grab the kayak and pull Nansen to safety. It was a remarkable example of human courage and endurance.

After Nansen had recovered from his near-death experience, they managed to push on along the coast. As they went they suffered attacks from walrus and polar bear. On 17 June they were once again camped on the shoreline of Franz Josef Land. Before setting out again Nansen decided to climb to higher ground to get a better view and establish their bearings. This decision led to one of the most remarkable meetings in polar history – his encounter with Frederick George Jackson and the members of the Jackson-Harmsworth Expedition.

Their description of this incredible meeting varies somewhat but the content is essentially the same. Jackson quickly realised this was to be a pivotal moment in history and would ensure his standing in polar folklore.

Dr Koettlitz wrote a clear description of the event. At around nine o'clock, just after dinner, Armitage had gone outside with his binoculars to search the horizon, as he now frequently did, looking for the *Windward* which they were daily hoping to see. Koettlitz recalls Armitage came in and said, 'Are we all here?' We could not understand what he meant, and said so. He then looked round, and seeing that everyone was within doors, said, 'I wanted to know because there is a man on the ice!' We could not believe him, and said he must be mistaken. No he was not. So out we rushed and then saw about three miles away, a black speck, standing upright and evidently moving in the south east, walking upon the white floe. Most certainly he was a man. Who could he be? Question and answer followed each other in rapid succession. All kinds of surmises were made.

'A shipwrecked walrus slooper'. 'The *Windward* had come to grief and this was a survivor', for no ship could be seen in the distance. 'Could it be Nansen?' No, impossible, etc., etc. Well, said Jackson, 'Whoever he is, I am off to see' and he went. We watched the approach of the two with the keenest curiosity.[5]

Koettlitz could not join Jackson as it was his turn to wash up the dinner things. Others followed Jackson, whose description of this event was far more dramatic – probably befitting such a historic moment.

Having agreed with Armitage from the roof that it was indeed a human, Jackson set off with rifle to meet the new arrival, Armitage being left on the roof to direct his course. En-route Jackson fired his weapon to attract the stranger's attention. After about three miles Jackson found a tall man in roughly made clothes and an old felt hat, covered in grease and oil and wearing ski. He assumed from the use of ski he was not an English sailor.

As Jackson approached, he noticed the man's hair was very long and dirty; he had a straggly beard and was generally filthy. They shook hands warmly and Jackson enquired if he had a ship close by? He replied sadly, he had not. It then struck Jackson from his features, and despite his filthy appearance, that this was indeed Dr Nansen whom he had met some years previously in London.

Jackson exclaimed, 'Aren't you Nansen?' to which he replied, 'Yes I'm Nansen'. They shook hands warmly once again, and Jackson said, 'By Jove I'm damned glad to see you',[6] and enquired from where he had come. Nansen's version of this event is rather more subdued but there was no doubting his relief at finding Jackson's expedition. He explained that his companion Lieutenant Johansen was at the water's edge with their kayaks. Nansen confirmed they had pushed as far north as 86°15N latitude and 90° east longitude, a magnificent achievement.

This was the Arctic's equivalent of Stanley's meeting with Livingstone but was perhaps even more remarkable. Stanley was searching for Livingstone but neither Jackson nor Nansen were looking for or expecting to meet each other. It was pure chance and possibly meant the difference between life and death for Nansen and his companion. Nansen later named the island on which he had over-wintered Frederick Jackson Island in honour of Jackson and the expedition that rescued them.

They returned to the hut, where Nansen was introduced to the other expedition members. Koettlitz, after congratulating Dr Nansen most heartily and welcoming him to Elmwood, set off to bring Johansen to their base. Nansen stayed with Jackson, recounting his exploits.

Koettlitz writes:

We took two light sledges and went to where Lieutenant Johansen of the Norwegian Army was waiting on the floe edge with the kayaks and other equipment. When we found Johansen

The meeting of Jackson and Nansen

we found he could not speak English, but I found he could German. We all then heartily welcomed and congratulated him; cheering him and the Norwegian flag he had flying lustily. Armitage gave him the first pipe of tobacco he had sampled in many a month. After hearing his news as to how they had left the *Fram* some sixteen months previously and providing news of our own, we packed the sledges with his and Nansen's gear. Transferring them all to Elmwood with some difficulty due to the rough terrain.

Our visitors were given a good meal, to which they did ample justice, for they had not had farinaceous food for quite a year, and they could not help expressing how delicious everything tasted to them. They were then photographed in their 'war paint', after which they had a bath, their hair which was very long was cut and they had clean clothes given to them. After shaving we made them comfortable.[7]

They listened through the night to Nansen and Johansen's extraordinary tale of survival. To Koettlitz's delight Nansen also showed great interest in the scientific and geological work carried out by Koettlitz and the other expedition members. Nansen was keen to explore the geological sections and exposures discovered by Koettlitz, which they spent the following weeks investigating.

Koettlitz described the time in Nansen's company exploring and examining the rocks of Cape Flora and the surrounding area as one of the happiest of his life. It was the start of a long-standing friendship and correspondence which would continue until Koettlitz's death.

For six weeks Doctors Koettlitz and Nansen spent every moment possible geologising on and around Cape Flora (at times to the annoyance of Jackson, who seemed to regard Nansen as his own personal property). This led to the most comprehensive assessment of the geological structures of Franz Josef Land ever made and eventually to members of the Royal Geographical Society accepting that Koettlitz's controversial scientific and geological papers were indeed correct, contrary to previous geological opinion.

Although Nansen was intrigued and challenged by the geological work at Cape Flora he was also impatient to return to Norway, to establish the fate of the *Fram* which he hoped had by now broken free from the Arctic ice and returned home. Jackson was also keen to remove a number of his expedition members. All were excited at the thought of letters from home which the *Windward* should be carrying.

On 26 July the *Windward* was sighted: news from the outside world at last. They all wrote their letters home and received news from their families, including that Armitage's mother had died.

Koettlitz described his unfeigned regret at the departure of Dr Nansen and his companion Lieutenant Johansen. Four of the resident party also returned with the ship, Fisher, Child, Burgess and Blomkvist, some relieved to do so. Two new companions had arrived, William Speirs Bruce, the acclaimed Scottish explorer and scientist, and Mr D. W. Wilton who had welcomed the expedition to Archangel when he was British Consul there. They were to begin their first year in the Arctic, with the veteran expedition members entering their third.

---

1. Koettlitz expedition journals retained in Koettlitz family archives.

2. Fridtjof Nansen – *Furthest North*, 1898.

3. *Ibid.*

4. Nansen and Koettlitz presentations at Manchester Geographical Society.

5. Koettlitz expedition journals retained in Koettlitz family archives.

6. Frederick G. Jackson – *1000 Days in the Arctic*, and Fridtjof Nansen – *Furthest North*, Vol. 2, page 279.

7. Koettlitz expedition journals retained in Koettlitz family archives.

13

The final year at Cape Flora

After Dr Nansen and Lieutenant Johansen had left, much work and research remained to be accomplished during the few summer months available. Zoological, meteorological, magnetic and geological observations occupied most days and in this Koettlitz found a valuable and knowledgeable companion in William Speirs Bruce. Bruce had already made a name for himself as a marine biologist and over the next 30 years was to become a polar authority. Bruce fairly rapidly came to regard the leader Mr Jackson as an 'ass'. He also possessed a short Scottish temper and Jackson was careful to allow him space and his own routine. Mr Wilton, who had been resident in Russia for many years and acted as Jackson's agent in Archangel, also decided, like Bruce, to remain for just one year.

The larder needed topping up for the impending winter and during this period at least 1,400 birds were shot and hung up around the outside of the house, just under the roof. This acted as a natural freezer and kept the game in good condition. Polar bears and walrus continued to be shot when the opportunity presented itself. Jackson had hoped to receive additional Russian ponies with the relief ship but had been sent five reindeer with harnesses instead. They did not prove successful as draught animals on the islands but could supplement the larder in times of hardship.

Whilst the daylight hours remained clear Koettlitz began to map the areas in which he had been geologising, and to prepare detailed geographical maps. In addition photographs were taken of the rock strata. Despite these there was no guarantee of his conclusions being accepted in London. By the end of August birds were once again beginning to head south and the weather was deteriorating, with more snow and ice at regular intervals.

Monday 7 September saw the second anniversary of their arrival on Franz Josef Land and a month since the *Windward* had departed. Their diet had improved with stores and foodstuffs which the ship had brought. Rum was the favourite after dinner tipple and sardines were eaten regularly, with a selection of vegetables to replace their daily scurvy grass.

Jackson was in chronic ill health, according to the doctor, with aching limbs, painful varicose veins, haemorrhoids and trouble with his teeth, which required regular stopping. Much time was spent that day bringing coal that the ship had dropped up to the house, not making for a very relaxed second anniversary celebration. Their third Arctic winter was approaching and Koettlitz was beginning to dread the monotony of continuous darkness coupled with the severe weather. When Jackson's infernal irritability and temper was thrown into the mix the three or four months of winter seemed to be a kind of purgatory.

Koettlitz endorsed the view put forward by Lieutenant Peary, the American Arctic explorer, who at a Royal Geographical Society lecture remarked, 'People at home seemed to think that the cold was the worst of Arctic experiences to bear, but that it was not so, the long, dreary, monotonous, maddening Arctic night was the worst by far'.[1]

As previously mentioned, Dr Koettlitz was an accomplished dentist, having studied the subject at Edinburgh University. However, he never envisaged having to instruct a third party on how to extract one of his own teeth. On Saturday 12 September, having endured days of intense pain, he gave Armitage a crash course in dentistry so that the offending tooth could be extracted. Armitage first practised by pulling a tooth from one of the dogs, in a very slow but methodical manner. Although Jackson insisted he was better qualified to pull the tooth, Armitage went ahead and slowly, painfully removed the tooth, much to the doctor's relief. It was normal practice before expeditions set out for all the members to have a thorough dental check, with all offending or suspect teeth being removed. This often led to explorers having a noticeable lack of teeth.

The following day, feeling much better, Koettlitz spent a fruitful day geologising at Shell Gully in the vicinity of Cape Flora. He was much excited by this trip and wrote in great detail of the day's work. On return to the hut he and Jackson spent a couple of hours skating on a nearby frozen pond, to his great delight. The following days were spent much as before, flensing bear and walrus skins, taking geological observations and adding to the winter larder.

Monday 21 September was a momentous occasion, bringing a change of underclothing, to Koettlitz's great relief. He had worn the same underclothing since June and felt it was time for a change. Considering he regarded other expedition members as dirty in their habits, the condition of *their* underclothing cannot be imagined.

The early days of October saw the continued gathering of migrating birds, who were ready for the dash south if the weather took a serious turn for the worse. Koettlitz noticed that the feather colours of the snow buntings were changing, no doubt to provide enhanced camouflage for winter. Glaucous and ivory gulls were also present in large numbers and although some specimens were taken for return to England and further study the majority passed by on their way south. Jackson confided to the doctor that he had a low opinion of Wilton, one of the newcomers, but thought Bruce a splendid chap, for a scientist.

Jackson spent much time dredging in the sea around Cape Flora, an occupation in which he had shown no previous interest. Bruce later informed Koettlitz that Jackson was trying to beat the number of specimens taken by Nansen. Koettlitz had constructed a new armchair for his own use from various materials he found around the hut. Much to his annoyance Jackson had taken to continually sitting in it, leading Koettlitz to write, 'Jackson cares nothing for his comrades and shows continually what a skunk he is'.[2]

Jackson had instructed Heyward to bring every tin of food he opened to Dr Koettlitz for examination before it was used. Whilst Nansen was staying at Cape Flora scurvy had once again been a subject of discussion. Nansen told Jackson and Koettlitz that in his view ptomaines (poisons found in decaying organic matter) might be the most probable cause of scurvy and that food contained in tin may be unfit for use. Thus Koettlitz had to authorise every tin as being fit for use. Despite Nansen's theory and the lack of scientific understanding, Koettlitz remained convinced that the daily consumption of fresh meat and vegetables when available was the only sure method of preventing scurvy.

October continued uneventfully, although Jackson fell into the sea whilst shooting birds and had it not been for Wilton's quick action would have perished. The group found time for ski races, much to Koettlitz's delight as by this time he was an accomplished ski runner. The sole remaining reindeer was put into harness in an attempt to pull a sledge; this proved totally unsuccessful and as a result it was destined for the winter larder.

This third Arctic winter passed much the same way as the previous two, although Koettlitz was grateful to have found a knowledgeable scientist and amenable companion in Bruce. Koettlitz worked on improving the expedition tents; he was an accomplished inventor and adaptor of expedition clothing and equipment and put this expertise to good use throughout the three years spent on Franz Josef Land. The final product was similar in all respects to the pyramid-shaped tent, with a secure entrance, that until recently was a common sight on polar and other extreme expeditions. William Speirs Bruce referred to the tents used on the Bruce-led *Scotia* expedition to the Antarctic as his 'Dr Koettlitz tents'. Koettlitz had also adapted and created face masks to prevent frostbite, as well as improved eye protectors and goggles to protect against both snow-blindness and the effects of wind and frostbite. He was experienced with the needle in stitching both clothing and humans.

They ate and drank well throughout this final winter, with no sign of scurvy or other ailments connected with a poor diet. It appeared that with Bruce as a member of the scientific team Jackson allowed more time for research and the collecting and recording of scientific specimens. With Bruce, Koettlitz prepared detailed geological maps of the area around Cape Flora. He spent much time writing up his extensive notes from his geologising activities, both those carried out alone and those wonderful days spent with Dr Nansen.

But everything has an end and the Arctic winter is no different. By the beginning of March 1897 the sun had returned, together with the birds and other wildlife. The sledges had been loaded but on this occasion only two of the expedition members could make sub-stantial journeys. The expedition was suffering from a shortage of both dogs and ponies, having been reduced to only a single pony and a few remaining dogs. This was sufficient to pull the stores and equipment for two men but no more. Accordingly, Jackson and Armit-age set out once more, on 16 March, heading west and north in an attempt to discover new lands and examine the extent of the Franz Josef Land archipelago. Once again Jackson left a series of instructions for Koettlitz and the others remaining at Cape Flora. Koettlitz and Bruce planned to carry out extensive scientific study of the area in which they resided, to make limited journeys on foot and to gather support for Koettlitz's theories on the age and structure of the rock faces in the region.

Koettlitz, Bruce and Wilton carried out a series of short excursions and achieved valu-able scientific results but they were hampered by a lack of animal transport which would have enabled them to explore more widely. The atmosphere at Elmwood was almost serene compared with that when Jackson was in residence. It was the sort of scientific environment that Bruce was keen to promote and he replicated it on his own *Scotia* expedition years later in the Antarctic – an expedition which Koettlitz always regretted not joining, despite having received an invitation from Bruce.

By around 1 May it was apparent that Jackson and Armitage were overdue. Although an exact return date had not been set, Koettlitz and the others were concerned for the safety of the men. In discussions with Bruce and Wilton it was decided that if they had not returned

The Koettlitz tents in use on the Scotia expedition

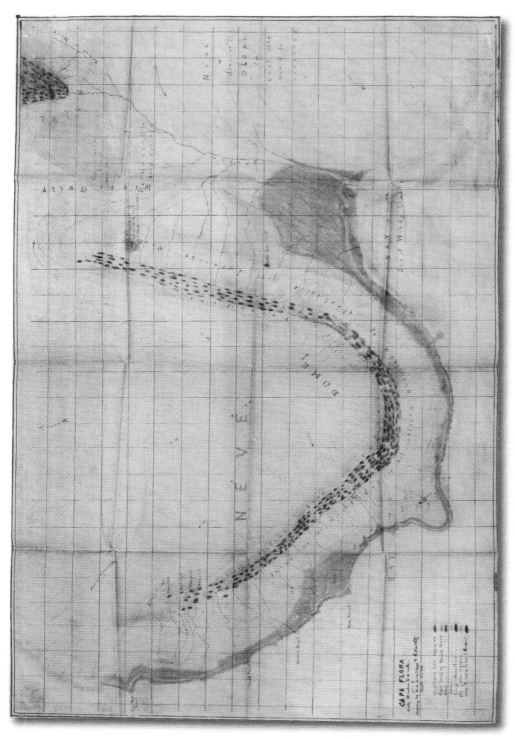

Koettlitz geological drawing showing geographic structure at Cape Flora

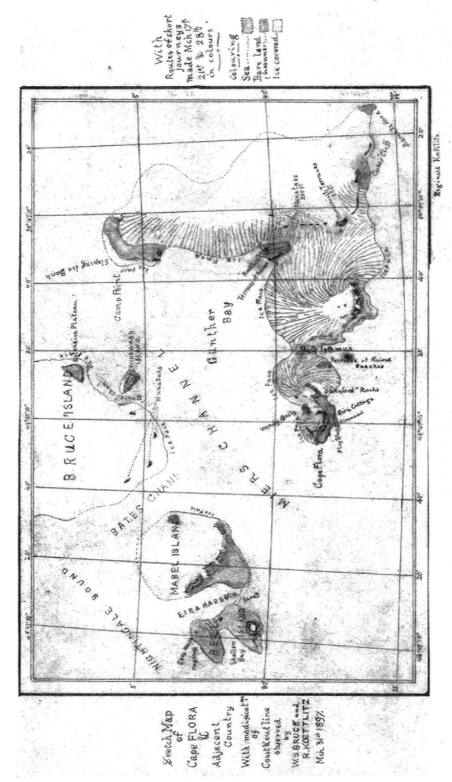

Koettlitz geological drawing showing Cape Flora and nearby islands

within seven days they would set out with relief supplies in an effort to trace them. This they duly did, pulling a sledge carrying 500 lbs of supplies, with Heyward left in charge at Elmwood. They found that using ski they could pull the sledge easily on smooth ice, and when this was not possible they man-hauled. Within 36 hours they had arrived at Eira Lodge on Bell Island, the lodge constructed by Leigh-Smith 16 years before. There they found Jackson and Armitage, who had recently arrived, in a dirty and grim condition having been forced to use bear oil for cooking when their fuel oil had run out.

Severe weather had delayed them for days at a time, confining them to their tent. The extreme weather had also killed their draught animals; the pony had died, together with nine of the dogs, leaving only five. This meant they had had to leave much of their equipment and supplies, which severely curtailed their marches and exploration. It also led to slow progress and the exhaustion of both men and the remaining dogs. The food and drink brought by Koettlitz and the others was gratefully received and consumed with much gusto and no little pleasure. They all remained at Eira Lodge for a further 36 hours due to bad weather and to allow Jackson and Armitage to recover their strength. Then together they set out for Elmwood, for the sheer delight of baths and home comforts, for Jackson and Armitage the first in weeks.

The date was 7 May 1897 and the two travellers had been away for nearly two months. Despite the handicaps of poor weather and the loss of the pony and dogs they had still covered a considerable distance. Setting out north and west alongside the British Channel they had managed to completely circumnavigate both Alexandra and Prince George's Islands, the largest in the archipelago, proving them for the first time to be separate islands. A journey of over 260 miles under often extreme conditions established them both as experienced polar travellers. Following these explorative journeys many islands and other features were named after the expedition members, including Koettlitz Island and Bruce Island which remain as lasting memorials to these early northern polar explorers.

A final short sledge journey was attempted in late May but was cut short by weak ice; one of their sledges fell through the ice and was lost. The rest of the summer was spent in and around Cape Flora carrying out further work for Koettlitz and Bruce's scientific studies, alongside all the usual duties necessary for survival.

Despite some later criticism of the scientific results there is no doubt the expedition made the greatest single contribution to the mapping of Franz Josef Land, laying the foundation for later expeditions. The expedition was to be described in later studies as 'the most innovative and successful British polar expedition for a generation'.[3]

By mid-summer the majority of the Cape Flora residents had decided they would not be remaining for a fourth year on Franz Josef Land. This included the two most recent arrivals, Bruce and Wilton, who wondered at times how Koettlitz and Armitage had lasted so long. So once again a lookout was kept for the *Windward*'s arrival from England, which would bring fresh stores and return expedition members to the United Kingdom.

On 7 July a ship was sighted but for an unexplained reason did not approach Cape Flora but continued up the Mier's Channel. It was later learnt that returning members of the expedition had spread word that the islands were inhabited by large numbers of walrus. The ship turned out to be the whaler *Baloena*, which had been whaling off Greenland and was returning via Franz Josef Land to hunt walrus, having heard from Captain Brown of

Map of central Franz Josef Land showing the extent of the expedition sledging journeys and discoveries

the *Windward* that it was an excellent and unexploited hunting ground. This coincided with the decline in whale numbers due to excess hunting and a concomitant dramatic increase in the price of whale oil, prompting walrus to become a profitable second option until their numbers inevitably also fell sharply.

On 22 July 1897 the *Windward* arrived at Cape Flora, closely followed by two other walrus hunting ships. It was apparent to Jackson that there was no support for staying a further year and that his attempt to gain the North Pole was over. During the following two weeks both expedition members and the crew of the *Windward* worked tirelessly to pack all their effects, scientific specimens and other equipment aboard the ship.

Koettlitz had endured three years in hostile polar lands with, at times, an unstable leader. In many areas his contribution had been an unqualified success, in particular his skill in keeping the entire land party fit and free from scurvy. In addition, he was confident that he had made important discoveries with regard to the age and structure of the islands of Franz Josef Land. He was impatient to return to England to prepare and present his findings to the Royal Geographical Society and the other eminent bodies in London. He had already been given crucial scientific support by Dr Nansen whilst they scoured the rocks and beaches around Cape Flora and was assured that his findings were sound. Nevertheless, some members of the expedition doubted his wisdom, pointing particularly to his lack of geological qualifications.

By 6 August they were ready to bid farewell to Cape Flora. As they left their home for the past three years the weather was good and the seas open. Jackson was keen to make further discoveries before leaving the archipelago and took them west in clear conditions then proceeded northwest to see if there was substance to Gillis Land which was supposed to be in that direction. They landed at Cape Mary Harmsworth and found a large, shingly beach on the west side of the Cape. Koettlitz carried out further geological study and in the process discovered the largest breeding colonies of eider duck and ivory gulls on the islands.

The *Windward* then headed northwest for a further 50 miles until she was stopped by thick and impassable ice. They saw no further signs of land in that direction; soundings showed that the depth of the ocean was more than 200 fathoms, indicating there was no land nearby. Jackson decided to turn back and set course for Johannan's and Andreasen's Islands but they found no trace of these islands which had been reported by previous travellers. They did not waste any more time looking for further land and set course for home. En-route they passed the Hope and Fear Islands, which afforded good views and a chance of landing, but all were impatient to return.

Stormy weather and adverse winds delayed their return but eventually the *Windward* arrived at Erith on the River Thames, after an absence for Koettlitz and the original expedition members of three years and two months.

One of the eminent people who greeted the *Windward*, and Koettlitz in particular, was Dr William Henry Neale from the *Eira* expedition. His views on preventing scurvy – lots of fresh meat and bear's blood in soup – had influenced the way Koettlitz dealt with the prevention of the disease on the expedition. In fact, Koettlitz had refined this advice by insisting on the daily consumption of fresh meat supported by whatever vegetable and fruit was available. Although lime juice was consumed its use was not compulsory. It transpired it was not required due to the high consumption of fresh bear, walrus and wild bird meat.

Koettlitz was convinced his theories were correct, with evidence provided by the death from scurvy of William Moatt, the only man involved with the expedition who refused to eat fresh bear and walrus meat. Koettlitz's experience also disproved the theory of Dr Almroth Wright, who believed that scurvy could be prevented by using sodium citrate and calcium chloride to create acid intoxication of the blood. Unfortunately, Wright's unproven theories were still accepted by some influential members at the time the National Antarctic Expedition set out in 1901.

As regards Koettlitz, he returned a man with greater knowledge in many areas, in particular with regard to survival on polar expeditions and to his geological and general scientific expertise. It was time to put this new-found knowledge to the test before the polar and geological experts in the institutions of London.

---

1. Koettlitz expedition journals retained in Koettlitz family archives.

2. *Ibid.*

3. Unknown source.

14

The geology of Franz Josef Land

D r Koettlitz concentrated on the preparation of his substantial paper to be presented at the Royal Geographical Society, London. The views put forward in this paper were complementary to the earlier papers and specimens he had sent back from Franz Josef Land with the *Windward*. His earlier reports had been subject to criticism by members of the Society, in particular Mr E. T. Newton and Mr J. J. H. Teall, both respected members. In fact, it was Newton who eventually communicated the paper before the Society on 22 June 1898.

As mentioned earlier, Dr Koettlitz had gained his geological knowledge from private study and extensive geological research in the area of County Durham when he was the resident doctor in Butterknowle village. Fridtjof Nansen was aware of this but still greatly admired Koettlitz's skill and scientific knowledge. He was in regular correspondence with Koettlitz on his return to Dover and on 30 October 1898, while aboard the *Fram*, he wrote a long letter concerning their findings on Franz Josef Land. This included the following comment, which should leave no doubt about his regard for Koettlitz's geological expertise:

> When this work is finished, which I hope will not take long now, I'm taking up discussion on some of the most interesting points connected with the geography and geology of that desolate little group of islands, where our friendship was first established, and the geological history of which we have so often discussed on our not-to-be-forgotten excursions together.
>
> You will, however, easily understand that I should not write on this subject without paying all possible attention to what you may have to say on the subject, on which you have laid down so much valuable work, and where yourself will be the authority.
>
> I am therefore looking forward with anticipation and impatience to your memoir, which I understood you were working on when we last met.[1]

This is a substantial endorsement of the geological expertise and knowledge possessed by Dr Koettlitz, something which others were not so willing to accept. The letter continued with many questions to Koettlitz concerning the geology of the islands and confirms the great esteem Nansen held for Koettlitz as a geologist.

Koettlitz had sent back with the *Windward* many samples of rock and fossils he had collected on the islands. With these samples were his initial findings and comparisons with other locations in the Arctic regions. His conclusions were widely disputed by the members of the Royal Geographical Society, in particular Messrs Newton and Teall as mentioned. Their judgement was certainly clouded by Koettlitz's lack of official qualifications. This was his opportunity to address these doubts and prove his findings were correct.

Koettlitz described the initial approach to Franz Josef Land as seen from the *Windward*, with cliffs rising to over 1,000 feet and snow- and ice-covered mountains to over 2,000 feet. They later found continuous ice faces which stretched down to the sea shore and completely covered entire islands, Bruce Island being one such example. The paper then sets out in detail the geological construction of each island visited or discovered by the expedition over the following three years. Geological examination of the available land was limited to a maximum of three to four months each year due to the Arctic winter and severe weather conditions. The paper was accompanied by comprehensive drawings prepared by Koettlitz whilst on the islands. More detailed study was possible of Northbrook Island and Cape Flora and the nearby islands due to their proximity to the expedition base, and these areas are discussed in greater detail.

Koettlitz's findings were supported by Dr Nansen following his time on the islands, as well as by the conclusions of the Swedish geologist Dr Alfred Gabriel Nathorst following his examination of samples taken by Koettlitz and Nansen. He showed that the rocks examined on Franz Josef Land were from the Jurassic period and not, as previously thought, from another geological period. Both Teall and Newton made their judgements from smaller samples brought back by the previous Payer and Leigh-Smith expeditions and the earlier, incomplete samples from Koettlitz sent back with the *Windward*. They could not accept that the unqualified geologist doctor could be correct in his findings. But Dr Nathorst was clear in a letter sent to Nansen, and included in Nansen's *Furthest North*, that these samples were from the Jurassic period.

Koettlitz set out in detail the reasons for coming to this conclusion:

The finding of ammonites macrocephalus in Franz Josef Land extends the range of this ammonite several degrees more to the north than it was previously known to occur, and the plant bearing beds, in association with those containing this ammonite, shows that a coast line at no very great distance must have existed.

These soft rocks therefore, known to be of Jurassic age, were subsequently covered up by successive flows of basalt, and the question arises as to when these flows took place, and whether they were deposited upon the surface as lava, or whether intruded between older strata, as intrusive sills.

Contrary, I believe, to the opinion of others who have examined the specimens brought home, I consider them to be of Jurassic age. Having had the advantage of examining the rocks in situ, I have gained a clearer conception of their conditions than can be possibly obtained by description.

My reasons for thinking them of this age, and not Tertiary like the basaltic formations of Scotland are as follows -

That the lowest bed of the series has tuff-like material underlying it, so have also other tiers, which proves the flow to have been sub-aerial and not intrusive.

The layers of basalt are vesicular on their upper and lower surfaces and compact in the centre, which also points to non-intrusion.

In the middle tiers of the basalt I have discovered large masses of fossil-wood enclosed in it, and also wood charred into charcoal.

The stratified rock between the tiers being only thin strata, continue so level, and show so little evidence of displacement, that they must have been laid down where they now are, and it appears impossible that the basalt could have been intruded underneath them.

That in association with these stratified beds are layers of tuff.

Where the basalt is in contact with these stratified rocks they do not appear to be materially altered by heat.

That in these strata I found fossil-plants which are considered to be of Upper Jurassic Age.

These reasons appear to me to be conclusive as to their age, if the date assigned to the fossil-plants to be correct![2]

The fossil-plants were of course examined by Dr Nathorst, so Koettlitz was confident of his findings, but the debate continued for a further 18 months and at the conclusion of the meeting at the Royal Geographical Society opinion remained divided. All agreed that Dr Koettlitz had carried out outstanding work under trying conditions. Mr Goodchild, a forceful member of the Society, spoke highly of the scientific value of Koettlitz's work, but still the paper was not endorsed by the members.

From the moment Koettlitz returned from the expedition until early in 1900 he kept up a constant correspondence with Nansen and, at times, Nathorst, concerning the age of the land mass on Franz Josef Land. This was particularly active before and around the time of the reading of his paper at the Royal Geographical Society. Nansen was also in correspondence with Nathorst, keen to get his public support for Dr Koettlitz. He had earlier identified the expedition leader Jackson as 'Having no scientific interest, in fact, completely lacking in all kinds of knowledge'.[3]

Finally, in a letter dated 8 December 1899 from J. J. H. Teall, Dr Koettlitz received the news and confirmation he had been working towards since walking the slopes of Cape Flora with Fridtjof Nansen:

My dear Koettlitz,

I have just received a paper by Hamberg on the basalt of King Charles Land. I am delighted to find that your opinion as to the age of the basalt is confirmed.

A weaker man would have been inclined to give way. You stuck to your guns and have won.

Hamberg describes fragments of basalt in a calcareous sand stone containing Mesozoic plants. I have re-read what I wrote at the conclusion of our first paper and am not ashamed of it. You will see I call attention to the absence of marine upper cretaceous in the Deccan and point at the possibility of the basalt being older in some places than in others.

It looks as if these eruptions began in the North Atlantic region, in Mesozoic times and continued right away down to the present (Iceland).

Hearty congratulations.

Yours faithfully,

J.J.H. Teall[4]

Koettlitz had been vindicated and had proved to the foremost geologists and other experts, in London and Europe, that his knowledge and expertise as a geologist was valid. It was a substantial achievement for a man whose medical skills were never in doubt but who had struggled to establish his geological credentials to all but his friend and confidant Fridtjof Nansen.

There is no doubting that Koettlitz would never settle back into the routine of general practice in the towns and shires of England. He had found his calling as an explorer, geologist and expedition surgeon. He lectured widely on his experiences whilst with the Jackson-Harmsworth Expedition and on polar exploration in general. He gave presentations at, for example, his old college in Dover, the prestigious Manchester Geographical Society, the Scottish Geographical Society and of course the Royal Geographical Society in London.

Although mentioned previously, it is worth examining the Dover and Manchester lectures in more detail because they showed an experience and foresight relating to the way possible future polar expeditions should be conducted. Koettlitz was anxious to be involved with, or lead, an expedition without delay.

His lecture in the Norman Hall of Dover College was given not only to the assembled pupils but also to the citizens of Dover. Dover at the time was a town and port of significance, with a colourful history dating back to Roman times. In fact, later excavations revealed Dover to be the leading port in Roman northern Europe and it still boasts the largest Roman remains in northern Europe. This ancient history has recently been enhanced by the discovery of an almost intact Bronze Age boat, possibly the best preserved ever found. It was within this historical context that Dr Koettlitz lectured.

At regular intervals he was loudly cheered by the assembled throng as he gave a concise history of Arctic exploration, mentioning Weyprecht and Payer who had led the Austrian expedition that had discovered Franz Josef Land, followed by the *Eira* expedition. He addressed the assembly with graphic details of the food eaten by the survivors of the stricken *Eira* – the meat of polar bears and walrus and broth made from their blood and boiled meat which had kept them free from scurvy and any major illness. He talked about the importance of dogs for hauling sledges and the use of clothing based on the design and type of the Samoyed and other Arctic peoples, and the benefits of ski and Arctic snow shoes – at which point he donned his Arctic clothing made from reindeer skin and fur by way of a demonstration, much to the delight of the audience.

The *Dover Telegraph* reported: 'He showed the garments worn, and a pitch of excitement was reached when, doffing a portion of his "evening dress" he donned them, and appeared as a fully-equipped Arctic explorer. The lecture was an outstanding success and showed that Dover College was privileged to have such an experienced polar explorer within its alumni.'[5]

The later lecture to the members of the Manchester Geographical Society (MGS) in the Coal Exchange was a far more serious affair and was given to a knowledgeable and influential audience. Between the two lectures Koettlitz had travelled on the Weld Blundell Expedition to North East Africa and had completed his solo trip up the Amazon River. His departure on the Scott-led *Discovery* expedition was to commence later in 1901. The Manchester lecture was therefore presented by a considerably more experienced doctor.

He commenced his lecture with these words:

Never be contented! Do not even wish to be! For an unsatisfied condition of mind, though consciously only vaguely realised by most people as the usual condition nowadays, and perhaps more rarely expressed in words, is nevertheless directly the origin and incentive

THE JOURNAL

OF THE

MANCHESTER GEOGRAPHICAL SOCIETY.

POLAR WORK: WHAT IT IS, WHY IT SHOULD BE DONE, AND WHAT IS STILL TO BE DONE THERE, ETC.

[Addressed to the Members in the Coal Exchange, Wednesday, January 16th, 1901, at 7-30 p.m.]

By Dr. REGINALD KŒTTLITZ.

DR. REGINALD KŒTTLITZ.

NEVER be contented! Do not even wish to be! For an unsatisfied condition of mind, though consciously only vaguely realised by most people as the usual condition nowadays, and perhaps more rarely expressed in words, is nevertheless directly the origin and incentive

VOL. XVII.—NOS. 4-6—APRIL TO JUNE, 1901.

Front page of the Manchester Geographical Journal

which impels the world towards progress, is the stimulus which causes men to think, and is the fountain of the ambitions which result in consequent action![6]

These few words at the start of this lecture encapsulate Dr Koettlitz's approach to exploration and scientific research. They also shed light on his impatience and occasional dislike of others who did not meet his expectations.

He continued to discuss the benefits of polar exploration, why Great Britain should be in the lead and that it was not necessary to wait for government assistance when supported by private individuals and business. There was no criticism of Nansen and other eminent explorers but he did question why Britain should stay quietly at home looking on whilst others were embracing polar exploration. He emphasised the importance of not only scientific but also commercial gain from such exploration, an interesting example being the use of walrus hide in making burnishers for bicycle production. He gave many examples from his experience gained on the Jackson-Harmsworth Expedition to Franz Josef Land, comparing it with exploration of the south and Antarctic regions.

Great attention was paid to the flora and fauna of these regions, in particular the north, with eloquent descriptions of the bird and animal life found on Franz Josef Land and new discoveries made there. He accepted that the south was largely unknown in geological, biological and botanical matters whereas the extensive plant, bird and animal life of the north was better known.

> Take, for instance, an example from my own personal experience again. At the present time trees do not extend further north in Europe and Asia, as well as in America, than some distance south of the shore of the Arctic Ocean – roughly, about 70 degrees north. Well, I have proved that in late Jurassic and early cretaceous times forests existed, bushes, ferns and other vegetation, which does not extend nearly so far north now, flourished luxuriantly in Franz Josef Land, which is 80 degrees north or 600 to 1000 miles further north. This proves that the climate was at least sub-Arctic there then and not Arctic. In other parts it has been shown to have been sub-tropical about there.[6]

It was an ideal time and place to display to such an audience the successful outcome of his geological and scientific research whilst on Franz Josef Land, which had been disputed by so many within the scientific community. It also showed his credentials for his selection as the geologist on the forthcoming *Discovery* expedition to the Antarctic.

Although a serious man Koettlitz still found time to admire the beauty of the polar regions: 'How can I, or indeed any one, describe to you the charm of the Arctic? A man must be a poet, an artist, and a musician all in one to be able to give an even imperfect idea as to its strangeness, its beauty and its grandeur.'[6]

Having travelled to both the tropics and the high north he thought the tropics did not compare with the Arctic sky in beauty and vividness of colour, but went on:

> The only horror and bugbear of polar travel is the long winter night. It is not the cold, for you soon get used to it. The dreary monotony, darkness and length of it – if one has already experienced one such night, causes him to shrink with a great loathing from the near approach of another. The darkness, being even at mid-day as profound as at midnight, prevents him from being able to take more than a most groping form of exercise, and then it

is that he looks forward most eagerly for each return of the moon, whose advent is a source of comfort and gladness.[6]

Koettlitz then spoke on the experience of living in polar conditions, amongst cold, bleak and desolate surroundings. He described the food, clothing, lighting and other essentials to life in these regions – even down to problems of keeping the pipe alight, 'which will generally freeze up unless one continually draws at it and afterwards keeps it in a warm place about one's person'.

He began his closing remarks by asking the question of whether any of this was essential or even worth the effort, and came to these conclusions:

Numberless are the questions which might, with some justification, be asked. I will answer this by another. Does anyone here doubt but that knowledge is a good thing? Who can know too much? Such a thing is impossible, and the more one knows, what does it teach him? Only how little he does know! Knowledge is power, it gives life a keener interest and enjoyment, is production and money when rightly made use of![6]

He then moved on to the crucial final section of the presentation, the idea formulated by Dr Nansen during their time together on Franz Josef Land:

With such knowledge and experience before us, therefore, is it not the duty of every cen-tre of education and commerce to take their part in promoting exploration and research wherever it can be undertaken? A centre like Manc^l ester, teeming with population, with its own university, its grand museums and libraries, schools, and other means of education, with its wealth, opportunities and enterprise, should therefore come to the fore and take its place in forwarding and promoting research, especially geographical. Might I suggest that there is a geographical feat well worthy of Manchester's attention? A feat which all the efforts of three centuries of men, from Baffin until now, have been unable, after repeated, gallant and persistent efforts, to perform, a feat, the attempts to gain which absorbed the attention of the world, and produced a great outlay of Great Britain's money, especially during the first half of the century just left behind. I speak of the making of the North-west passage.[6]

He emphasised the words spoken by Nansen when they were discussing the making of the Northwest Passage while on Franz Josef Land. Nansen felt strongly that after the amount of labour, lives and money Great Britain had expended on the enterprise, her task was to bring it to a successful result.

Why should not Manchester step in, take up the task, and gain the glory of at last accomplishing it? Koettlitz had given the subject, together with that of taking the North Pole, much thought and believed that £80,000 and four years could accomplish these tasks. He encouraged the well-heeled businessmen of Manchester to back these ideas and bring further glory to the city. He made mention of the other two British expeditions in the planning stage, the Scott-led National Antarctic Expedition to Antarctica and the W. S. Bruce-led Scottish scientific expedition also going south. Although Koettlitz had already been selected as a member of the National Antarctic Expedition, his later letters written from South Africa showed he would have gladly led, or jointly led, an attempt on the Northwest Passage. But, as with his attempts to gain financial backing for a long-term scientific expedition to the south whilst living in South Africa, the funds were not forthcoming.

The lecture given at the Manchester Geographical Society brought to an end Koettlitz's involvement in and further discussion concerning the Jackson-Harmsworth Expedition, but its importance in shaping his polar credentials is not in doubt.

---

1. Letter from Nansen to Koettlitz dated 30 October 1898, written from Lysaker, Norway.

2. Koettlitz statement on the geology of Franz Josef Land (Appendix to *1000 Days in the Arctic*).

3. Koettlitz expedition journals retained in Koettlitz family archives.

4. Letter from J. J. H. Teall to Koettlitz dated 8 December 1899 – Koettlitz family archives.

5. *Dover Telegraph* article dated 3 November 1897 – Dover Museum archives.

6. Manchester Geographical Society presentation by Dr Koettlitz, Wednesday 16 January 1901.

PART 3: THROUGH AFRICA AND SOUTH AMERICA

15

Weld Blundell Expedition to Africa

The expedition to the far north had imbued in Dr Koettlitz an appetite for further travel and a desire to carry out more scientific research whilst on expeditions to the wild and unexplored corners of the globe. His time spent at the Royal Geographical Society in London and other such bodies in Manchester, Glasgow and Edinburgh, presented him with opportunities to meet others planning such expeditions.

One such person was Herbert Weld Blundell, who in the spring of 1898 accompanied Captain J. L. Harrington on his journey to Addis Ababa (Addis Abbeba) to take up his appointment as the first diplomatic representative in the capital of Abyssinia (now Ethiopia). Their route took them from Zeila on the coast via Harar to Addis Ababa. Mr Weld Blundell thought Abyssinia a land of great opportunity. Prior to his departure in May, before the rainy season, he had sought permission to return in the following November. Immediately on his return to England he set about planning his expedition and choosing its members.

Dr Koettlitz's skill as an expedition surgeon and geologist was well known within the expeditionary circles of the time and he was duly appointed as doctor, geologist, anthropologist and field manager with responsibility for stores and transport. The other expedition members appointed by Weld Blundell were Lord Lovat (his nephew), Mr Harwood (a taxidermist), and a valet to act as camp superintendent, making five in total. They would be supported by numerous locally hired attendants of varied expertise and tribal backgrounds. The means of transport was to be camels and horses on the initial section, departing from the coastal port of Berbera on the Somali coast.

The expedition objectives were clearly defined: to map the country, especially the portions not previously visited by 'white men'; to investigate the geological formations; and to make zoological collections, especially ornithological ones, and as many anthropological and ethnological observations as possible. It was proposed to travel continually so that the expedition could be completed in six months. Weld Blundell had the experience of his previous brief visit so had clear ideas about what was to be achieved.

Travelling independently they met up in Aden at the end of November 1898. Several days were spent hiring Somali servants, obtaining the final stores and a few luxuries and writing letters home before crossing the Gulf of Aden to Berbera. There they hired camels, ponies and mules for the caravan and by 6 December were ready to set out for the first objective, Harar. The caravan finally consisted of 35 pack camels and mules, 18 attendants to the pack animals, ten personal servants and four Sudanese soldiers who had fought at the Battle of Omdurman, for protection, plus a head man. In addition to the ponies for the Europeans, a donkey and sheep were taken along as bait for lions in case any were encountered.

Dr Koettlitz did not waste the short time in Berbera and made a thorough exploration of the town and its surrounding area. Berbera at the time was split into two sections: an area for the European occupants, which included a barracks, post office, shops, a hospital and a number of foreign consular offices including the British residence; and another for local inhabitants. A fine harbour divided the two. In the limited time available Koettlitz made a number of scientific observations, including the discovery of an interesting mollusc which when later examined at the Natural History Museum was classified as a new species, *Sepia Koettlitzi*. He regarded this as a fine start to the expedition, although of course he was unaware at the time of the importance of his find.

Berbera was chosen as the departure point rather than Zeila because it was hoped they would pass through more fertile and more easily travelled country. Finally, on 6 December the expedition set off early to prevent the native porters disappearing into town to sample the available human pleasures. The immediate countryside was fairly barren, with little grass or other vegetation, but game was often spotted. Eventually the landscape improved and the flora and fauna accordingly, especially the bird life. Caravans were often seen passing in the opposite direction carrying all manner of goods, including food and ivory, with large families in attendance.

The doctor's skills were soon put to the test when the following day one of the men was stung by a large scorpion. While the insect is known to have been promptly placed in a bottle for preservation, the fate of the native is unfortunately not recorded. Their choice of route proved a good one and the vegetation became luxuriant with many palm trees, meadows and attendant bird life and large flocks of goat. By now they were already 2,740 feet above sea level. They passed through a small town, Addi Adeya, meaning 'white with flocks', an apt description.

On the march they shot partridge, guinea-fowl and the occasional bustard, keeping the larder well stocked, so they ate well. The collection of wild birds to be used for scientific research on return to England was already growing. These included parrots, toucans, partridge, bustards, rollers, sunbirds, weaver birds, shrikes, doves, Egyptian vultures, golden eagle and beautifully coloured starlings. Most remarkable to the ear was the bell-noted shrike or anvil bird, which made a noise similar to the blacksmith striking his anvil. The expedition was ultimately to collect 520 specimens, representing 299 species. This included 11 new species unknown to science at the time. The expedition was congratulated by the Ornithological Club in London in an address given in November 1899 celebrating their achievement.

They had to be continually vigilant both on the march and in camp as wild animals were common and not afraid to approach. For example, when they were camped at Jummat early

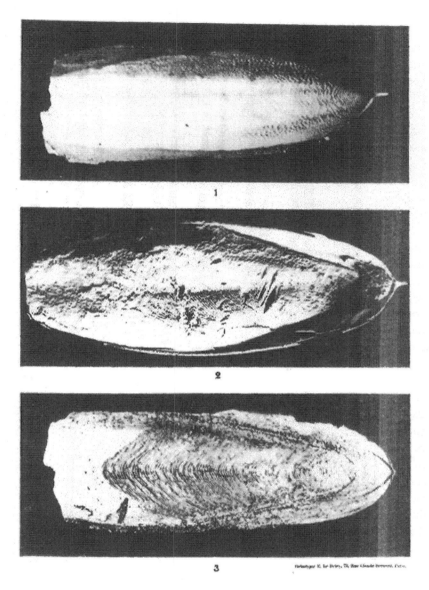

The mollusc Sepia Koettlitzi

in the journey a leopard leapt into the animal compound in the middle of the night and made off with a sheep before the guard could stop it.

At every opportunity Koettlitz made geological observations of the areas through which they passed. He was intrigued by the number and size of the obelisk-like white ant and termite heaps often attached to dead trees or rotting wood; he was amazed at the industry of these tiny creatures. The group occasionally diverted from the planned route to hunt for game, which at times was plentiful; this included the beautiful oryx and many antelope. This was sometimes necessary for the larder but also to procure trophies to exhibit on return to England.

They were impressed with the number of domesticated animals being herded by the local Somalis, including cattle, sheep and goats in large numbers as well as tame ostriches, which were kept for both food and feathers. After a short break in the area of Jefr Medir to allow Mr Weld Blundell to hunt (unsuccessfully) for lion, they crossed the Meran prairie, heading for Jig-Jigga at a height of more than 5,300 feet above sea level.

The wooded terrain populated with cedars, thorny acacias and other trees came to an abrupt end. The next 40 or so miles consisted of flat grassland, where mirages were common – visions of large lakes where none existed. Antelope were also common and many fell to their rifles, both for food and for trophy. Whilst the others spent time hunting Koettlitz made geological notes and studied the rock formations. The expedition continued to climb the extensive plain and the nights became increasingly chilly, in sharp contrast to the daytime temperatures. The Somali servants felt the cold keenly and were described as pitiable objects, a description not unusual for the time.

They arrived in Jig-Jigga, a town situated on a small river marking the boundary line between British and Abyssinian territory, during the evening of 22 December. Although many antelope had been shot, Weld Blundell was disappointed that lion, elephant and other big game had not been taken. It was at Jig-Jigga that they encountered their first Abyssinians, at a stockaded military post in the town. The local chieftain and other leading officials lived in large houses, called toukuls, in the town. At a meeting with the local chief, accompanied by many armed warriors, gifts of eggs, sheep, goats, fowls and tedge (local mead) were exchanged. After this exchange, permission was granted to travel through the country of King Menelik, and thus there was no opposition to their progress.

After a short stay in Jig-Jigga the expedition set off for Fiambiro, a market town and trading centre some two days march away. The terrain was very different, more difficult to traverse, with many streams and rivers to cross. The villages they passed appeared to be more permanent, with well-constructed, circular huts with conical roofs. It was harvest time and large heaps of grain were seen in each village. The well-cultivated hillsides reminded Dr Koettlitz of the vineyards of the rivers Rhine or Mosel.

They reached the plateau on which Fiambiro is located, and measured the height as 6,403 feet above sea level. Fiambiro was a small market town in which sheep, goats, cattle, donkeys, camels and many foodstuffs were traded between Somalis and Abyssinians. Koettlitz took advantage of their short stay to make a study of the geology of the area, taking samples of the rock formations for scientific examination on return to England. The party spent Christmas Day at Fiambiro. Here they also paid off their Somali camel drivers – the countryside from here would prove unsuitable for camels. Mules were now to be the means of transportation.

Many of the mules were in fact owned by Weld Blundell, who had purchased them following his previous short visit with Captain Harrington. They had been brought here from Addis Ababa by an extraordinary figure named McKelvey, who was known as the Abyssinian Englishman. Koettlitz wrote:

McKelvey, although being white was attired in every respect just the same as an Abyssinian, his head was shaved, and as so common with Abyssinians, bound up in a white cotton cloth, upon which was the usual terrai-like hat so frequently used by these people, the shamma or long cotton cloth worn as a shawl, or toga fashion, over his shoulders, the short narrow-legged cotton pantaloons and nothing upon the lower legs and feet. Under the shamma he also wore a cotton shirt and that is all! This man was now one of the interpreters of the British Agency.[1]

It transpired that McKelvey had been one of the original prisoners taken following the battle at Magdala. He had been tortured like the rest and retained the scars. Having been rescued and returned as far as Alexandria he had elected to return to Abyssinia, where he had remained for over 37 years, living as a native Abyssinian. When Captain Harrington first located him in Addis Ababa he had forgotten his native English tongue but soon picked it up again when he heard Harrington and others speaking.

Koettlitz continued:

All these years he had lived in the barbarous fashion of the natives. He had served King Theodore and King John as a soldier, but most of his time had been spent making a living as a merchant, a kind of hawker who takes his wares upon pack-mules from place to place and attending the markets. In this practice he had travelled across wide tracts of the country. Needless to say, his moral conditions had sunk. Not only has he the vices of the Abyssinian, but combined with these are some European ones, and there are no redeeming qualities. He is most unreliable, a perfect yet plausible humbug and cheat.[1]

Whilst in Addis Ababa the doctor visited McKelvey's house, which he described as 'worse than some of the natives'.[1] There was no furniture or bedding and one squatted and slept on the floor upon a goat or cow skin. He had many children from many wives, the most recent being nine months old and as white as a European child.

Despite having passed this damning judgement on McKelvey, Koettlitz accepted that he was of considerable use to the expedition. He had superb knowledge of the country and its population. He was also adept at negotiations with local chieftains.

Like the bulk of the Abyssinian population McKelvey was a Christian, although Koettlitz thought this was more in name than fact; they took great pride in calling themselves Christians. He thought it remarkable that Christianity was widely practised, so surrounded were they by 'Mohammedan and other heathen' neighbours – although it did appear that only the wealthy attended church as the priests seemed to charge for attendance. He recorded that the quality and quantity of agricultural farming was less in Abyssinia than in Somalia, noting that it was the women who worked the fields as the men appeared to see themselves as warriors, not farmers.

As the group approached the outskirts of Harar, an Egyptian-built walled town situated on a rise in a fertile valley, some of these cultural observations began to change. Harar is a town of regional importance. As they made their way they travelled through well-irrigated gardens; the water was being fed to the fields and gardens by rough wooden aqueducts and gutters. The gardens were numerous and contained cotton, red pepper, tobacco and coffee, as well as other vegetables and fruits. It was truly a prosperous and fertile region, which supported a thriving commercial community. The town buildings were mainly of mud-plastered construction; there were narrow streets and terraces and both churches and mosques. It was a multi-cultural society – native Abyssinians, Greeks, Indians and a number of French citizens resided there. The walled town was guarded by gates, manned by a motley collection of soldiers whose duty was to impose a tax upon the traders passing back and forth.

The grandest building in town was occupied by the Governor, Ras Makonnen, on whose behalf the taxes at the city gates were being raised. His house was built in fine red granite and was surrounded by bazaars and shops selling merchandise of every description.

The expedition spent a few days in Harar writing letters home, hiring additional pack-mules and acquiring stores for the next section of their journey. On 31 December they left the pleasures of Harar and set off again, following a mountainous route via Kunnie to avoid the hot desert, although the desert route would have been more direct.

Whilst in Harar, Dr Koettlitz wrote a long letter to his brother Maurice, who continued as a doctor in general practice in Dover. Dated 29 December 1898 and addressed from the 'Doctor's tent, the camp near Harar, Abyssinia',[2] it gives an interesting insight into a Victorian-period African expedition on the march. It also highlights the marked contrast between the Abyssinia of that period and Ethiopia at the end of the 20th century, a country ravaged by regular famine and war.

My dear Morry,

I am just sending you a line, as there will be no caravan to Zeyla tomorrow, to let you know that all's well so far. We start tomorrow for Addis Abbaba a 3 weeks' journey from here. We started on the 6th inst from Berbera and have come S.W. from there, over the extraordinary barren, dry, rough country of Somaliland. We got to Jig-Jiga the frontier of this country on the 22nd and entered Abyssinia on the 23rd, my birthday.

The country quite changed there, more mountainous, and more water, so more vegetation. The people are also not nomads like the Somalis of Somaliland, more industrious, till the ground and live in rather better houses. As we neared Harar the cultivation increased, and beautifully kept gardens and banana palms, cotton and coffee became very frequent. Fields of dhumha (or millet) and other similar grain are everywhere.

This grass grows like maize to quite ten & twelve feet high. Piles of the ears of grain without stalks (which are left standing in the fields) were outside the villages and it looked more civilised. Yet the people are a neer-do-well, conservative, villainous looking lot, but smarter on the whole than the Somalis – who however are a miserable looking race of men.

Whilst writing this letter the flies which are a perfect plague here (about Harar) will not leave me alone. I have to stop writing continually to drive them away from my face, head, eyes & hands. The sun has been simply scalding by day, and the nights sometimes down to freezing point. We are 6000 feet above the sea. This altitude as well as latitude causes the heat of the day to be tempered by the cool north east trade winds, so that one does not feel the sun so much here as lower down in Somaliland.

My nose, hands and neck have been so affected by the sun as to cause these parts to feel as if frostbitten. They are also peeling in the same way as after frostbite.

I have not needed to take any precaution to avoid fever so far, except that I use your Pasteur filter for my drinking water every day. (I do not trust Blundell's filters). This is because there are no mosquitoes so far, and they are no doubt the principal cause of fever. I saw and felt one or two at Aden, and Berbera, but have not seen any since, though Lord Lovat says he has seen some in his tent.

I have a large tent all to myself, and am on the whole pretty comfortable. Have also my own pony to ride, and own seyce or groom.

Blundell however I do not care for nor also much for Lord Lovat. They are a bit too stand-offish for me. Quite what I should have expected of "nouveau riches".

I am sending back two more rolls of exposed films. Please have them carefully developed, or if you can, do them yourself and keep them numbered. I am getting 3 more complete sets of Abyssinian postage stamps with postcards & will retain them with me until I return. It appears that though printed (in France) and issued, they are not used.

Now give my love to all, especially mother, tell her that if I can I will write to her from Addis Abbaba. I hope Mabel and the baby are flourishing. Don't forget to give my greetings to the aunts and cousins.

Your affectionate brother

Reginald Koettlitz.

PS. Letters will find me if addressed to – c/o Messrs Cowasjee Durshaw Bros, Aden.[2]

The letter was received in the Dover Station Office at 10.30 p.m. on 22 January for delivery to his brother's address the following day. Considering the distance from a remote town in North East Africa and means of travel (foot, mule, camel, sea and rail) it reached Dover with commendable speed.

The letter also highlights once again the problem Dr Koettlitz had in relating to establishment personalities and his distaste for the English class system so prevalent and influential at the time. Koettlitz was a genuinely caring person who disliked abuse in all its forms.

On 31 December they set off once more by way of the longer, mountainous route via Kunnie to avoid the desert. This route led through more fertile country with much cultivation. Dr Koettlitz made frequent notes about the flora and fauna en-route and was much impressed with the colourful Quolquol tree, which possesses beautiful rose-coloured bunches of flowers hanging like candelabra arms. He also recorded many plants now common in the United Kingdom, among them jasmine, wild clematis, laburnum and the mountain ash or rowan tree.

On reaching Lake Hanamaya they discovered a great number and variety of birds and Blundell decided to delay for a day to make a collection for returning to England. They spent New Year's Day doing so, making an impressive and extensive collection which included warblers, grey wagtails, ducks, teal, coots, pochard, geese, white and black ibis, stilts, sandpipers, knots, grebes, swallows, martins and finches. Many of these birds were also common in Britain but there seems to have been no discussion regarding their migration from this region of Africa to and from Britain. In this period, despite hunting on a grand scale both at home and in Africa, the birds remained common and present in vast numbers, with just a few exceptions. The doctor again spent time examining the rock formations around the lake and immediate area, which he found consisted primarily of red granite with huge gullies formed by rain erosion over many centuries.

Their route took them into deep valleys, with precipitous descents which caused the doctor to wonder how laden mules would ever progress – but they did so without major mishap. He continued to make geological observations, comparing the area with the rock formations he had studied on the Isle of Skye and Franz Josef Land. The hills were formed almost entirely of basaltic material with the thick layers of basalt inter-bedded with a yellowish grey-coloured agglomerate and scoriaceous rock. Koettlitz came to the conclusion that their formation had been caused by extreme weathering conditions and noticed similar results as found in northern regions.

Following these few days of research and collecting they pressed on along the Arosso and Itu range of mountains, at heights of between 7,000 and 8,000 feet. Steep wooded slopes abounded in apes. There were great temperature variations between night and day; the native bearers shivered in their light cotton clothing and longed for the sun to rise to warm them up and make them more mobile. The English members of the expedition were of course comfortable in their tents with warm clothing and bedding.

1. Koettlitz paper for the *Scottish Geographical Magazine* No. 8, August 1900.
2. Letter from Koettlitz to his brother in England dated 29 December 1898 – Koettlitz family archives.

16

For England and St George

On arriving at Lake Chercher Weld Blundell again delayed to obtain more examples of the local bird life, which was found in abundance, together with crickets and grasshoppers in vast numbers and varieties. From here the journey continued via Laga Hardim, following the telegraph line that had been installed between Harar and Addis Ababa. This was a single line of wire elevated on posts and trees and had been erected by a German company with the assistance of King Menelik. It was not well maintained and was often out of commission. The operating stations were at distances of two or three days march. Normally placed within well-stockaded compounds, they consisted of a few huts with limited furniture and an electric battery to activate the system. Great patience was required before a message could be passed along the line – but this was the expedition's first opportunity to pass a message to Addis Ababa.

The following days involved much hot and dusty travelling in difficult countryside. As temperatures in the daytime were so high, it was decided to travel in the evening to ease the burden on both men and animals. The expedition was in the country of the Galla and Danakil tribes, which caused their Abyssinian porters some alarm. These people had a hostile reputation. On one occasion a group of warriors were seen approaching and Weld Blundell formed an armed ambuscade on some high ground. When challenged by Blundell it transpired they were an elephant hunting party and they were allowed to pass. News of Blundell's approach to such matters must have been passed around the region's tribes as they were not troubled in any way during the rest of the journey to Addis Ababa. They continued to traverse the Fantalle Hills and Kassim Valley, which formed parts of the great Hawash River Valley, with Koettlitz making comprehensive geological observations as usual. He described the valley they had passed through as being studded with beautifully preserved extinct volcanic craters, both large and small, and observed that in his opinion they were of quite recent formation in geological terms.

After traversing this valley the expedition arrived at the fortified town of Godoburka, which was surrounded by a basaltic wall and ramparts with an imposing fortified entrance. From his geological observations at Godoburka Dr Koettlitz believed this range of volcanoes identified a line of weakness in the Earth's crust that stretched southwest to northeast from Lake Rudolph passing north to the Red Sea and Aden, and even as far as the Dead Sea in Palestine.

From Godoburka they ascended to Balchi and the high plateau. After three days' march through this thinly populated region the expedition arrived in the capital of Abyssinia, Addis

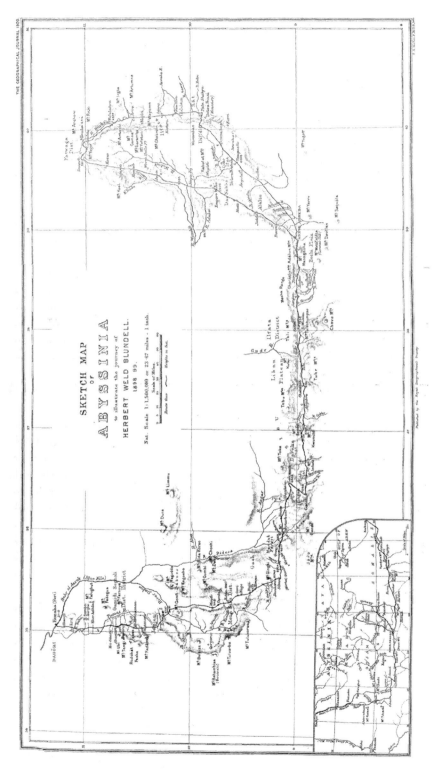

Weld Blundell Expedition route map

Ababa. Koettlitz's initial impressions were not favourable; he described the place as being scarcely worthy of the description 'town' for it consisted of nothing more than a vast number of toukuls (huts) scattered singly or in groups over a stretch of undulating countryside some six miles in extent. The area was cut through by a number of streams which no effort had been made to bridge. The King's compound, known as a Gebbi, occupied a prominent position in the centre and included a small number of stone buildings recently constructed by Indian masons with the help of some Italian and French merchants.

Britain of course was represented by Captain Harrington who had arrived in the previous year accompanied by Weld Blundell. There were other representatives from France, Russia and Italy, the Russians having the largest establishment including a medical team. The bulk of the trade both locally and internationally was carried out by Indians, Greeks and Armenians. There were numerous markets throughout the town, which sold the agricultural goods produced by the Gallas. Koettlitz described the main market as 'being occupied by a large, motley crowd who squat on the ground with their wares spread out before them'.[1] There was a medley of buyers and sellers dealing in every type of commodity including foodstuffs, mules, donkeys, cattle, sheep and goats.

Also in the capital were a small number of conical, thatch-roofed churches surmounted by the characteristic Abyssinian or Coptic cross. The British government compound at the time consisted of a number of tents and temporary huts surrounded by a mud wall which provided a limited amount of security. As mentioned, the resident consul was Captain Harrington who was supported in manual labours and with local contacts by the somewhat dubious Irish-English trader McKelvey.

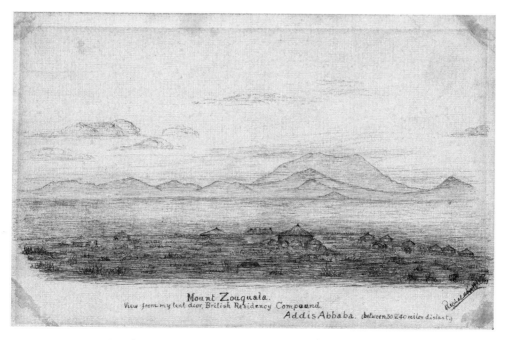

Mount Zouquala.
View from my tent door, British Residency Compound.
Addis Abbaba. (between 30 & 40 miles distant.)

Koettlitz painting drawn from the British Residency compound

The stay in Addis Ababa was to be a prolonged one as Blundell, accompanied by Lord Lovat, had to travel to meet the King to gain his permission to travel further. The King's camp was some 180 miles to the north near Magdala, where he was located with his army to receive submission of a rebel subject Ras Mangasha.

Dr Koettlitz remained in the capital in charge of their main camp, making the necessary preparations for the continuation of their journey. As always he spent his time wisely. He made a journey of some 40 miles south to visit Mount Zouquala, the famous holy mountain of the Abyssinians, shown on his detailed painting drawn from the British compound. As always he had an eye for the geological features of the mountain, describing it as a lofty mass of some 2,000 feet which forms one of a series of perfect extinct volcanic craters in the region. On the lower slopes were scattered villages, whilst the upper portion was densely wooded. On the summit there was a flat-bottomed valley partially filled by a lake. The total altitude was approximately 10,000 feet, resulting in a cold and bracing climate.

The local population regarded this place with a certain amount of superstition and believed that by bathing in and drinking the waters miraculous cures were wrought. Thus pilgrimages were made to the holy site by the sick, maimed and diseased from all parts of Abyssinia and beyond. These journeys depended on the state of security at the time, as is still the case. Water from springs falling from the rocky walls was believed by local women to be a cure for sterility and the whole mountain was dedicated to the Virgin Mary.

A number of priests and religious hermits were resident in the area and had formed a monastery. The men lived in isolated huts, sometimes hidden in the forest, or in small churches, also often concealed. All spent their lives in prayer and self-mortification. The doctor witnessed rigorous religious exercises which often took the form of severe floggings with hippopotamus hide whips until much blood was drawn. He thought the priests had a wild, half-maniacal appearance. Whilst wandering in the area Koettlitz came across a church within a small compound where a number of priests were engaged in casting out evils and associated religious acts. Their aim was to cast out the devil and other evil from sick and maimed people gathered before them. Many people were waiting in line to be treated.

Koettlitz gained entry to the church, leaving his Islamic attendants outside. Here the most amazing set of circumstances occurred, which are worth setting out in detail. It transpired that Dr Koettlitz was the first British national these priests and other church members had seen at this most holy of locations. It seems he was the first Western European, or one of the first, to explore this sacred mountain. The priests doubted his authority and his assertions that he was indeed a Christian. The Russians had for some time had considerable influence in the area and within the Abyssinian church, and the religious buildings held sacred items similar in appearance to the Russian Orthodox Church.

Therefore, the orthodoxy of any non-Russian claiming to be a Christian was doubted and very much questioned. It was believed that no other peoples apart from Abyssinians and Russians were Christians. Thus Dr Koettlitz found himself in the position of having to prove his Christian belief. He was shown a large number of Christian relics and paintings and closely questioned by the assembled priests as to their identity. The doctor passed with flying colours – the priests were delighted but still not wholly satisfied. On approaching the door of the holy of holies he was shown a great treasure, a double folding panel which depicted the annunciation of Mary and St George and the Dragon, who was the patron saint of both Abyssinia and its church.

Koettlitz pointed out that St George was also the patron saint of England and to prove the point he produced a gold sovereign from his pocket which displayed St George. It was rapidly and excitedly compared by the priests with the panel; their delight, wonder and excitement was unbounded. Dr Koettlitz was indeed a Christian and one of some considerable standing as he carried the proof in his pocket – a true Christian talisman to guard against all evil.

Koettlitz was subsequently granted full access to the churches and their treasures. It was a great privilege, not previously granted to any Englishman nor possibly since. If only he had been aware of the great unsolved mystery of the 'Ark of the Covenant', which is thought to be located in the very area where he was given such unprecedented and privileged access he may have investigated further.

It was a memorable and outstanding personal exploration and yet another example of Dr Koettlitz breaking new ground. This achievement has subsequently disappeared into the files of history and is being recorded here for only the second time.

Koettlitz returned to Addis Ababa with great satisfaction. Next he visited a series of hot springs close to the town which were much used by the sick, especially those suffering from rheumatism and skin complaints of every description. He wrote that the springs bubble up through the mud and rock in a close-by valley and flow into a rivulet nearby. He took the temperature of the springs and found them to be 170 degrees Fahrenheit (76.3°c).

People of both sexes stripped naked and, without any regard for decency, sat in the small basins made by the water and mud, in full public view. The only restriction on which basin to use was because of the extreme temperature emanating from the earth. Such bathing was also carried out on the summit of Mount Zouquala, where similar claims for the curative properties were made. Dr Koettlitz found these treatments of great interest and was impressed with their apparent success. He was determined to bring such treatments to England on his return, even if a man-made environment was required.

Since arriving in Aden, and during the land journey, Koettlitz had kept up a correspondence with Dr Nansen, despite the remote location and complexities of delivering the letters by mail. Their content was mainly connected with the expedition to and the geology of Franz Josef Land. Nansen held Koettlitz's geological observations in great regard. The final letters from Koettlitz written in Harar and Addis Ababa ran to 17 pages. This detailed information assisted Nansen's research and some of it was included in the subsequent journals concerning the journey of the *Fram* and Nansen's stay on Franz Josef Land.

At the beginning of March, Blundell and his companions returned from their prolonged diversion to see the King. He had granted permission for the expedition to continue on its route to the Blue Nile. Therefore, on 2 March they bade farewell to Addis Ababa and Captain Harrington, leaving him once again as the sole British representative in the capital. They travelled west through hilly and varied country along the base of the Metcha range of hills, crossing the Hawash, Guder and Gibbe rivers before arriving in the town of Bilo in the district of Leka. Bilo was an important trading town which housed the residence of the local chief or 'Choom' who controlled the region. Dr Koettlitz's reputation had preceded him and when he pitched his tent it was mobbed by the sick seeking treatment. His tent was overwhelmed and he was forced to instruct the Sudanese soldiers to 'lay about them' with hippopotamus hide whips to regain some order. However, he did his best to examine and treat all who attended for their many ailments, some of a quite personal nature. This experience also allowed him to record particular details of the natives of the region.

Despite a minor problem with the Choom concerning their continued progress – he was questioning the legality of the letter from the King and in particular the authority relating to the use of rifles to hunt elephant – the expedition pushed on to Gatamma, making good time. They proceeded through stunning, hilly countryside dotted with the many small villages of the Galla tribe en-route to Mendi.

Koettlitz was impressed with the Galla people, who had recently been subjugated by the Abyssinians. He described them as a fine-featured, well-formed, agricultural and pastoral race. They were kept in abject subjection by their conquerors by not being allowed to possess fire-arms or other weapons. The Abyssinians were thus able to rob and ill-treat them and tax their produce, without mercy. As a result the tribe was left in a very unhappy and perilous state.

On arrival in Mendi the expedition party was delayed and held captive by the deputy to the local Choom, Dejadge Demis, who was away on a distant raid. A runner was sent to the Demis to confirm their identity but a delay of almost three weeks ensued. Food was in short supply for the local population due to Abyssinian raids. The delay did however allow the doctor time to continue his study of the local people.

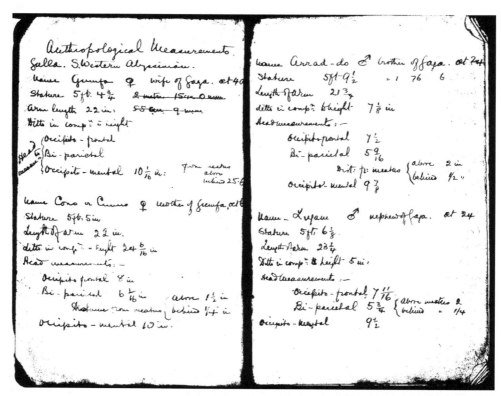

Medical notes from Koettlitz journal

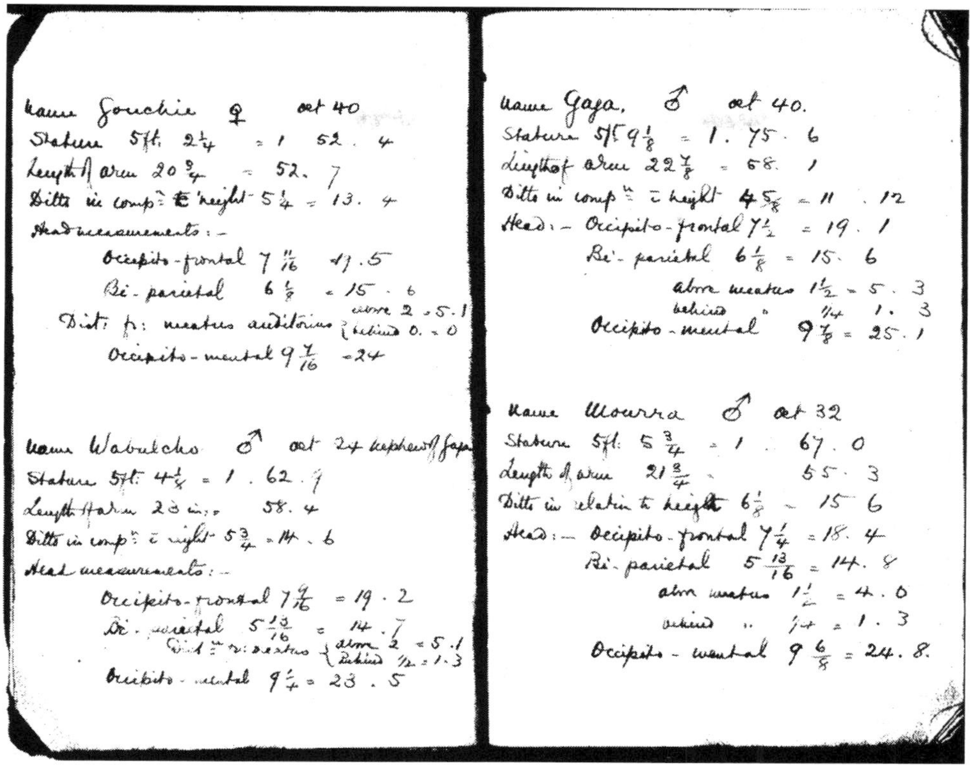
Name Gouchie ♀ aet 40
Stature 5ft. 2 1/4 = 1 . 52 . 4
Length of arm 20 3/4 = 52. 7
Ditto in comp: c height 5 1/4 = 13. 4
Head measurements: –
Occipito-frontal 7 11/16 = 19.5
Bi-parietal 6 1/8 = 15 . 6
Dist: fr: meatus auditorius {above 2 = 5.1, behind 0. = 0}
Occipito-mental 9 7/16 = 24

Name Wabutcho ♂ aet 24 nephew of Gaja
Stature 5ft. 4 3/8 = 1 . 62 . 9
Length of arm 23 in: = 58. 4
Ditto in comp: c height 5 3/4 = 14 . 6
Head measurements: –
Occipito-frontal 7 9/16 = 19 . 2
Bi-parietal 5 13/16 = 14 . 7
Dist: fr: meatus {above 2 = 5.1, behind 1/2 = 1.3}
Occipito-mental 9 1/4 = 23 . 5

Name Gaga. ♂ aet 40.
Stature 5ft 9 1/8 = 1 . 75 . 6
Length of arm 22 7/8 = 58. 1
Ditto in comp: c height 4 5/8 = 11 . 12
Head: – Occipito-frontal 7 1/2 = 19 . 1
Bi-parietal 6 1/8 = 15 . 6
above meatus 1 1/2 = 5 . 3
behind " 1/4 1 . 3
Occipito-mental 9 7/8 = 25 . 1

Name Mourra ♂ aet 32
Stature 5ft. 5 3/4 = 1 . 67 . 0
Length of arm 21 3/4 = 55 . 3
Ditto in relation to height 6 1/8 = 15 6
Head: – Occipito-frontal 7 1/4 = 18 . 4
Bi-parietal 5 13/16 = 14 . 8
above meatus 1 1/2 = 4 . 0
behind " 1/2 = 1 . 3
Occipito-mental 9 6/8 = 24 . 8

Eventually they were permitted to proceed and crossed the Dabus River into the country of the Shangalla, or Berta people. Koettlitz described them as being quite different from the other tribes:

> They are true Negroes, while the Somalis, Abyssinians and Gallas, so far encountered have almost European features and stature. They are never seen without their extremely dangerous throwing knives, swords, barbed spears and throwing sticks, similar to a boomerang. Both men and women are also extensively covered across their bodies with gashes to the skin which are arranged in intricate patterns. Despite this frightening, well-armed appearance it had not stopped the recent Abyssinian attacks.[2]

The expedition continued towards the Blue Nile which they crossed by flimsy ferry boat from Fasok to Famaka. At the time Famaka was the most advanced outpost of the Anglo-Egyptian army. They were kindly received here and benefited from the limited hospitality that could be offered. Without delaying to prolong the enjoyment they continued by camel and mule caravan with their, by now, extensive specimen collection to Rosaires. Here they boarded a gunboat for the journey to Sennaar.

Upon arrival at Sennaar they were welcomed by Colonel Lewis, the hero of the Dakla uprising and other notable battles. He was delighted to see them and entertained the expedition members as well as he could considering the location whilst Blundell considered the next phase of the journey down the Nile.

At Sennaar the river was very low and the gunboat could travel no further, forcing them to take a slow, clumsy, barge-like local boat to continue the journey. They were cooped up in this boat for a further ten days, confined to an 8ft² rough-hewn cabin. At least the cabin prevented the beating sun from causing further sunburn to the Europeans.

Blundell and his expedition arrived in Khartoum on 1 June, where they were lodged in the Kalifa's palace and entertained by Colonel Maxwell and the officers of the garrison.

The new environment more than made up for the confines of the barge, with Blundell writing fondly of this stay: 'On the 1st June we passed under the facade of the rapidly growing governor's palace among the palm trees of Khartoum, and that night we lodged in the Khalifa's house, I sleeping in his state bedroom with bathroom attached'. A luxury indeed after many months on the march!

The Battle of Omdurman had taken place here only nine months before. This conflict resulted in the defeat of the Mahdi army of Dervishes, numbering in excess of 50,000 men, by the combined British force of just 8,000 soldiers. Many thousands of warriors were slaughtered. The battle saw the last ever regimental-size cavalry charge by the British army, conducted by the 21st Lancers light cavalry regiment. Three Victoria Crosses, the highest British award for bravery, were awarded to soldiers of the regiment. During the three days the expedition members stayed in Khartoum they took the opportunity to visit the battlefield accompanied by officers of the garrison – but time was pressing for their return to British shores.

The party boarded another native boat, a 'nuggar', and headed up the Nile towards Atbara, successfully navigating the Shabluka rapids. On arrival at Atbara they were able to switch to more efficient modes of transport, and by boat and train had soon made their way to Cairo. On arrival in Cairo the expedition members made their own arrangements for the return to London, where the expedition papers would subsequently be presented to the Royal Geographical Society by Herbert Weld Blundell and Dr Koettlitz.

Before any of this could be accomplished Koettlitz had first to return to England.

---

1.   Koettlitz paper for the *Scottish Geographical Magazine* No. 8, August 1900.

2.   *Ibid.*

17

Homeward bound

K oettlitz was to travel from Suez, Egypt, on the S.S. *Britannia*, departing on Sunday 18 June 1899. This left a short time to explore Cairo and the Pyramids of Giza before boarding the train to the Suez Canal and Port Said. As always the doctor kept a detailed diary, both whilst waiting to board the S.S. *Britannia* and during the journey across the Mediterranean to France. The entries include a comprehensive description of the buildings, trees and flowering plants in the area of the Suez Canal.

Eventually, the ship arrived offshore. Koettlitz boarded a large steam launch which took passengers and baggage to the ship. He was accompanied by two other passengers: Miss Jackson, a meek-looking lady, possibly a maid; and an army officer departing on leave. In total there were only seven passengers on board the *Britannia* for the journey. After tea on deck and dinner, Koettlitz turned in early. He was keen to purchase a deck chair for the trip the following day as items of comfort seemed in short supply. Despite being much bothered by mosquitoes during the night he rose early. This enabled him to bargain with a vendor who came aboard, and purchase lace and some items of jewellery. At 8 a.m. the *Britannia*, after further coaling, headed off for Marseilles via the Straits of Messina and Carpentaria. It took two hours before Egypt slipped over the horizon with the ship on a calm sea. The doctor spent the remainder of the day reading on deck.

The days that followed highlighted the difficulty Koettlitz had in adjusting to a sedentary routine. He still rose early as if on the march and always took a cold shower or bath despite hot water being available. As the *Britannia* journeyed into rough waters he was reminded, to his great discomfort, that he was a very bad sailor in such conditions. It appears he was not alone, as the lady passengers were also very sick for extended periods. However, this did not prevent the doctor from sketching distant islands such as Crete as they passed the coast.

There was no let-up in the sea conditions, and at times the ship rolled at an angle of 45 degrees. It was a struggle even to stay put in one's bunk and much damage was caused to property around the ship. Koettlitz said Mrs Carew, one of the lady passengers, was driven to a fit as she was sure the *Britannia* would capsize. Fortunately, as they approached the Italian coast with Sicily in sight, the sea abated. By breakfast on Thursday 22 June they were approaching the Straits of Messina and calm had been restored. Mount Etna was clearly visible through occasional fog, with snow covering the summit. The towns and villages of Sicily and the Italian mainland were seen in all their splendour together with the classic whirlpools of the Scylla and Charybdis Straits. The ship passing over these caused some excitement for the doctor if not the other passengers on board. The *Britannia* survived these engulfing whirl-pools and headed past the volcanic Lipari Islands and Stromboli. With his great geological passion Koettlitz studied these islands in detail but was disappointed that he could not examine the smoke and steam seen issuing from secondary craters at close quarters.

After dinner the sea rose once again, resulting in a most uncomfortable night for all. The sea was so rough that Koettlitz stayed in his bunk all day. Much damage was caused to the exterior fittings of the ship, deck ladders and other equipment being swept away.

In spite of the appalling weather conditions they passed close to Elba then Sardinia and Corsica, but were unable to pass between these dramatic islands. Koettlitz thought he was getting to grips with the conditions and even decided to turn up for dinner on Saturday evening, but by 8.45 p.m. he was regretting that decision and was once again confined to his bunk. As dawn broke on Sunday 25th the coast of France was visible but the mistral continued to blow, with huge seas crashing over the ship. As they approached the islands of Marseilles a pilot boat was able to come alongside, towing them to calmer water closer to the shoreline where they awaited a doctor to come aboard to give them a clean bill of health. There followed a procedure that Koettlitz described as a 'ghastly and totally unnecessary farce'.[1] Whilst the passengers were examined their cabins, luggage and clothing were sprayed with a solution of chloride and lime.

At 2.30 p.m. the *Britannia* was eventually allowed to proceed into the harbour. Viewing it from the ship on approach, Koettlitz was impressed with Marseilles, its fine Byzantine architecture and church surmounted by a huge golden statue of the Virgin and Child. After a brief trip ashore to purchase film for his camera, Koettlitz spent a restful night on board, at last in calm, peaceful conditions.

This was to be a short stopover in Marseilles so Koettlitz was determined not to waste a minute. It was time to explore before the ship set out once more for England and home. The ship's doctor, Dr Cook, knew the city and area well. Over the following three days, at times with Dr Cook and at times alone, Koettlitz explored Marseilles and its environs, visiting churches, public buildings, museums, parks and the coastal region. Even a visit to the zoological gardens was on the agenda and all were photographed. Unfortunately these early images of the region have long since disappeared.

The ship was due to depart on Friday 30th at 4.30 p.m. Postcards were dispatched overland to friends and family in England and elsewhere. As Koettlitz headed back to the ship a fine group of battleships passed close to the shore, clearly displaying the massive guns and turrets which would pose such threats in the not too distant future. On leaving Marseilles the *Britannia* passed close to the assembled battleships. By the following morning the ship was sailing close to the Spanish coast off Barcelona. The sea was calmer and the ship lighter having off-loaded cargo in Marseilles, so good speed was made along the coast. By late afternoon of the Monday they were passing through the Straits of Gibraltar with Africa once again to one side and the Sierra Nevada in the distance on the other.

A stop was due to be made in the port of Gibraltar for coaling and taking on additional passengers. A further two ladies and three men joined the ship. Koettlitz was pleased to have additional passengers for conversation and an exchange of stamps. The Koettlitz family were all keen stamp collectors and by the time he was resident in South Africa Koettlitz possessed an impressive collection.

By Tuesday the ship was passing Cape St Vincent and soon land was out of sight as they proceeded into greater seas. The Atlantic seas were huge and much more impressive than the Mediterranean, alarming many on board. The doctor was keen to watch storm petrels and other seabirds gliding close to the enormous waves. This led to a return of his sea-sickness, aggravated by intense earache that required self-treatment. He spent time in the chart room with the captain plotting their course past Cape Finisterre and towards the English coast. The sea was beginning to abate but two lady passengers, Mrs Carew once again and a Mrs Ketchen ('a nice Baptist woman'),[2] remained in bad condition, suffering severe sea-sickness. In addition, Koettlitz's ear was increasingly painful and the doctor decided action was required. He asked a steward to make up a bucket of salt and hot water and put a sock to soak in it. The sock was then placed over the affected ear overnight, bringing some relief. Calmer waters soon allowed deck games to be played. Koettlitz also had long, religion-themed talks with Mrs Ketchen, whom he found most knowledgeable on the subject.

By Saturday 8 July the *Britannia* was passing the Pembrokeshire coast at Cardigan Bay, heading for the port of Liverpool, its final destination. They sailed into port without further mishap. The assembled passengers bade their farewells and it was time for Koettlitz to head for Dover and London to prepare his expedition reports and presentations before the learned institutions of London and Edinburgh. Already he was thinking of the next expedition in which he could take part. He was keen to continue his travels and improve his skill and knowledge in the subjects in which he had become so adept. Despite the obvious problems he had when relating to other expedition members, in particular the English upper classes, he realised they were essential in obtaining funds and backing for travel to these extreme and unexplored foreign regions.

The African expedition was lauded as a great success by the scientific community in London. Besides the extensive geological, botanical and geographical evidence collated by Dr Koettlitz, a very large number of animal, bird, reptile and other specimens had been collected. This included 18 species of antelope, ten elephants, many rodents and two lions; plus 523 bird specimens collected by Lord Lovat and Mr Harwood, including 11 new species. The whole collection was presented to the British Museum for further study.

The anthropological and ethnological observations and studies collated by Dr Koettlitz were laid before the Royal Physical Society together with his geological specimens and research. His invertebrate collection, consisting mainly of insects, was handed to his former colleague from Franz Josef Land, Mr W. S. Bruce, for further study in Edinburgh. The collection was of great interest to Bruce and his colleagues, including as it did the land Mollusca and marine specimens from the Somali coast. His meteorological observations were entrusted to the Scottish Meteorological Society for further study by Mr R. T. Ormond, a member of that institution. These observations were included in the paper presented to the Royal Geographical Society. It was agreed by all that the expedition had made significant advances in the scientific knowledge and appreciation of the region.

---

1. Koettlitz journal written on journey to England, June 1899 – Koettlitz family archives.

2. *Ibid.*

18

Planning for the Antarctic

Whilst Dr Koettlitz and Herbert Weld Blundell worked on their successful presentations and reports for the Royal Geographical Society, others were concentrating on mounting an English expedition south to the undiscovered lands of Antarctica, perhaps even the South Pole itself.

At the forefront of this adventure was Sir Clements Markham, who had dreamt of such an expedition since the mid-1800s. He had limited personal experience in Arctic exploration but was at the centre of all expedition planning, being President of the Royal Geographical Society. He also had unrivalled contacts within the Royal Navy and government which put him in touch with many sources of funding – essential to all polar expeditions. His initial objective was the North Pole and the surrounding seas and lands, as well as transiting the Northwest Passage, the alternative route to the east. These had been goals of many previous – unsuccessful – British expeditions. Many of these adventures had stirred the imagination of Victorian England – especially the expeditions of Sir John Franklin, which had ended in disaster. This attitude of the Victorian and Edwardian populace towards their heroes was to endure for many years to come, with the concept of 'glorious defeat' being a curiously English phenomenon.

By 1885 Clements Markham had turned his full attention to the Antarctic. Towards the end of the century the successful exploits of Fridtjof Nansen and of the Jackson-Harmsworth Expedition were answering many of the questions relating to the north. Markham formed the first of many committees to examine the issues which would lead to success on the Antarctic continent. This was always seen as a Royal Navy expedition, led by naval officers and consisting mainly of naval personnel with a scientific element in support. By the time Weld Blundell and Koettlitz returned from Africa, the planning of the National Antarctic Expedition to the south was well advanced – and Koettlitz, now well known in the institutions of London, Edinburgh and Manchester as a successful if slightly eccentric expedition surgeon, geologist and botanist, was determined to be part of it.

Throughout 1899 Sir Clements Markham worked tirelessly raising funding for the expedition, which by now was a joint enterprise between the Royal Geographical Society and the Royal Society. The politics of this union were dubious and at times devious, with Markham becoming annoyed and frustrated at the participation of the Royal Society. This led to many disputes – staffing, funding, participation of both scientists and naval staff all became controversial topics among those involved. Markham strongly wanted the expedition to be naval-led and managed, while the Royal Society preferred a scientific-led expedition. There was a total clash of objectives and personalities and the feathers of the leading participants were at times severely ruffled.

By the turn of the century funding had been obtained and final recruitment of the leader, naval staff and scientific members was well advanced. In Markham's view the English had a right to explore and control the Antarctic continent. In true Victorian fashion he divided the continent into four quadrants: Victoria, Ross, Weddell and Enderby, named after the Queen and previous famous explorers to the region. He decided that the National Antarctic Expedition would explore the Victoria and Ross quadrants and that the Germans, who were also mounting an expedition, would be allowed the Enderby quadrant. He also decided that the expedition would consist of a Royal Naval commander, navigator, three executive officers, an engineer and two surgeons with a ship's company of 26 men. There would be three scientific civilians and perhaps a scientific director. Dr Koettlitz had been active in gaining support for his application as senior surgeon and geologist.

By this point Koettlitz had an impressive record on both polar and African expeditions and was strongly supported by others, including Alfred Harmsworth. He was also backed by the respected scientist Sir Archibald Geikie, who provided a glowing testimonial setting out Koettlitz's achievements with an unqualified recommendation.

Based on these recommendations Sir Clements Markham, in the late spring of 1900, appointed Dr Koettlitz as senior surgeon with the additional responsibilities of expedition chemist and other scientific duties as required. Markham wrote:

> I selected Dr Reginald Koettlitz as surgeon. He had served during three Arctic winters in Franz Josef Land in the Harmsworth Expedition with Armitage, and therefore has considerable Arctic medical experience. He is anxious to do his best, zealous, and painstaking and will, I believe, be a success. His mind perhaps works rather slowly, and he has no sense of humour; but on the other hand he is thorough and persevering.[1]

This was a fair assessment but Markham had confused Koettlitz's lack of humour with his serious, professional attitude to work, both medical and scientific, as shown in Franz Josef Land and North East Africa. This attitude would have been familiar to Lieutenant Albert B. Armitage, who having been recently given the Murchison Award for his scientific observations during the Jackson-Harmsworth Expedition, was appointed as navigator aboard the *Discovery*. Having spent three years in the company of Dr Koettlitz on Franz Josef Land he was very well aware of his attitude to scientific research and the work ethic.

By June 1900 the senior naval and scientific appointments had been agreed, although the terms and conditions of their appointment were still the subject of much debate. Ultimately Professor Gregory, one of the outstanding scientific expedition leaders of the time, stood down, primarily due to the restricted conditions of his appointment and the fact that he had not been made overall leader of the whole expedition. This role had already been given to Lieutenant (later Commander) Robert Falcon Scott, a man who had no previous polar experience or much specialised scientific knowledge. He was nevertheless an experienced naval officer with varied experience on board Her Majesty's ships in both UK and foreign waters. Interestingly, Scott considered himself to possess a competent scientific mind.

Earlier, in March 1900, in anticipation of his appointment (which was confirmed on 23 March), Dr Koettlitz had been drafted by Clements Markham to be a member of a small committee of experts. This included his namesake Admiral Markham, who had many years' experience travelling in northern polar regions. In addition to his skills as an expedition surgeon, Koettlitz was also an expert on the most suitable provisions for men to survive and work in the environment expected in the south. Working as a member of a small committee with the Markhams was a daunting experience but the doctor threw himself energetically into the task. He soon sought the advice of his friend and advisor Dr Fridtjof Nansen.

In fact, he had written to Nansen earlier, in January, when he had been approached informally by Markham about the task. In a letter from the family address in Dover he wrote:

> No doubt you have heard that the Geographical Society together with the Royal Society is getting up a National Antarctic Expedition. They have done me the honour of asking me to sit on the sub-committee of Hygiene which includes such men as Lord Lister, Sir Michael Forster and other celebrated men for the regulation and planning out of matters connected with the health of that expedition.[2]

He went on to ask what precautions Nansen took in the preparation of the tinned and dried foods, and in the ventilation, warming and keeping dry of his ships; what proportion, per man, Nansen allowed in weight of food for each man per day; plus if he had advice on any other matters that had a bearing on the maintenance of the health of the men. Koettlitz also voiced the fear to Nansen that the National Antarctic Expedition would be sent out without a 'proper scientific staff'.

Koettlitz's appointment to the sub-committee followed a successful presentation he made before the British Association for the Advancement of Science, which had included a section on polar exploration. Koettlitz had highlighted the success of Nansen's expedition, whose members had survived over three years in the Arctic without a sign of scurvy, backing it up by his personal experience in Franz Josef Land. The fact that these expeditions had remained largely scurvy free was in marked contrast to a recent British Government expedition which had gone down to a man with the disease and had been forced to return home.

Nansen replied promptly with the information requested, in a letter dated 27 February from Lysaker, Norway. He detailed the amount of food each man was given on sledge journeys and whilst aboard the *Fram* and emphasised: 'Give the men good healthy food and I guarantee you will have no diseases; ventilation, warming etc., is very easily arranged, and need no special study.'[3] This of course is exactly the procedure Koettlitz had already followed whilst on Franz Josef Land and which had kept the land party in such robust health.

Whilst engaged in these preliminary planning activities in the lead-up to the Antarctic expedition Koettlitz still needed to make a living. He was not a rich man and did not possess independent funds. He was currently without a medical position, a situation that could not continue for the whole planning phase of the expedition as it would be financially untenable.

Koettlitz had been seeking a short-term position as an expedition doctor, or as a doctor who could travel to foreign lands. This search was satisfied, much to the dismay of Sir Clements Markham, when he was appointed ship's doctor on a Red Cross Line steamer. The vessel, the steamer *Sobralense*, was to voyage across the Atlantic Ocean and up the River

Amazon to Manaos (as far as ocean-going steamers could travel at this time). For the past 30 years trade between the British Isles and the Amazon basin had been steadily growing, and Dr Koettlitz wrote: 'I have long held a wish to see this famous stream, the most magnificent in the volume of water that it brings to the sea.'[4] Koettlitz was also secretly hoping the opportunity might arise for him to invest in the fast-growing rubber industry that was beginning to flourish in the Amazon basin. For the forthcoming weeks the committees of the National Antarctic Expedition would be without their most recent polar traveller.

---

1. Sir Clements Markham RGS – *Antarctic Obsession*, page 16.

2. Letter from Koettlitz to Fridtjof Nansen dated 9 January 1900 – addressed Pencester Road, Dover.

3. Letter from Nansen to Koettlitz dated 27 February 1900 – Koettlitz family archives.

4. Koettlitz paper for the *Scottish Geographical Magazine*, January 1901, pages 11–30.

19

Liverpool to Manaos

Manaos, situated nearly a thousand miles up the Amazon River, had for many years been the furthest upstream that ocean-going steamers could travel. But by early 1900 both the Booth Line and the Red Cross Line were sending steamers as far as Iquitos, a distance from the river mouth of over two thousand miles. Trade was opening up the river, in particular the fast-expanding rubber industry.

Boarding in April as ship's doctor, Koettlitz joined the *Sobralense* as it travelled from Liverpool to the Amazon via Madeira before returning via New York and the West Indies. Koettlitz expected his medical duties to be light, which would enable him to carry out scientific and maritime studies for the duration of the trip. After ten days at sea the ship approached the Brazilian coast at Salinas, where a pilot was taken on board to navigate the sand banks on the final leg to the port of Para. These banks with a mass of other debris are formed from the huge amount of material brought down the rivers which converge to create the Amazon Delta. Thus the banks are continually moving and a specialist pilot is essential.

The approach to Para is long and slow, passing many islands, with small villages set amongst a luxuriant jungle scene. The river was busy with craft of all types and sizes, both fishing boats and vessels carrying commercial cargo. Having been cleared by the Para quarantine station – and flying the approved health check flag – the ship dropped anchor two to three miles from the port. In earlier times ships could lie close to the port but the silting of the river now prevented this. They were further delayed by additional checks by local government officials, whom Koettlitz described as 'a self-important, lazy lot of people, that private individuals are at their mercy, and their morals are very elastic',[1] indicating that an exchange of money would achieve the necessary permission to proceed.

Para, also known as Belem, was a large and important port, with a population of some 100,000. The city was located on a site reclaimed from the forest and had a tropical climate, with high temperatures and regular rainfall, although it also benefited from cooling sea breezes. There were many large, handsome public buildings and churches, as well as fine gardens, plazas and a theatre, and well laid out residential streets lined with imposing dwellings. There was even a rapid tramcar system traversing the city. It was a prosperous place, with many of its residents profiting from the vast natural resources of the Amazon basin. Koettlitz noted that the tramcar operatives held the notes taken from customers between their teeth, which must have been a fertile source of contagious diseases!

Shortage of time meant that Koettlitz was unable to make an in-depth study of the local people as he had done in northern Russia and North East Africa, but he described in detail the physical appearance of the residents of Para. This was a population of great variety: Americans, native Brazilian, Portuguese and other Europeans, Indian, Chinese, native Indian tribes and a substantial African population who had been transported to the area as slaves. It was a population made up of people from many countries and the results of liaisons between these peoples. Para was a large frontier town with constant movement of trade and people, where many steam vessels traded with the rest of the Brazilian coast and up river.

The steamers ferried the people in the most deplorable conditions – always overcrowded, sitting in filth and dirt. Many people would die on these river boat journeys; on a single trip sometimes scores of passengers would perish from accidents and disease. Yellow and malarial fever was common and took their toll among locals, especially new arrivals from Europe and North America. Europeans and Americans dominated the substantial trade offices and warehouses in the city. The principal export was rubber and Koettlitz thought the town's very existence depended on it, but nuts, cocoa and other vegetable products were also exported in huge quantities. Because of the silting up of the river, lighters were used to transport the goods to the waiting steamers lying offshore. Koettlitz thought that the very slowness of this process would eventually damage the port's viability.

After a three-week stay in Para it was time to push on up river. Under the guidance of the river pilot, without whose knowledge the run to Manaos would be impossible for an ocean-going steamer, the *Sobralense* negotiated the maze of low-lying, densely wooded islands which lie at the confluence of the Para and Tocantin rivers. After some five hours they passed through the ever-narrowing channels of 'The Narrows'. The country here was thickly wooded tropical forest, which could be observed clearly from the bridge of the ship. The channels were intricate and ever changing, requiring the skills of highly skilled navigators, appointed only after many years of training. Whilst traversing the Narrows they passed the town of Breves, the principal rubber collection point for the area.

Koettlitz marvelled at the wonders of the vigorous tropical vegetation, the huge forest trees and the creepers in full bloom. He described how the water itself was invaded by luxuriant water weeds, grasses and blooms, giving the appearance of a river meadow. The bow wash from the steamer caused them to rise and fall and revealed the home of the sea-cow or manatee. This silent, harmless and shy water beast was then common, not yet an endangered species as it is today along with many others within the Amazon River complex. Wonderfully coloured birds, parrots and butterflies inhabited the forest canopy and river banks. The whole scene was punctuated by the screeching of monkeys and parrots; the night was accompanied by the buzzing of all types of insect, with moths flying in great numbers.

Rubber trees were plentiful along the banks and, although they were restricted to certain districts, this area of the river contained large numbers of these highly productive and financially rewarding trees. Rubber tappers, known as 'seringueiros', lived in huts dotting the river bank. These huts, called 'baracas', were raised on stilts to escape the river in flood, and were where the rubber hunter's family would spend their time when not tapping rubber. Canoes were used to transport the rubber to the nearest collection point. The huts were left open at the sides to benefit from what breeze there was, but it was a hard, isolated, unhealthy existence. Malaria was a common visitor, killing young and old alike. The rubber workers were generally of mixed Portuguese and local Indian extraction. They drank large amounts of raw rum, named locally Cashasse, which was brewed in huge quantities in the region. Each hunter generally managed and tapped around 100 rubber trees in his area. Tapping was done during the drier seasons. A precise V-shaped incision was cut into the tree and the latex collected in a small tin. The trees were cut early in the morning and the latex collected around midday. The latex would run from the trees for approximately four hours before sealing itself. The process was completed by treating the latex over an open fire, which removed the liquid, leaving a rubber ball collected around a stick shaped like a paddle. When large enough the stick was removed, and the rubber was then collected by traders who visited each site.

Once again Dr Koettlitz made a photographic record of his travels. He was an accomplished photographer and created a substantial collection of photographs from his expeditions to polar and tropical regions. He collected butterflies, moths, beetles and other insects of every size and species at every opportunity. He found the butterflies difficult to catch compared with British varieties due to their swifter and more erratic flight patterns, but many were taken as they passed over and around the ship.

It took a further six hours before the channel widened once again, as they entered the three-mile-wide Huguara River. A further three hours steaming brought the *Sobralense* to the main Amazon itself; here the river's width was between eight and ten miles. The mighty river held the doctor in awe as it moved silently and steadily towards the open sea at an average speed of four miles an hour, bringing with it not only millions of tons of sediment to enrich the communities along the bank but also such dangers to river users. He found it difficult to comprehend that waters rising in the Andean mountains 3,000 miles away could still be travelling at such a speed at this distance from the source.

His religious instincts were aroused: 'The contemplation of so great and magnificent an evidence of the almighty power which governs such glorious works as these compels one to reverence the Author of it all.'[1]

As they entered the main river the pilot took the steamer from one side to the other to areas where the current was less powerful, thereby avoiding sand banks and keeping the *Sobralense* on the move upstream. This allowed Koettlitz to examine both sides of the mighty river, at times very close to the bank. The number of tended rubber trees gradually decreased but groups of huts still appeared in clearings on both banks where cocoa plantations were being developed. The settlements appeared to be in a general state of neglect and the inhabitants living in a state of poverty, although food seemed plentiful.

Koettlitz was not impressed with the attitude of the locals, in particular their lack of industriousness: 'The ordinary Brazilian loves laziness and is so indolent that he will rarely do a stroke more work than he is compelled to do.'[1] If he had resided in the country, with its extreme tropical conditions, for any length of time might he have formed a less judgemental opinion.

The settlements seemed to become more numerous as they approached Cocoa Grande, a small thriving township. Substantial cocoa plantations were found here and the residents lived in more substantial dwellings with large numbers of domesticated animals. The *Sobralense* did not delay but pressed on up river to the confluence with the Rio Tapajos, described as 'a fine river'. Here they made a short stop at the small town of Santarem. The town, with a population of over 2,000 inhabitants, stood on slightly higher ground, avoiding the worst of the river flooding. It was a bustling place trading in Brazil nuts, sarsaparilla and copaiba, the last two used for the preparation of medicinal products then as now.

Continuing along the vast river, still many miles in width with no discernible banks, the *Sobralense* passed Obidos, a small town similar in importance to Santarem. Santarem is the only place over the lower 1,000 miles of the river where true river banks can be seen. The Amazon narrows at this point and the depth becomes approximately 100 fathoms. Although Koettlitz was impressed with the scale of the Amazon he was disappointed by the lack of wildlife that could be seen from the ship or on the nearby banks and in the jungle, and the inaccessibility certainly compared with the Blue Nile. The high water and the density of the jungle around the Amazon accounted for this, while the area abutting the Nile had been developed over thousands of years and it was more accessible.

Nevertheless, he continued to collect a variety of marine and other specimens when the opportunity arose. He recorded a good variety of bird life including ibis, herons, ducks, partridge, terns, darters, macaws, parrots, hawks and vultures, some of which were taken as specimens. After the steamer had passed Obidos, the Parintins Hills appeared. These mark the boundary of the Para and Amazonas regions – Manaos, their eventual destination, being the capital of the latter.

The *Sobralense* had now been steaming up river for over four days. Once again they were entering an area where the gathering of rubber was the main source of income and employment. As they passed the frontier town of Itacoatiara the *Sobralense* left the main channel in order to avoid strong currents. This brought the ship closer to the banks and allowed Koettlitz to add to his growing collection of insects, including beautifully coloured dragonflies, beetles, grasshoppers and other insects that landed on deck or flew close by.

They were approaching the confluence of the rivers Amazon and Rio Negro, the latter named after the deep black colour of its water when seen from above. It produces a reflection as good as looking in a mirror, yet when taken from the river in a glass the liquid is perfectly clear. At the junction the two powerful rivers produce whirlpools and swirls as they compete for dominance. The *Sobralense* left the Amazon and proceeded five miles up the Rio Negro, to arrive in the thriving, bustling capital city of Manaos.

The state of Amazonas equals in area all the remaining states of Brazil put together. Manaos was the centre of the commercial, political and intellectual life of the state. It was the seat of the state governor and home to 40,000 people of many races and descriptions.

Considering its location so far up the mighty River Amazon, Manaos was a remarkable city. The streets and building were well built of stone, the streets lit by electric light, and there was an excellent tram service driven by electricity. There were several imposing churches, a fine, domed theatre, well laid out public gardens and various monuments, giving a feeling of prosperity, order and wealth. The majority of merchants were European or American, with a sizable British community. In fact, British capital controlled much of the local industry, which was based principally on the production of rubber but also on trade in Brazil and other types of nuts and vegetables. There was also employment, on a smaller scale, in the hunting of wild deer, catching fish for drying and killing herons for their plumes, which were destined for the European and American fashion industries. It was here that Koettlitz was hoping to get a stake in the burgeoning rubber market which would provide a profitable financial return with minimum risk.

117

There remained a major problem with the location of Manaos: its disrupted communication with the major markets of Europe and North America. A telegraph wire had been laid along the river bed to Para and other towns at the Amazon's mouth but it was continually broken by the volume of the river and the debris carried within it. There was no overland route through the dense tropical forest on which a telegraph line could be erected, so the main means of communication remained the river and the boats that plied continually along its length. Ultimately, Koettlitz's objective of getting a stake in the growing rubber industry didn't materialise.

Whilst the *Sobralense* discharged her cargo and loaded the goods for the return journey Koettlitz took the opportunity to travel up the Rio Negro to explore the river and its environs. He travelled by steam launch, rowing boat and canoe. As it was the rainy season the river was over 50 feet higher than its normal base and in places allowed a view into the tree canopy. They used the branches of the tree tops to propel themselves forward, in the fashion used by the local Indian tribes when hunting. During this trip Koettlitz added to his collection of insects, birds and small mammals.

Time was short and soon he was back on board the *Sobralense* for the return journey down river towards the open sea. Because of the force and speed of the current, the return journey to Para takes half the time of the trip up river. From Para the *Sobralense* headed north towards its next port of call, New York. When they were approximately 250 miles from the mouth of the Amazon, Koettlitz noticed a massive area of almost black water, through which they steamed for over 12 hours at 11 knots. He consulted the skipper about it and discovered it was known as 'Humboldt's Black Water', although there was no further explanation. Koettlitz was convinced it was the influence of the Amazon and showed the great power of that river so far into the Atlantic Ocean. Compared with the short excursion up the Amazon the return journey was routine. Koettlitz continued to collect marine specimens and birds at every opportunity, all of which later made their way to the University of Edinburgh.

It was a short but productive journey for Dr Koettlitz. His medical duties had been light, allowing him to further enhance his botanical and marine scientific knowledge. His study of the native Amazonians had been restricted but he made accurate notes when possible. It was time to head back to London before travelling south to the Antarctic with the *Discovery*.

Upon his return he presented his research material and specimens to the University and Museum in Edinburgh. They presented Koettlitz with an outstanding scientific endorsement, asserting 'that they had never seen such a large entomological collection made by one man in such a short time, let alone on a single journey'.[2]

---

1. Koettlitz paper for the *Scottish Geographical Magazine*, January 1901, pages 11–30.

2. A. G. E. Jones, biography of Koettlitz dated 11 August 1986 – Koettlitz family archives.

20

The Antarctic beckons

hile Dr Koettlitz had been travelling up the Amazon the political and personal machinations between the Royal Geographical Society and the Royal Society had been continuing. As Clements Markham put it: 'Whilst in charge of the executive work between April 1899 and November 1900, I had been worried and hampered by the Royal Society's committees.'[1] This of course was a prelude to personal and professional disputes and disagreements that would occur throughout the expedition and even as far as the preparation of the expedition scientific reports in the years following the *Discovery*'s return.

In one area at least great progress had been made: the construction of the expedition ship, the *Discovery*. Attempts had been made to find a suitable working vessel but it became evident that a purpose-built expedition ship would have to be constructed. The *Discovery* was to be built in Dundee, one of the few remaining shipbuilding ports in the British Isles capable of building a wooden-hulled ship of the required size and strength. The keel was laid in March 1900 and the ship constructed to a very precise specification, built to operate and survive in the severe Antarctic conditions.

Following his return to the project, Koettlitz pressed on with his duties in relation to the provisions and equipment sub-committees, all the while keeping in regular contact with Dr Fridtjof Nansen. Remembering always this was an English, Royal Navy-led expedition, Markham pressed on with a matter of utmost importance: designing the officers' sledging flags and the flag to be flown by the *Discovery*. In this he was following the tradition of earlier polar expeditions. Markham had previously designed the sledge flags for the officers of the 1875 Arctic Expedition.

The unsettling disputes between the two powerful scientific societies continued until November 1900. Finally, following the publication of a comprehensive report which he prepared, Scott gained approval for his plan. Scott was to be in overall, unhindered control of the expedition – albeit always under the watchful eye of his mentor Sir Clements Markham. Each of the appointed officers and scientific staff pressed on with their respective duties.

Koettlitz, in addition to the responsibilities already mentioned, began personal research relating to bacteriology and phytoplankton (see later in the chapter). It remained a disappointment to him that he had not been appointed as expedition geologist along with his medical duties. He was by 1900 a very experienced polar expedition geologist and had received the support of Nansen, Sir Archibald Geike and Teall, all eminent persons in the field of geology. In fact, in a letter to Professor Gregory, at the time still head of the proposed scientific staff, Markham had praised Koettlitz's medical and geological skills, finishing with: 'He is a good and genial messmate and I do not think a better man could be found.'[2]

This opinion was supported in a letter to Gregory from the eminent zoologist and Royal Society member Edward Bagnall Poulton, who wrote: 'The point in his (Koettlitz's) favour is that he is qualified and has had experience of scurvy. He is as you know a geologist and if Miers came that would be rather superfluous, but if he could be turned to other things it would be alright if he is readily led and capable of other work.'[3] He asked for a reply by return if possible with regard to the appointment of Koettlitz, Armitage and Hodgson and was of the opinion that Dr Koettlitz should be appointed at once. The pressure by both Markham and Poulton to officially appoint Koettlitz continued through April into May 1900.

In April 1900, Professor Gregory agreed to the appointment of Koettlitz, writing to Clements Markham: 'Dr Koettlitz seems to me to be the most suitable man of the three. I had mentioned him as an alternative to Hodgson in my last letter to Professor Poulton. If he is to be appointed as doctor to the expedition, then I suppose he must stop with the ship. Koettlitz's Arctic experience would be most useful on land. In Franz Josef Land he acted as geologist and there is no need of a second geologist.'[4] At that time Professor Gregory was still a crucial and leading member of the expedition management; he was expecting to lead not only the scientific aspects of the expedition but the expedition itself.

The political manoeuvring between the Royal Geographical Society and the Royal Society continued, proving increasingly disruptive to the expedition planning. On 6 May 1900 Professor Poulton had written to Gregory confirming the appointment of Koettlitz as expedition surgeon but added in a section marked 'Private':

> Clements M is terribly difficult to work with. We had a fearful row last Weds & if he had not climbed down the R.S (Royal Society) would have withdrawn from the whole thing & the Treasury would probably have withdrawn their vote & the whole thing comes to an end. The other three members of the Exec C (executive council) all agreed that they wanted a naval commander, I always doubted. Well C.M (Clements Markham) on this alone wrote to the Admiralty what he says is a private letter & also a letter suggesting names no one else had ever heard of even as standing. Well Goschen took his letter as official (no doubt it was on RGS paper) and appointed the men – A Lieut Scott of the Majestic & a Lieut Royds as second in command. He brought this before the Ex C as an accomplished fact.[5]

The letter continued in a similar vein, indicating that the Royal Society was most annoyed and unhappy with the way the appointments were made and with the conduct of Clements Markham in particular. Poulton hoped that because Scott was from the scientific side of the navy and not the surveying side he might prove a competent commander but stated firmly that 'His (Scott's) chance and that of the whole expedition was nearly wrecked by the absurd behaviour of CM (Clements Markham)'.[6] Poulton hoped such behaviour by Markham would not occur again and that the expedition would be able to progress without more disruption. He continued to discuss the appointment of the scientific staff; he was of the opinion that Gregory should approve such appointments and was hoping for his consent to the appointment of Dr Koettlitz.

On 26 May 1900 Markham confirmed that Dr Koettlitz had been appointed as the expedition surgeon and reserve geologist and that he was ready to undertake other scientific duties as required. This saga was to run for many months and led to a most unsatisfactory conclusion, according to Poulton. It was clear to him and the other Royal Society members of the expedition committee that Gregory was by far the most suitable candidate to lead the expedition, particularly with regard to its scientific aspects. He had successfully led a scientific expedition to North East Africa and had gained ice experience in both Spitzbergen and the European Alps. He was eminent in the field of geology, a subject of the utmost importance to any Antarctic expedition. Scott had no polar or ice experience and, although possessing a scientific mind, did not compare to Gregory.

The continuing pressure from multiple interests ultimately led to Professor Gregory resigning as head of the scientific team on the expedition, with Scott taking overall control. The treatment of Gregory led to much dissent within the Royal Society, particularly from Professor Poulton and Captain Tizard. Both were well aware of the lack of polar explorative knowledge within the naval element of the expedition, with only Koettlitz and Armitage having had direct experience of polar survival for any length of time. They regarded Markham as being too enamoured with naval lore and the heroic power and courage of the Royal Navy, its officer class in particular. Although Markham had spoken with explorers who had survived in the far north, including Fridtjof Nansen, he largely disregarded their advice.

Markham's attitude is shown clearly in a letter he wrote to Professor Gregory in June 1900 while Gregory was still a member of the expedition. After discussing the age of expedition members and equipment to be carried Markham wrote:

> Dogs are useful, when well fed, to the Eskimos on the smooth ice of the Greenland coast and to the Siberians over their hard snow. They have also been found useful for short journeys over smooth ice in Arctic Expeditions. For real polar work they are worse than useless and their employment is horribly cruel.[7]

He mentions their use by Peary in the north and then Nansen, continuing:

> With Nansen very poor work was made with the dogs, they got weaker and weaker, were killed to feed each other and all perished. Over rough ground they are an intolerable nuisance, cause endless delay and are worse than useless. Nansen's skis were not much better: in soft snow and rough ground he longed for Canadian snow shoes. Better with neither. Look at what men have done without all these new-fangled contrivances.

In conclusion, he advised that man-hauling was the most successful way to travel and haul loads in polar conditions, referring to naval expeditions in the past.

Markham's description of Nansen's use of dogs and skis on his arduous journeys across the Arctic wastes and in Greenland bore no resemblance to the facts. Markham was wrapped up in the glory of man-hauling, with Englishmen, preferably Royal Naval Englishmen, doing the hard work. It was a method ultimately doomed to failure, as proven on Scott's second expedition to the Antarctic. It stands in stark contrast to the methods employed by Roald Amundsen who conquered the ice and glaciers en-route to the South Pole by the use of dog and ski.

Koettlitz informed Nansen that Professor Gregory had indeed resigned from his position within the expedition, offering his views as to the possible causes and result:

> There is no doubt that he has been far from well treated by the two Royal Societies. The Royal Society has not been consistent through its representatives upon the committees, in upholding the rights and dignity of science and thus has failed in its duty. On this account the Royal Geographical Society has had its own way and gone back on its original offer to Dr Gregory and now offers him only a secondary part which he will not accept.[8]

Koettlitz continued with his duties with regard to the provisioning of the expedition and the acquisition of scientific and other equipment, for use not only when sledging but when living in the hostile conditions expected in the Antarctic regions. In this he used not only his own knowledge and experience gained in Franz Josef Land but the ultimate source of polar experience, Dr Fridtjof Nansen, with whom he was in continual correspondence.

His personal medical and scientific equipment for travelling was financed by a collection made by the students at Guy's Medical School where Koettlitz had studied and qualified. The most up-to-date travelling medicine chests for expeditions were produced by Burroughs Wellcome of London. Koettlitz had used one of their medicine chests during the Jackson-Harmsworth Expedition and it had proved robust and the finest available at the time.

By November Koettlitz was asking Nansen's advice on sourcing additional equipment – sledges, ski, sleeping bags, gloves, footwear, in particular the reindeer fur boots called finesko. The list even included the wooden snow goggles used by the Eskimo. Koettlitz was concerned at the way the expedition planning was progressing, telling Nansen:

> I am not at all satisfied with the way the R.G.S and Royal Society are planning our National Antarctic Expedition, it is a case of 'too many cooks spoiling the broth' and all being novices or old fashioned.[9]

The chaotic state of the expedition planning was highlighted when Koettlitz, in a letter to Nansen on 19 November, apologised on behalf of Scott for putting him to so much trouble.

Despite this Nansen continued to research on Koettlitz's behalf and supplied him with contacts and information as requested. The relationship formed on the slopes of Franz Josef Land while examining the geological structure of those islands was strong and Koettlitz would write to Nansen in complete confidence. There is no doubt Koettlitz was in awe of the great explorer-scientist, one of the foremost geologists of his time. They shared a profound, professional attitude towards the importance of science in polar exploration as well as towards the planning and personnel required to achieve their aims. It was apparent that Markham and Scott were not aware of – or did not understand – the relationship between the two men.

In December 1900 Koettlitz sent his most critical letter to date to Dr Nansen. He was already having doubts on the leadership of the expedition and his role and participation in it:

> Sir John Murray and other friends of mine, besides Bruce and myself are however far from satisfied with the plans and course things are taking. As I feared, yet scarcely expected to

Burroughs Wellcome medicine chests and contents

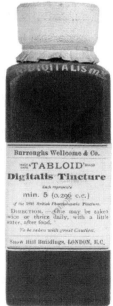

Koettlitz – Microscope and medicine bottles

be so marked as it is, after all the experience of others, notably yourself, these plans and preparations are largely governed by the precedents of British expeditions, as ignorantly and blindly followed by men of the official class (I mean men in, or have been in government service, more particularly Naval) especially the old, such as compose by far the greater percentage of those who form the committees and who have the management of the matter. Again, I think it is a great pity also that a man should be placed in command who has had no experience, or has no knowledge of the kind of work which he is expected to do.

How much better it would have been if someone had been placed in command who had former experience! Or, if not was at least a man who had been trained in science and who had scientific instincts!

The course and final result of this matter, as at present constituted, will, I fear, be much blundering, waste of time and money, as well as not half being done which should have been done, in a word, it will be muddled through 'a l'Anglais' as so much undertaken by the official class (in England at least) is muddled and blundered through.

To give you one instance, among many, it had been intended to take no dogs, or other animals at all, but to use men only, as traction power when upon sledge expeditions, and it was only, as a grudgingly given concession to the representation of Captain Scott, who cannot explain their value, that permission has been given to take twenty (20!!) dogs and I expect that Captain Scott has done this only because of what you have said to him when talking to him!

To think that men can be such fools, after the remarkable object lesson which has so recently been given them, by the success which has attended the Duke of Abruzzi's expedition which took over a hundred of these animals!! Such blindness has indeed a tendency to disgust and weary one with the whole business, and would, if it were not for the hope that one may be able to do some good work in the south not withstanding.[10]

These letters nearly always ended with discussion on the geological formation of Franz Josef Land and the specimens they found together whilst Nansen and Johansen were waiting for the return of the *Windward*. It was a period of pure geographical science in Koettlitz's life that he valued greatly.

The build-up to the departure of the expedition continued. The *Discovery* was nearing completion, much to the satisfaction of Clements Markham. Her sea trials were completed in May 1901 before departure for London.

In the meantime, Koettlitz had a pressing personal engagement. For some time he had been courting Marie Louise Butez, a 38-year-old French citizen, and he felt it was important to marry before he departed south on board the *Discovery*. Marie was born in Calais, France, but had lived in Dover and London for some years. They both resided in London at the time and on 2 March 1901 they married at the Chelsea Register Office.

In attendance was a member of the National Antarctic Expedition by the name of Ernest Henry Shackleton, master mariner and soon to be appointed third lieutenant aboard the *Discovery*. Koettlitz and Shackleton were both professional in their attitudes to exploration and the aims and objectives of the expedition. Although they expressed this differently they nevertheless possessed an excellent understanding of each other. Shackleton was to be the signatory to Koettlitz's will prior to departure. This relationship was seriously compromised later on the southern continent, an unfortunate development that lay in their future dealings. After the *Discovery*, Shackleton would go on to become one of the most renowned and successful polar explorers. One of the first people to be informed of Koettlitz's marriage was Nansen.

It had been confirmed in February that Koettlitz, in addition to being the senior surgeon, was also responsible for botany and bacteriology. Despite his recent marriage he spent the majority of his time in the British Museum working on the scientific aspects of phytoplankton with George Murray and in the bacteriology department at Guy's Hospital.

As far as was possible considering the power politics at play, Koettlitz had followed Nansen's advice with regard to the tinned and fresh provisions and to maintaining the strength of the expedition members to prevent the onset of scurvy. His own experiences in Franz Josef Land gave him additional confidence in making the correct health-related decisions. His views regarding the causes of the disease are now known to be flawed but at the time there was no better authority on its prevention available to Scott. The provision lists were extensive and included fresh, dried and tinned vegetables; fresh, tinned and bottled fruits; tinned meats and fish; plus supporting foodstuffs which would be used to prepare fresh bread, cakes and puddings. If daily use was made of the fresh meat available from the abundant wildlife in the Antarctic regions, scurvy should not present a problem. Koettlitz was sure of this.

The real challenge was one of personalities, not science: would Scott listen to the advice Koettlitz presented?

Some interesting items were listed under 'Medical Comforts': 27 gallons of brandy and whisky, 60 gallons of port wine and 36 gallons of sherry with a similar amount of champagne. How would English polar expeditions manage without being able to pass the port and toast all and sundry in champagne? An essential element in maintaining good morale was tobacco and 1,800 lbs was carried for both the mess deck and wardroom.

Whilst transiting New Zealand Dr Koettlitz was confident scurvy could be avoided and wrote an article for the *British Medical Journal*, asserting: 'If as is possible there will be a sufficiency of fresh game in the shape of penguins and seals we can take it as certain that no scurvy will be heard of.' He confirmed this statement in a letter to his brother Maurice written in New Zealand in December 1901, obliquely indicating that his views might be ignored and that he wished to clarify his intent before the *Discovery* headed south. If scurvy appeared it would not be the fault of the expedition's doctor.

A large quantity of lime juice – as opposed to lemon juice – was carried, despite Koettlitz's known reservations about its efficacy in scurvy prevention. Navy-led expeditions still issued lime juice rather than the lemon juice which had been successfully used within the Royal Navy for many years. In fact lime juice has a low vitamin C content compared with lemon juice.

The long, convoluted debate as to the causes and the best prevention of scurvy had continued for 200 years. In 1734 the Dutchman John Bachstrom proposed that scurvy was the result of a deficiency of fresh vegetables in the diet. Others disagreed. In 1746 the Scottish physician James Lind prescribed the use of regular lemon juice by long distance sailors. He disagreed that the lack of fresh vegetables was the cause as his fellow countrymen were deprived of fresh green vegetables for half the year and had no scurvy. He had not recognised that the continual consumption of potatoes, carrots, onions and turnips was replacing the green vegetables as a scurvy preventive. But he was on the right track.

Lind was made physician at the naval hospital in Portsmouth where he continued his experiments. Unfortunately, he failed to provide a general theory and clear guidelines at a time when theory was becoming more important than effective practice. So when Nathaniel Hulme took up Lind's recommendations in 1768 (Proposals for Preventing Scurvy in the British Navy) they were not acted upon.

The discovery that air was a mixture of gases led to the theory that air might be a cause of scurvy, which in turn led to proposals for better ventilation on ships. There was a debate on this subject on board *Discovery* at its Antarctic base over 100 years later. Meanwhile, Cook's voyages on the *Endeavour* (1769) and *Resolution* (1772), made without outbreaks of scurvy, proved the efficacy of sauerkraut as a preventative, but still the connection to the use of vegetables and fresh meat was not made. An Edinburgh surgeon's mate, Thomas Trotter, wrote a paper in 1786 suggesting a link between lemon juice and oxygen, as the gas is found in all acid fruits and the blood of scurvy sufferers showed a lack of oxygen. Gilbert Blane, another Scotsman who in 1786 had been made Physician to the Fleet, put forward Lind's recommendations to the Admiralty. Unfortunately, they had to pass the matter on to the Hasler Naval Hospital Sick & Hurt Board who saw no need to test it and no further action was taken.

Investigations into the causes of scurvy continued into the early 19th century when a number of scientists realised that when vegetables were scarce cases of scurvy erupted, both at sea and on land. These outbreaks were not confined to Britain; the Californian Gold Fields suffered in 1848, as did Russia when food was scarce. Soldiers in the Crimea and the combatants in the US Civil War in 1860 were also afflicted. In London, Thomas Buzzard, having examined the disease over many years in many countries, wrote a paper concluding that the 'lack of fresh vegetables really was the cause'.[11] There was added confusion over the use of lemons or limes. Citrus juice was currently out of favour. A Professor Parkes favoured the use of citrus fruits as he thought the disease was caused by an acid imbalance in the blood. The majority of these papers were constructive but there was still not a tested cure or definitive cause.

In the 1850s the British navy firmly believed that lime juice was the answer to the problem of scurvy, but outbreaks still occurred. In 1876 an attempt on the North Pole by the Nares expedition saw four deaths from scurvy. The expedition was led by Albert Markham, cousin of Sir Clements Markham, and on their return Parliament ordered an enquiry. From this enquiry a whole new list of possible causes arose: darkness, damp clothing, an excess of carbon dioxide below decks, heavy labour and stress – all health-related issues, but none of them linked to the genuine reason for scurvy outbreak. Nares was blamed for not taking either lemon or lime juice whilst sledging, even though he wasn't the expedition leader. The Markhams and the old polar admirals within the Royal Geographical Society closed ranks for protection, protesting that they 'never took juices to the Arctic'.[12]

As Commander Scott had Clements Markham as his mentor it is not surprising that he saw no need to take at least lime juice on his sledge journeys during the *Discovery* expedition. It was a mistake, as big as the insistence on man-hauling. It added another out-dated and thoroughly inefficient legacy from earlier naval exploration to an already chaotically planned expedition.

Koettlitz was influenced by Dr W. H. Neale, the surgeon on the *Eira* expedition to Franz Josef Land. Neale rightly believed that lime juice on its own was not sufficient prevention against scurvy and that fresh meat and blood were essential. As described during the Jackson-Harmsworth Expedition, Koettlitz insisted on the daily consumption of fresh bear meat, walrus and birds, all of which supplemented the provisions they had taken with them. Although the expedition had lime juice it was not compulsory to take it. Not one member of the shore party suffered from scurvy, despite spending three years in the Arctic.

The worst of all scurvy theories came from Dr Almroth Wright of the British Army Medical School, following his examination of scurvy deaths during the Boer War. His view was that scurvy was caused by acid intoxication in the blood and he forbade the taking of lemon or lime juice. This led to the regular taking and testing of blood during the National Antarctic Expedition. Frederick Jackson, a British army officer, accepted Wright's theory, which led to his comment that 'The use of lime juice neither prevents nor cures scurvy'. This is true, but he also did not fully understand the significance of Koettlitz's insistence on the consumption of fresh meat. Koettlitz was caught between the views of Wright, Jackson, Markham, Neale, Scott and Oslo's Professor Torup who suggested that eating tainted tinned food was a possible cause.

Research continued by other prominent scientists, including Lord Lister, President of the Royal Society, and Professor Vaughan Harley. Harley consulted Frederick Jackson, and with the support of Lister they tested the tainted food theory on monkeys. They concluded that tainted food may be a cause of scurvy, despite this theory having been disproved by earlier expeditions in Africa and India. The research was incomplete but the theory had gained credence.

Koettlitz remained convinced that eating fresh meat and vegetables when available was the preventative required, but acquiesced to the view that tainted tinned food was a possible cause. He even wrote that the consumption of tainted tinned, preserved or salted meats is practically certain to be linked with scurvy.[13] Like others before him he knew how to prevent the disease but could not discern the cause. The debate would ramble on throughout both the *Discovery* expedition and Scott's second expedition to the south on board the *Terra Nova*. Of course, when scurvy hit the National Antarctic Expedition, both at the base and in those returning from sledge journeys, it was the daily introduction of fresh seal meat and other game by Koettlitz and Armitage that cured the affected personnel – although others tried to take the credit.

The tainted food theory continued up to and following the return of the *Discovery* expedition. Despite the lessons learnt on the expedition, the surgeon on Scott's second and tragically final expedition in 1910–1913, Dr Atkinson, lectured approvingly on Almroth Wright's acidification of the blood and Dr Coplan's tainted food or ptomaine poisoning theories. Scott noted this view and approved of Atkinson's conclusion.

1. Sir Clements Markham RGS – *Antarctic Obsession*.

2. Letter from Markham to Professor Gregory dated 16 March 1900 – Koettlitz family archives from A. G. E. Jones.

3. Letter from Poulton to Professor Gregory dated 23 March 1900, written from Barcelona – A. G. E. Jones research papers.

4. Letter from Professor Gregory to Sir Clements Markham dated 30 April 1900, written from Melbourne – A. G. E. Jones research papers.

5. Letter from Poulton to Professor Gregory dated 6 May 1900, written from Oxford – A. G. E. Jones research papers.

6. *Ibid.*

7. Letter from Sir Clements Markham to Professor Gregory dated 16 June 1900, written from London – A. G. E. Jones research papers.

8. Letter from Koettlitz to Fridtjof Nansen dated 21 May 1901, written from London – Koettlitz family archives. Original in Norwegian National Library.

9. Letter from Koettlitz to Fridtjof Nansen dated 5 November 1900, written from Dover – Koettlitz family archives. Original in Norwegian National Library.

10. Letter from Koettlitz to Fridtjof Nansen dated 8 December 1900, written from Dover – Koettlitz family archives. Original in Norwegian National Library.

11. Scurvy-related research by Don Aldridge – file in Koettlitz family archives.

12. *Ibid.*

13. Koettlitz expedition journals from Jackson-Harmsworth Expedition – Koettlitz family archives.

PART 4: ANTARCTICA

21

To the south

Whilst moored in East India Dock the *Discovery* was visited by sponsors, establishment figures, past polar explorers and many others who had an interest in the expedition. There were many dinners to attend, people and institutions to thank. But by Monday 5 August 1901 the crew had returned from leave, the scientists were as well prepared as they could be and the ship left her moorings, heading for Cowes on the Isle of Wight. Here the King and Queen and other dignitaries inspected the ship, after which the King made a short speech wishing the expedition God speed and a safe return. Markham returned late that evening to say his farewells, hoping that the expedition into which he had put so much time and energy would end in success – and in the process bring glory not only to Scott and the expedition members but the country as a whole. The *Discovery* departed Cowes the following day, Tuesday 6 August 1901, at 11.45 a.m. and proceeded down the English Channel, heading south.

Scientific research was to be a crucial part of the journey south, with stops being made at Madeira, South Africa and other islands en-route to New Zealand. The scientific officers on board would make continual observations whilst transiting the Atlantic and Southern oceans and gather as many specimens as possible. Continual deep sea sounding and dredging would be undertaken. Fresh provisions and the sledge dogs would be picked up in Lyttelton, New Zealand. From Lyttelton the *Discovery* would head south towards the Antarctic continent and further explore the regions discovered by James Clark Ross, before setting up safe winter quarters as soon as practicable. The main objective of the expedition was the exploration of the interior of the Antarctic land mass which was at the time mainly unexplored, coupled with scientific endeavour. The plan of operations did not envisage the *Discovery* being locked in the ice for almost three years until the arrival of the relief ships, *Morning* and *Terra Nova*.

Polar explorative experiences and discussion aboard the *Discovery* as it headed south were minimal. Importantly, Commander Robert F. Scott had no previous experience working and surviving in the polar environment. A number of the officers and the crew were experienced sailors but only three men aboard had survived winters in the severe polar cli-

Scott and officers/scientists on board Discovery. *Note Koettlitz*
tall and serious as explained in the MacPhee introduction

mate. And of the three only one of them had experienced the Antarctic continent – Louis C. Bernacchi, the expedition physicist, Australian born, who had wintered on Cape Adare with the Southern Cross expedition in 1899. The other two men were the first officer Albert Armitage and Dr Reginald Koettlitz. These three men brought with them considerable knowledge of the problems of over-wintering in the severe conditions that would be encountered on their arrival in the Antarctic. Although it was already known that the area in which the expedition would be based was mountainous, with huge glaciers close by which would need to be traversed to travel inland, not one member of the expedition had mountaineering experience or experience of climbing in ice conditions. Despite the wealth of mountaineering experience within the great institutions of London, Markham had been blind to this requirement on the southern continent.

It was not known at this stage of the voyage whether the leader would be prepared to listen to and learn from the more experienced men on board; Koettlitz was already doubtful. Scott was hoping that the expedition would further his naval career; he admitted that he possessed no knowledge of, or particular interest in, the techniques of polar travel and survival. The other naval officers and scientists with the exceptions mentioned above were in a similar situation. They were essentially enthusiastic amateurs, encouraged by the view in Edwardian England that English manhood would overcome all adversities – hence the keenness on the naval tradition of man-hauling. The departure of Professor Gregory ensured Scott's complete control over all affairs and that the expedition would run on naval lines.

As the *Discovery* headed south towards Madeira it was realised that she was a slow ship in most conditions and that the journey to New Zealand would take much longer than anticipated. This would also restrict the use of the new dredging and tow gear which was essential to the gathering of scientific specimens for the scientists on board. By the evening of 14 August they were anchored off Madeira. This presented an opportunity for sending letters home and allowed the departure of Dr H. R. Mill, who had been on the *Discovery* to assist with the meteorological and oceanography aspects of the voyage. He also instructed the scientists who were to use this specialist equipment.

During this section of the voyage George Murray, Acting Chief of the Scientific Staff, wrote that the 'Baiting of Koettlitz had already begun – already he is showing his serious professional approach to the whole situation including his objection to a joke about the whale and her babies'. It was to be a long three years for Koettlitz. On leaving Madeira the 'Koettlitz baiting' continued, including to a lesser degree Hodgson and Ferrar, the official expedition geologist. Normally it was enacted by the Royal Naval and junior scientific staff.

Koettlitz and Dr Mill had been close confidants for some time. In April 1900 Koettlitz had confided to Mill 'that either him-self or Armitage should be the Chief of the Scientific Staff',[1] stating that all the others including Gregory were novices in this area having not endured polar winters and lacking the knowledge of 'all the scientific activities'.[2] He even asked Mill to support an application to the committee along these lines.

Once replenished with essential provisions the *Discovery* resumed the journey south, crossing the line with the usual antics amongst those for whom it was a first crossing of the Equator. This did not include Koettlitz, who frowned on such activities and regarded it as yet another excuse to stray from the real purpose of the voyage – gathering specimens for the advancement of science. Murray had previously instructed the other members of the ex-

Koettlitz on board Discovery *(sitting by the hydrogen tanks for the balloon ascent)*

pedition 'not to have horseplay with Koettlitz when crossing the line but do what they want with the younger men'[3] – although when the line was crossed and it came to Dr Koettlitz's turn Neptune said, 'Here Dr Koettlitz lean and tall forthwith into my bath shall fall' but he was let off lightly.

By early September they were heading for South Trinidad where a landing was planned. *Discovery* arrived off South Trinidad on 13 September. In a letter to his brother Maurice Dr Koettlitz confirmed that he had felt squeamish most of the time due to the continual rolling of the ship. After a hazardous landing six hours were spent looking for new specimens. One of the most notable results from this was the discovery of a new petrel, Wilson's petrel, named after Koettlitz's assistant surgeon and zoologist, Dr Edward Wilson. Wilson was a fine artist and throughout the expedition he recorded most of the specimens caught. His drawings are some of the finest ever completed in polar exploration. For Koettlitz, apart from getting relief from the ever present sea-sickness, the most interesting spectacle was the multitude of land crabs that inhabited the island, numbering in the thousands – but not as many as those described in the *Cruise of the Falcon* by E. F. Knight.

Whilst in the region of South Trinidad Murray wrote: 'Dr Koettlitz has found a new "Peridinium" and is beside himself over his first "babe", he couldn't leave it alone. Dr Wilson had to watch it while he was at tea. Royds then found many more specimens.' This sums up the Koettlitz attitude to the scientific aspects of the expedition; to him, scientific discovery should always be the primary objective.

From South Trinidad the *Discovery* headed for Cape Town where it was hoped leaks to the ship could be repaired and the ship refitted and coaled. Because of the slow speed of the ship under sail, the engines had to be used more than expected increasing coal usage. Cape Town was also an important stop in that magnetic observations were carried out there; these proved successful if time consuming. Cape Town saw the departure of Mr George Murray of the British Museum, who was leader of the scientific team. Murray had been due to stay with the ship until Melbourne, but this stop had been cancelled and the next port of call after South Africa would be Lyttelton, New Zealand. The change of plan was the explanation given by Scott for Murray's early exit but it was not the only factor.

Since the resignation of Professor Gregory, the debate as to who should head the scientific team had continued. Scott was adamant that he had the scientific knowledge to lead this aspect of the expedition in addition to the naval ones. George Murray thought otherwise, but following a meeting between himself, Scott and Armitage it was agreed he would leave the ship in Cape Town. This was on the understanding that Koettlitz would take over as scientific director. Murray wrote in his journal on 30 September: 'Shortly arriving in Cape Town, much to be done and get things squared up on board. There is still a lot to be done in handing over my duties to Koettlitz as Scientific Director.'[4]

Murray confirmed this in a letter to Dr Koettlitz:

Discovery at sea

1 October 1901

My dear Koettlitz,

133

For dutiful reasons well known to you I am about to return to England, and with Captain Scott's concurrence, I desire to inform you that you will in future be recognized on board as the 'senior member of the Civilian Scientific Staff'.

The duties of the members are defined by order of 18 August 1901, of which I hand you a copy, and since these are being performed faithfully and with full understanding I do not find it necessary to leave you with any other parting message than the earnest request that you will maintain by all means in your power the cordial relations that exist among the officers of the expedition.

I am
Yours very truly

George Murray
Chief of Scientific Staff[5]

The letter conferred on Koettlitz the title 'Chief of Scientific Staff' and gave a warning to the doctor to be more forgiving in his attitude to the other expedition members. It seems that Murray already feared that not all expedition members would be able to adapt to Koettlitz's professional attitude.

This was a major change in the management structure of the expedition scientific staff. But Scott, in his book *The Voyage of the Discovery*, makes no reference to Murray's letter and the appointment of Koettlitz as Chief of Scientific Staff. It is obvious from this and from the letters subsequently sent home by Koettlitz that Scott disregarded Murray's letter and Koettlitz's appointment. Scott was now not only expedition leader but also the self-appointed head of the scientific staff, despite a lack of suitable qualifications and experience.

Both Mill and Murray returned to England and the *Discovery* headed on for New Zealand. Koettlitz had lost not only his confidants but two scientists with similar understanding of the expedition's scientific objectives. En-route to New Zealand the *Discovery* performed better and the scientific staff continued to take marine and other specimens at every opportunity. In particular, fine bird specimens were caught at regular intervals. On 22 November Macquarie Island was sighted and a landing made in Fisherman's Cove. The island had two large penguin rookeries, which included the large and impressive king penguin. Koettlitz was later to write up his views on Macquarie and compared it with the Falkland Islands.

After a short stay the *Discovery* headed for Lyttelton, New Zealand, where it berthed on 30 November 1901. Further examination of the ship's hull was required, to try to finally resolve the problem of leaks. There were large quantities of foodstuffs, including a flock of 45 sheep, coal and other equipment, to be taken on board. The small number of dogs that had arrived in New Zealand from Russia were awaiting their arrival. The entire expedition – officers, scientific staff and crew – were made most welcome by the residents of Lyttelton and nearby Christchurch.

Koettlitz was very impressed by the reception, writing to his brother Maurice in Dover: 'We have had a grand time in New Zealand and I have almost decided that, should no difficulties arise, I shall come and settle down here.'[6] He was confident of getting a practice in Christchurch. He confirmed this view in a letter to his mother, adding:

Discovery *departing New Zealand*

What I like about the colonies, especially colonies like New Zealand, is that there is less class prejudice and littleness which is so obvious and ineradicable in the people at home, and on that account, if no other, I am sure you would soon feel much more at home than at home itself.[7]

Koettlitz felt suffocated by the class system in England, which was mirrored on board the *Discovery*. The great journey had hardly begun, with years still to come on the Antarctic mainland, but he already doubted the wisdom of being a member of this Scott-led expedition.

Whilst in New Zealand Koettlitz made four speeches and attended many dinners, both private and public. He spoke at the Philosophical Society and Citizens of Christchurch dinner and at both Girls' and Boys' High Schools end-of-term gatherings. Together with five other *Discovery* crew members he also visited a Maori village some 18 miles from Christchurch where he addressed the entire community. Following this he was presented with a Maori cloak, a tradition reserved for honoured guests.

His time in New Zealand was busy and, apart from attending the many functions, he also prepared botanical and other specimens he had collected on Macquarie Island ready for dispatch to England. He compiled an important article for the *British Medical Journal* on scurvy, insisting that scurvy would be avoided if his advice was followed.

Koettlitz was most excited at the contents of a letter from Weld Blundell concerning results from some of the geological specimens he had found in South West Abyssinia: these had been confirmed as gold. Blundell had formed a company with the objective of mining for gold in the region, with Koettlitz as a shareholder. But, as with many grand plans, this never came to fruition.

The stay in New Zealand had been very satisfying for Koettlitz; he was impressed with the country and in particular the people and looked forward to returning.

First, however, there was the small matter of breaking through the Antarctic pack ice and reaching the Antarctic continent without mishap. The *Discovery* was packed to the gunnels with every type of stores, equipment and animal needed to survive in the extreme conditions of Antarctica. The residents of Christchurch and the surrounding region gave the *Discovery* a rousing send-off at 2 p.m. on Saturday 21 December. All went well until the excitement of the occasion got the better of Seaman Charles Bonner, who fell from the mainmast and died instantly. This led to a short delay whilst he was buried with naval honours. The *Discovery* took on further coal supplies at Port Chalmers, making a total of 330 tons, and by Christmas Eve 1902 the lights of New Zealand were slowly fading away as the ship headed south.

---

1. Letter from Koettlitz to Dr H. R. Mill dated 13 April 1900, written from Dover. Original in Scott Polar Research Institute (SPRI) Cambridge.

2. *Ibid.*

3. Mentioned in *Two Years in the Antarctic* by A. B. Armitage and journal of George Murray, Acting Chief of Scientific Staff, 29 August 1901.

4. *Ibid.*

5. Letter from George Murray to Koettlitz dated 1 October 1901, *Discovery* – Murray collection, SPRI.

6. Letter from Koettlitz to his brother in England dated 23 December 1901 – Koettlitz family archives.

7. Letter from Koettlitz to his mother in England dated 21 February 1903, *Discovery* Winter Quarters – Koettlitz family archives.

22

Through the Southern Ocean

Despite all the stores and equipment being carried by *Discovery*, the weight of which caused some instability, the ship made good progress south towards the Antarctic pack ice. In the heaving, rolling sea Koettlitz continued to suffer from sea-sickness, which he now regarded as little more than an occupational hazard. The ship was followed by many species of bird, including fulmars, petrels and the aggressive skua. Specimens were taken at every opportunity for research on board and to return to England. As the ice thickened penguins were spotted on the floes, wary of the many seals and killer whales that inhabited the region but tolerant of man, who was not regarded as threatening. Seals were shot, both for research and for consumption, with seal meat advocated by Dr Koettlitz as an essential source of fresh food for combating scurvy. Seal meat was an acquired taste – strong, game-like and not pleasant to the eye – but Koettlitz hoped that by introducing it early the crew would become accustomed to the taste before it became a necessity. It was not easily consumed by some who had been used to an English diet of domestic cattle, sheep and fowl.

Time was even found, whilst tied to a large ice floe, to try out the skis that should be an essential element in any successful polar expedition. There were two experienced skiers in the party, Koettlitz and Armitage, both of whom had made long journeys in the Arctic using skis. Koettlitz in particular was a very competent skier and should from the outset have been given the task of training the others. But, as with other key aspects of the expedition, it was not deemed sufficiently important.

The *Discovery* continued south, with stops made to 'water ship' – this involved cutting large blocks of ice to bring aboard, to provide a continual supply of fresh water. The tow-net was also used at every opportunity, as it had been throughout the journey; this was the responsibility of Koettlitz. The myriad of sea creatures known as phytoplankton were brought aboard for scientific examination under the microscope of the ever-serious doctor. He took great delight in showing these discoveries through the microscope to anyone who had the patience to withstand his scientific deliberations. However, it soon became apparent that some members of the expedition had little interest in such things. Koettlitz's frustration, which had begun to build during the chaotic preparations before they had even left England, was building.

Soon clear water was ahead and the *Discovery* with steam and sail made good headway to the south. Getting through the pack ice was cause for celebration, and at dinner the champagne was opened and a toast drunk to the future of the expedition – just a small amount of the many gallons of champagne that were aboard. They also had the first sight of land at about this time, adding to what Scott described as a 'joyful frame of mind'.[1]

This frame of mind was not shared by all the sailors aboard the *Discovery*: they were already fed up with the daily inspections, deck scrubbing in freezing temperatures and other traditions carried out on the ships of the Royal Navy. It was another example of the captain being unable to adapt to the different environment of an expedition ship traversing dangerous polar waters. A brief stop was made in Robertson Bay, part of the Cape Adare Peninsula, where the Borchgrevink-led expedition over-wintered in 1896 (the first party to over-winter on the Antarctic continent). As mentioned, a member of the current expedition, Mr Bernacchi, had been part of that previous landing. The huge numbers of Adele penguins first discovered on that expedition were still present in their thousands. The expedition hut and remaining provisions were found to be in excellent condition.

The stay was short, with the *Discovery* pushing on south and east towards the Great Ice Barrier. On 30 January 1902 the party sighted – and named – King Edward VII Land at the eastern end of the great barrier. This was an exciting new discovery, which with good cause led to some satisfaction on board. En-route a number of locations had been examined with a view to setting up winter quarters but Scott's opinion, initially kept to himself, was that they should find a location further south. Up to this point he had still not confided to the other members of the expedition that he intended to over-winter on the continent. Messages had been left for possible relief ships at locations including Cape Crozier, where a number of the crew had received a freezing drenching leaving the beach to return to the ship. Whilst transiting the barrier they were surprised by the irregular height of the ice cliffs, which at times exceeded 200 feet.

Later Koettlitz, ever the faithful correspondent, wrote to Nansen setting out his views on the construction of the barrier and describing its shrinkage since the visit of Ross many years before. He thought the barrier face had shrunk by as much as 30 miles or more, and came to the view that the numerous ice island structures found often many miles offshore were not icebergs or ice islands but sections of the barrier that had broken off. Furthermore he wrote:

> I noticed from the first, and drew Armitage's and Captain Scott's attention to it, that these Antarctic bergs – ice-bergs – at least most of them, and indeed all the typical Antarctic large, flat-topped ones that we have seen, are not ice-bergs at all but are composed of compressed snow, so also is the whole of the barrier face. None of it is ice.[2]

He also stated that glacier ice might be below the compressed snow but the vast bulk is snow – which was not proven until many years later. Koettlitz would be forever the frustrated and unrecognised geologist during the National Antarctic Expedition.

Following a period when the *Discovery* was in danger of entrapment in the ice, Scott decided to turn and head back in a westerly direction, retracing their steps. En-route, the ship stopped and attached ice anchors to the ice barrier at a suitable inlet, from where they were to raise a captive balloon to allow extended views of the great barrier. The balloon had been supplied by the War Office and a number of the crew had received specific training with the army at Aldershot. Once the balloon had been filled Scott made what he described as 'somewhat selfishly the honour of [making] the first ascent in the Antarctic regions'.[3] Shackleton also made an ascent and took the first photographs from a balloon in this area.

Whilst Scott and the others were struggling with the balloon ascent, Armitage was leading a small team of six men south across the ice barrier. Surprisingly, considering Armitage's previous Arctic experience, the group was ill-prepared; a sign of things to come. They had a tent unsuitable for three men, insufficient food and no means with which to heat it. They also had no support from the dogs carried on board. Luckily the weather was kind and they managed to man-haul over 30 miles and temporarily held the record for travelling the furthest south.

While on the Jackson-Harmsworth Expedition Koettlitz had developed the pyramid tent, which is still in use in a modern version in polar exploration. Yet he was not consulted regarding the correct equipment they should have carried on this short journey. Armitage was well aware of the difficulty of survival in these conditions and the success of the 'Koettlitz tent' on Franz Josef Land. He should have known the group was ill-prepared. Perhaps the balloon operation meant the first short overland journey was of secondary interest.

On 4 February the *Discovery* cast off from what was later named Balloon Bight and headed west. By the 8th they were back in McMurdo Sound which they had briefly entered on the outward journey, anxiously looking for somewhere to spend the winter. Scott had previously consulted Hugh Robert Mill, the respected geographer, as to the best location to over-winter, and Mill had recommended this area if a landing was possible. By 9 February the *Discovery* had worked her way up McMurdo Sound and at its head found a suitable place to over-winter. The location was overlooked by the two great volcanoes Mount Erebus and Terror. Here the expedition hut was erected and the ship secured for winter. The hut had been ordered in Australia and was suitable for Australian conditions but not entirely compatible with the Antarctic weather. Again it would appear that survival information had either not been sought from the available sources or not heeded when given – a hut that is ideal for the Australian outback is not generally suited for over-wintering in the Antarctic in temperatures that regularly drop well below freezing. Nevertheless the hut proved useful as a storeroom and emergency accommodation. Smaller huts were also erected for scientific purposes.

By 14 February, building was progressing well and emergency stores had been landed, including kennels for the few dogs. Scott was delighted to have them off the ship as it meant the deck could return to an appearance of cleanliness. 'A good riddance to them,' he wrote. Perhaps this was what led to his dislike of using dogs for haulage and his pref-erence for man-hauling, by far the most ineffective and inefficient means of transport in polar regions.

With these duties completed all hands needed to concentrate on polar survival. In par-ticular, training in the use of skis, dog handling, the erection of tents, efficient use of the cooking apparatus and dressing oneself in confined tent spaces. All these tasks would need to be accomplished in often extreme temperatures. The Koettlitz tent was excellent in its construction, but when occupied by a number of men in bulky, frozen clothing space was limited. This was basic but essential life-saving training activity.

Recreational pursuits, such as a football match between 'officers' and 'men' on 13 February, seemed to take precedence over serious polar study and preparation. Crucially time was found to name the various landmarks in the vicinity: Cape Armitage, Observation

Hill, Hut Point, Arrival Bay and many more. In addition to the sense of conquest, it made the men familiar with the area in case of future emergency.

The initial sledge journey made by Shackleton, Wilson and Ferrar highlighted the lack of preparation. They experienced great difficulty erecting the tent in bad weather and then found themselves unable to use the cooking apparatus. They all suffered frostbite due to the length of time it had taken to erect the tent and because they had carried on marching in storm conditions. This limited first adventure could have easily ended in death or serious injury to the party. These problems were caused by a complete lack of training combined with the attitude shown by the leader and officers of the expedition.

Armitage and Koettlitz had both survived in these conditions in the northern polar region for three years; Bernacchi also had previous experience, albeit not on this scale. It was unwise not to use these skills in both the training and early sledge journeys. Nansen had emphasised to Scott the essential use of ski and dogs, together with other crucial survival issues, during their meetings in Norway. His book *First Crossing of Greenland* should have been required reading for all concerned. Either this information and advice had been forgotten, or it was assumed that the Royal Navy way was best.

It was important that a message be left for the information of the relief ship. A location had earlier been agreed, at Cape Crozier on the eastern side of Ross Island, a distance of approximately 40 miles. Scott had injured his leg whilst trying to improve his skiing and instructed Royds to lead the journey. Consisting of four officers and eight men, crucially, Koettlitz was included, meaning that there would at least be one experienced polar traveller and skier among the enthusiastic beginners. Unfortunately only three were using ski; the rest were man-hauling with the assistance of a number of untrained dogs and handlers: potentially a recipe for disaster. Koettlitz wrote that a naval executive officer was always given command despite being young and inexperienced, as was the case with Royds.

Koettlitz was given the opportunity to provide a crash course of instruction in polar survival to the ship's company, officers, scientists and men. He addressed them all on the mess deck. He covered how to avoid becoming a victim of frostbite and snow-blindness and other perils encountered whilst sledging in such a climate. He also attempted to explain the remedies to such conditions, emphasising the need for great care to be taken. This late attempt to explain the dangers that would be encountered was woefully inadequate. Scott later wrote:

> I am bound to confess that the sledges when packed presented an appearance of which we should afterwards have been wholly ashamed, and much the same might be said of the clothing worn by the sledgers. But at this time our ignorance was deplorable; we did not know how much or what proportions would be required as regards the food, how to use our cookers, how to put up our tents, or even how to put on our clothes. Not a single article of the outfit had been tested, amid the general ignorance that prevailed the lack of system was painfully apparent in everything. Though each requirement might have been remembered, all were packed in a confused mass, and, to use a sailor's expression, 'everything was on top and nothing handy'.[4]

Why this state of confusion, why this shambles which would put the travellers' lives at risk and risk total failure of the expedition? Scott writes as if their ignorance was unavoidable.

Yet Armitage and Koettlitz had both carried out long polar journeys under extreme conditions and survived; they were both experienced users of ski; even the tents were based on the Koettlitz design. They had both travelled much further than the distance to Cape Crozier whilst in the north; packing a sledge in the right order was second nature to them. They had prepared food under worse conditions and had used both dogs and ponies to assist sledge hauling. It was months since the expedition had left the shores of England and they were into their second month on Antarctica, yet still a training schedule had not been prepared.

Within a short time of the Crozier sledging team's departure the lack of training in both men and dogs, as well as the poor equipment, was hindering their advance. As mentioned, only three of the party were using skis: Koettlitz, Royds and Skelton. Many within the expedition still doubted the advantages of skiing, preferring to stumble along as best they could in deep snow while pulling sledges. It didn't take long for the non-skiers to realise their error but it was too late now – the skis had been left at the base. Progress was so slow that after three days out, and on the advice of Koettlitz, Royds decided to press on to Cape Crozier with Koettlitz and Skelton whilst the rest of the party returned to the ship under the command of Lieutenant Barne.

The returning group encountered the first death in Antarctica, when Seaman Vince fell over an ice cliff and perished. The inadequate training, clothing and footwear, coupled with a team suffering from frostbite, meant that an accident had been almost inevitable. Barne's report on the incident sets out these failings in detail. Vince and others had been wearing fur boots which were unsuitable for the ice-covered ground. Considering the slipping and sliding which ensued, Barne's team were lucky to experience only a single death.

Royds, Koettlitz and Skelton, despite making good progress, were hampered by very low temperatures, at times down to minus 42 degrees Fahrenheit. The weather was severe and the terrain difficult even with skis, and after 15 days on the march they returned to the *Discovery* with the post undelivered. They had made three further attempts on foot from a distance close to Cape Crozier and would have succeeded under more favourable weather conditions, but each was sabotaged by inappropriate footwear and clothing. To Koettlitz the signs were clear: the expedition lacked just about every skill requirement for polar travel and survival.

Having recovered from his skiing injury, Scott was determined to make one more sledge journey before the winter set in. The intention was to lay a depot on the barrier to assist the following season's exploration. He left his experienced travellers behind, possibly to prove that despite his total inexperience of surviving in such conditions, other factors could lead to success. He went without skis and intended to man-haul the sledges on foot alongside the out-of-condition dogs. Man-hauling was of course the traditional naval method of polar travel, advocated by Sir Clements Markham and the old, out-dated English Polar Hands. After three days of endurance, having travelled barely ten miles, with the conditions even colder than those experienced by the Cape Crozier party, he returned to the ship, having deposited their provisions.

Experienced polar travellers would use the winter season for training and adapting the clothing, footwear, sledges and other equipment essential to survival. It would be necessary for the sledging parties to become familiar with the use of the Primus cookers which were vital when on the move. Naval traditions such as daily inspections of the men outside in freezing conditions would also need to continue, as this was accepted practice.

It was not to be a happy winter on board the *Discovery*.

1. R. F. Scott – *The Voyage of the Discovery*, first published 1905, Vol. I, Chapter IV.

2. Letter from Koettlitz to Nansen dated 29 August 1904, *Discovery*, North Atlantic – Koettlitz family archives. Original in Norwegian National Library.

3. R. F. Scott – *The Voyage of the Discovery*, first published 1905, Vol. I, Chapter V.

4. *Ibid.*, Chapter VI.

23

The first winter on Antarctica

For Koettlitz, his first winter on the Antarctic continent was a time to make comparisons with his winters spent on Franz Josef Land. He was surprised by the conditions. In a letter to his mother in Dover he wrote:

> By the 13th April the long night was upon us, the weather though not as bad as in Franz Josef Land, there not being so many gales, was nearly always windy and the blizzards when we got them were more smothering and blinding. The lowest temperature recorded at a thermometer I established one and a half miles away to the south and which I visited nearly every day, during the dark as well as when the light returned, this was −62 degrees or 94 degrees below freezing Fahrenheit.[1]

This contrasts with descriptions given by Scott, who wrote that the weather restricted most outdoor activities apart from the occasional game of football.[2] He was writing as an inexperienced polar traveller; if he had taken the time to speak to Koettlitz and Armitage he might have understood that the conditions were not as severe as he assumed and that training could and should have continued.

Lectures by the scientific staff on their specialist subjects became part of weekly life. Many board games were played by the lower deck and amateur theatricals were staged, as advocated by Sir Clements Markham. The ship carried grease paint and other items essential to putting on a full stage show. Such activities were thought by some to help reduce the onset of scurvy. The expedition even included a troupe of performers named the 'Nigger troupe' who put on performances in one of the huts adjacent to the ship. As Scott himself wrote, 'There is no doubt the sailors dearly love to make up; on this occasion they had taken an infinity of trouble to prepare themselves.'[3] I doubt Nansen whilst crossing Greenland or heading for the North Pole, and later Amundsen when relieving Scott of the glory of being first to the South Pole, were overly concerned about the wearing of grease paint, or how to best construct a joke in 'Nigger language'!

Scott and Koettlitz, both accomplished chess players, often did battle over the chess board, causing Scott much annoyance when he was beaten by the eccentric surgeon. As with all things, Koettlitz took a pride in his ability, even at board games. Heated debates were held amongst the wardroom members, covering all manner of subjects. At times music would ring out from the pianola, which was often played before dinner to soothe the mood of the wardroom members.

Every Sunday, the ship was scrubbed down and a formal inspection of the men held on deck under the awning, even in severe weather conditions, resulting in the threat of frostbite without having been anywhere near a sledge journey. Following this inspection Sunday service was held, with Royds playing the harmonium and Koettlitz reading the lessons. The remainder of the day was kept free.

The midwinter festival was celebrated in some style on 23 June. The ship was decorated throughout and when Scott and the officers did their rounds confectionery treats were handed out to the men together with an extra tot of grog, before the wardroom sat down for dinner. Considering the location and the circumstances it was an extravagant affair and worthy of note – a great deal of planning had been put into this event. A turtle soup starter was followed by mutton donated by the New Zealand farmers, with vegetables, and plum pudding, mince pies and jellies all washed down by excellent dry champagne. This was followed by crystallised fruits, nuts and raisins with port and liqueurs. An English gentleman would not forsake his standards even in the Antarctic. It was an important morale booster that was much needed by some. Their spirits were boosted even further by a stunning showing of the Aurora Australis that night, watched by the entire ship's assembly and serving as a head clearer for many.

The other notable monthly event was the measuring of height, chest, waist, biceps, forearms and weight, and the taking of blood, of all the expedition members by Doctors Koettlitz and Wilson. Koettlitz was the main blood taker and some suspected he had an unquenchable thirst for the substance. The samples were taken from the little finger. At times he missed on the first prick whereupon he would make a more aggressive jab in order to make the blood flow, and then suck it into a small glass tube for testing.

It did not follow that the more muscular men withstood the Antarctic conditions better than slighter men; Koettlitz was often asked later in life how 'one so tall and thin'[4] could survive life in polar conditions. He spent a great deal of time hunched over his microscope, part of the bacteriology equipment presented to him by the students of Guy's Hospital, examining both the crew's blood samples and the specimens taken from dead seals, penguins and other creatures. These were both part of his duties as botanist and bacteriologist to the expedition.

He made delightful sketches of his discoveries and many of the team were interested to take a look through the microscope for themselves. Koettlitz was a serious-minded surgeon and scientist, at times not willing to be the butt of the officers' jolly japes. If a derogatory remark was made and the culprit was a scientific colleague, Koettlitz would comment, 'So and so, you surprise me! I would not have expected it of you.'[5] However, if the comment was by an officer or seaman he would not be allowed to visit the laboratory again to peer through the microscope; he would be greeted by silence from within.

Armitage understood Koettlitz, having spent three years in his company on Franz Josef Land, and wrote: 'Soon our good natured surgeon would relent, and again allow us to share his interest in the fascinating work that he had undertaken, and showed some of the younger members of our mess, who were most persistent in their chaff, that he also was capable of a jest, for he created the "Order of the Ass" and classified them according to their respective merits.'[6]

In fact, as Koettlitz wrote to his brother, he 'found the whole business unedifying and very frustrating'.[7] The majority of the specimens and the meticulous records mentioned by

Armitage were somehow lost on their return to the scientific establishments in London, much to Koettlitz's disappointment and dismay. Perhaps some never forgot being presented with the 'Order of the Ass' whilst in Antarctica.

Meals in the wardroom were formal, especially dinner. An officer or one of the scientific staff was elected president of the mess on a weekly basis. It was the president's duty to ensure that all were seated before grace was said, with any absentees instructed to apologise to the president and account for their absence. At the end of dinner grace was said once more and wine passed round to drink the King's health. This was common practice within the Royal Navy and although Koettlitz had to take his turn as president he found the whole business too formal and at times unpleasant. It did not fit with his idea of a scientific expedition living in the polar regions. To Koettlitz it was a distasteful aspect of the class-ridden English society which he so abhorred. His idea of emigrating with his new wife to New Zealand at the end of the expedition to avoid this type of suffocating snobbery was becoming increasingly appealing.

Whilst this bout of gaming, reading and theatricals had been going on, Scott had been harbouring and planning his desire to make an attempt at the furthest south, even the pole itself if possible. He confided this to Wilson, along with his intention to take both him and Shackleton on the journey. This showed his inexperience once again, in excluding his experienced polar travellers, Koettlitz, Armitage or even Bernacchi. By his own admission he was 'woefully ignorant'[8] of Arctic literature, which as leader of a polar expedition he should have studied in great detail. Nansen's *Furthest North*, his account of his experiences on the *Fram* – which some might consider the polar traveller's bible – was not even in the *Discovery*'s library. Koettlitz had a personal, signed copy of the book gifted from the great explorer and could soon have improved Scott's knowledge even at this late stage, if he had been of a mind to listen.

It was not until August that attempts were made to get the dogs, essential to success, into efficient teams. But, as Koettlitz often wrote, the attitude of 'make do', the use of 'common sense and muddle through' would suffice. It should have been obvious that this traditional attitude so beloved within the navy would not work in the hostile and unusual conditions encountered on the Antarctic continent. Nansen, Peary and later Amundsen studied the survival practices and skills of the native peoples in the polar north. Even Frederick Jackson, leader of the Jackson-Harmsworth Expedition and an Englishman who thought he was superior, had sufficient respect for the environment to take the time to study the Samoyed people and their methods of survival. Scott had done none of this and did not take advice from experienced members within his team, thereby endangering all those who travelled with him.

Planning went ahead not only for Scott's journey to the south but also for other sledging trips by other members of the expedition in areas closer to the expedition base. These early trips soon encountered a serious problem commonly suffered by inexperienced polar travellers but which should not have been an issue on this expedition: scurvy.

Whilst in New Zealand Koettlitz had written for the *British Medical Journal* that scurvy should not be a problem to the expedition due to the amount of fresh game available. He followed this up in a letter to his mother, after the discovery of scurvy:

We got through the winter all right, but during the early spring sledging it was found that some of the men were suffering from scurvy, and when I came back from a trip and examined every member of the ship's company I found that practically everybody, officers and men, were tainted with the disease, of course myself included. Stringent regulations were enforced which I had advised repeatedly long before – about the frequent consumption of seal meat (fresh meat) and we soon got rid of it.[9]

This confirms the assertions made by Roland Huntford in his work *Scott and Amundsen*, that despite the pleas of Koettlitz since the expedition had arrived on Antarctica that game should be slaughtered on a daily basis for consumption by all throughout the winter, Scott refused to sanction such a policy. Scott had disliked Koettlitz from the outset and ignored his proven experience and sound advice.

Scott thought that killing seals and other animals for food, as distinct from for science, was 'cruel'.[10] In fact, he disliked the sight of blood and this, coupled with his disrespect for Koettlitz, skewed his judgement. Koettlitz and Wilson had continued to examine the tinned food at the expense of the men's health throughout the previous winter. Only after Armitage and Koettlitz cured the scurvy outbreak by the use of fresh meat and improving the culinary skills of the cook did Scott sanction a limited killing of seals for consumption, thereby improving the strength of the team before the sledging operations resumed. For the moment, Scott accepted the Koettlitz theory concerning fresh meat being essential in the prevention of scurvy.

The dogs should also have been on a diet of fresh meat; instead they were forced to live on biscuits and foodstuffs brought on-board ship from New Zealand or even further afield. As a result they were under-fed and ill-trained.

Another example of Scott's refusal to take advice was the placing of the ship's boats on the ice prior to the first winter taking hold. Armitage, Scott's second in command and an experienced polar traveller, already had personal knowledge of the folly of doing this. The very same mistake had been made by the Jackson-Harmsworth Expedition on Franz Josef Land, and had resulted in many backbreaking days digging the boats out of the deep snow and ice. Armitage advised Scott not to do this but he was overruled, and the *Discovery*'s boats were in an even worse state than those on Franz Josef Land, buried far deeper and completely frozen in. It took many men and hours of work to retrieve them, but fortunately they were not badly damaged. However, the boats were unavailable for use in case of emergency, and demonstrated once again a lack of foresight and polar experience.

The winter drew to its close with the routine seldom changing. The monthly edition of the *South Polar Times*, edited by Shackleton, continued to appear, including sketches by various officers and scientists and containing the superb drawings of Edward Wilson. These included caricatures of each member of the team. Koettlitz had gained the nickname 'Cutlets', and his picture showed a rather strange, gangly individual, and was the subject of much derision by some members of the wardroom.

Koettlitz's obsession with precision often caused him to clash with other members of the expedition. Scott once described a person's breath freezing while exhaling, when ice crystals seem to form in mid-air, as similar to the movement of sand on a beach when washed by a wave. Koettlitz responded that the correct, scientific description of the phenomenon was like the 'minutest crepitation'.[11] Scott wrote that few knew what the word meant until they had consulted the dictionary but that description was adopted.

By 25 August the sun had returned and an excellent dinner was held to celebrate 'The Feast of the Sun'. Turtle soup, tinned fish, seal cutlets and mutton were all washed down by a fine Heidsieck '95: nothing better to stir the English explorer's soul before the imminent sledging season. Their clothing and equipment had been adapted and improved following the previous sledging efforts. The use of ski and dogs in place of the slow, inefficient and laborious man-hauling was still debated, with the following sledging season set to be the test.

1. Letter from Koettlitz to his mother in England dated 21 February 1903, *Discovery* Winter Quarters – Koettlitz family archives.

2. R. F. Scott – *The Voyage of the Discovery*, first published 1905, Vol. I, Chapter VII.

3. *Ibid.*, Chapter IX.

4. Sam Bergman article in Adler Museum Bulletin, South Africa, November 1979.

5. Albert B. Armitage – *Two Years in the Antarctic*, page 99.

6. *Ibid.*

7. Letter from Koettlitz to his brother in England dated 21 March 1904, *Discovery*, Port Ross, Auckland Island.

8. R. F. Scott – *The Voyage of the Discovery*, first published 1905, Vol. I.

9. Letter from Koettlitz to his mother in England dated 21 February 1903, *Discovery* Winter Quarters.

10. Roland Huntford – *Scott and Amundsen*, Chapter II, page 165.

11. R. F. Scott – *The Voyage of the Discovery*, first published 1905, Vol. I, Chapter VIII.

24

Sledging season 1902–1903

Scott wrote extensively about the history of sledging in polar regions, having studied the journals of past British polar explorers, particularly that of Sir Leopold McClintock, the doyen of English polar travellers. McClintock had travelled substantial distances in the Arctic regions. The method revolved solely around the naval tradition of man-hauling, without skis, drawing heavy loads at a very slow pace. It is brave, courageous even, but laboriously inefficient. Scott had visited Fridtjof Nansen in Christiania, Norway, with the intention of acquiring not only knowledge but equipment for the expedition. Nansen was at the time the undisputed authority on modern polar travel in terms of both what equipment to take and the best means of travel. Scott's visit was too short and probably too late to influence already ingrained views, and the National Antarctic Expedition fell back on the Royal Navy tradition of brute force and guts. They were confident that, when combined with the superior attitude of the Englishman, this would be enough to carry them through.

Apart from the limited experience gained since his arrival on Antarctica, Scott's knowledge was scant. The three experienced travellers' views should have been constantly sought, but were not. Koettlitz had long been excluded from Scott's inner circle, despite Armitage describing him as being 'Over 6 feet tall, spare and hardened by his previous polar experience'.[1]

Apart from the means of haulage the other essential aspect of polar kit on which advice should have been taken was the standard of clothing. The Antarctic is colder over longer periods than the north, so the quality and suitability of clothing for sledging would be a matter of life and death.

Nansen, the members of the Jackson-Harmsworth Expedition and later Amundsen had all based their clothing on the materials and methods used for millennia by the local northern peoples. Instead of the integrated militza or anorak-type outer garment based on reindeer and other animal skins used successfully in the north, the men of the *Discovery* were primarily kitted out in London with canvas outer garments which did not breathe. They also used hats that did not protect the neck. Both were ineffective against the low temperatures encountered by the sledging parties.

There were some successful innovations: the sledges were of Norwegian design and construction, and the tents were based on the Koettlitz design so admired by the Scottish explorer William Speirs Bruce. Even Scott agreed that the Nansen Primus cooker for heating food whilst on the march was essential, even if during the early journeys they didn't know

Koettlitz in northern polar attire with pipe and gun as used on Jackson-Harmsworth Expedition

how to operate it. Another early lesson was learnt in relation to storage of paraffin in the tin containers used whilst sledging. The cork bungs were prone to leaking and evaporation. If, on a long march, the supply of paraffin was reduced to such a degree that it was not possible to prepare hot food, serious repercussions were inevitable.

Great debate surrounded the use of dogs as a means of sledge hauling. Nansen and other experienced polar travellers had used them with great success. Unfortunately, Scott's judgement had once again been clouded by the opinions of Sir Leopold McClintock, who did not favour the use of dogs, preferring instead to use the strong backs of the men of the Royal Navy. It seems that Scott regarded the dogs as 'man's best friend'[2] to be treated as pets and not as work animals under conditions which at times involved harsh treatment and sometimes death.

His knowledge of leading dog teams was as scant as his use of skis. He had never seen them in the hands of an expert and did not understand that at times they needed a leader out front to follow. They could not just be driven from behind as you would an oxen or respond to the constant lash. They needed a diet as good as a man's to be fit and strong enough to meet the demands of sledge hauling. Scott's dogs had been on a diet of biscuits and later rotten stock fish brought from Europe, which led to even greater decline in their health and strength. Scott later wrote proudly of his humanity towards the animals,[3] but his general ignorance actually led to greater abuse of the dogs, before he formed his ultimate aversion to using them at all.

The omens were not good for the commencement of the first main sledging season, but with the 'forever forward' attitude of the English gentleman explorer it was assumed that success would surely follow. All the Antarctic could throw at the men of the *Discovery* would be overcome by true grit and naval muscle.

During this period a series of journeys were to be carried out in various directions. Scott was to head across the ice barrier on a southern reconnaissance while Armitage was to head west on a similar journey, both with a view to greater exploration later.

The first team to leave was led by Royds and consisted of Koettlitz, the powerful duo of Evans and Lashly, with Wild and Quartley. They were to head in a southwesterly direction towards Mount Discovery, which would provide Koettlitz with a good opportunity to geologise. By common agreement this was a well-balanced team and fit for purpose. As they posed for photographs they were indeed the 'A' team. Both Wild and Evans were to be involved in far greater and riskier journeys in later years with Shackleton and Captain Scott. Scott wrote:

> The party looked very workmanlike, and one could see at a glance the vast improvement that has been made since last year. The sledges were uniformly packed. Everything was in its right place and ready to hand, and all looked neat and business-like. One shudders now to think of the slovenly manner in which we conducted things last autumn.[4]

Armitage was to leave the following day and Scott a few days later. Scott's journey was to last only two days before very low temperatures and bad weather, accompanied by major problems with the tent, drove him and his two companions back to the ship.

The journey made by Koettlitz and his companions was to last nine days. They encountered similar storm conditions as Scott, including a minimum temperature of minus 53 degrees, but they weathered the conditions much better. There was an experienced polar traveller amongst them and their tent posed no problems at all, with the skirt well secured by snow at the base. Despite encountering severe conditions and losing a sleeping bag, fortuitously later found on the return journey, they returned looking fit and well, if a little battered. They had made good progress towards Black Island, covering very rough ground, and Koettlitz reported he was confident that the island could be circumnavigated when conditions eased. He obtained authority to make this journey later in the month.

In fact, after a few days' recovery, on 23 September 1902 Koettlitz led a small party consisting of himself, Bernacchi and Dailey, the carpenter, to explore the areas surrounding

Brown and Black Islands and if possible to circumnavigate both. They carried provisions for ten days and hoped to carry out geological surveys on the islands. After crossing much rough terrain, with ice debris reaching 160 feet in height, their course was set direct for the centre of Brown Island. This took them, unknowingly, across the outlet of a huge glacier that would soon bear Koettlitz's name. They were obliged to turn south towards Black Island, which was reached on 27 September and where camp was made. On 29 September Koettlitz ascended the northwest promontory of the island where he saw a channel between Brown Island and Mount Discovery, full of broken ice and rock debris, and another channel separating both from Black Island.

Beyond he could see a huge glacier which came down from the mountains behind Mount Discovery. He considered this to be the source of the huge ice deposits upon which he gazed. The glacier was ultimately named the 'Koettlitz Glacier' and to this day remains of immense size and the subject of continued study. This was a new discovery.

After further examination of Black Island, making a collection of geological specimens and morainic deposits, they completed its circumnavigation in a newly found channel. The three then headed back, arriving safely on 2 October 1902. Koettlitz thought further sledging access to Brown Island would be almost impossible as it was surrounded by huge ice and rock debris about three miles out from its base.

It was a short but successful journey of discovery made without mishap or incident by two explorers with previous polar experience, conclusively proving the value of such expertise. On their return Armitage was in command, as Scott had not returned from his depot-laying journey.

Scott returned the following day and after a welcoming dinner was informed by Armitage that scurvy had again struck a number of the expedition members. Armitage and Koettlitz had already taken action to cure the outbreak, which had been caused by ignoring the Koettlitz fresh meat strategy. Armitage described in detail in his book *Two Years in the Antarctic* how he changed the previous food regime, insisting on daily fresh meat consumption accompanied by what vegetables were available, and daily porridge.

Scott wrote:

> Koettlitz has only been back a few days from his second trip, but has made an examination of everyone on board. He tells me there are signs of scurvy in a good many, but in most cases it is only the merest indication, and probably we should not have known anything about it had it not been for this searching examination. The worst cases are those which I have named and they, as well as the rest are improving by leaps and bounds – in fact, the disease is vanishing rapidly. He confesses himself unable to suggest any cause for the outbreak.[5]

This statement is at complete odds with the previous advice provided by the doctor and Armitage. It forgets to mention that Koettlitz had advocated the banishment of tinned meats, a strategy later introduced, as confirmed in a letter to his family in England. Koettlitz had even taken advantage of the improved light and warmth to grow a crop of mustard and cress using Antarctic soil and as an alternative some flannel. Unfortunately, it was not possible to grow enough to act as the equivalent of the scurvy grass found in Arctic regions, but it was enough to provide mustard and cress sandwiches to all hands. This was the first time that soil from the Antarctic continent had been used to grow a crop of any kind, and shows once again how the eccentric doctor was pioneering ideas and methods for the prevention of scurvy. It also earned him a rousing three cheers from the ship's company.

Dr Koettlitz was to make further sledge journeys during this season, in particular supporting Armitage in leading the western support party. But the main thrust was to be made by Scott, Shackleton and Wilson with the southern sledge journey to explore new territory to the south. This involved crossing the great Ross Ice Shelf to achieve a new furthest south and perhaps the pole itself.

Two support parties set out on 30 October to lay depots in support of this venture, with Scott and his two companions leaving the *Discovery* on 2 November. They took 19 dogs to assist with hauling the sledges and would use skis when appropriate; all three still lacked training in the use of both. Royds, Koettlitz and Skelton had previously proved that sledges could be hauled using ski, but all three of these parties preferred to man-haul, with skis carried as little more than extra baggage. They had no real alternative, as they had had so little practice and their ski fittings proved inadequate.

During this journey south there was friction between Scott and Shackleton, with Wilson becoming a peacemaker. The dogs were gradually killed and fed to their mates or died of exhaustion, but somehow the trio managed to make a new furthest south. Wilson became concerned that they had already passed the point of no return, with their failing health and poor physical condition potentially leading to serious problems on the return journey. Having passed the 82nd parallel by 28 December, Scott and Wilson ventured a little further south before Scott gave the urgent order to turn back.

The subsequent race for home turned into near disaster as the weather worsened, food ran low, dogs died or were killed one after the other. They had to make the main depot more than 100 miles from the *Discovery* or die of hunger and exhaustion, compounded by the onset of scurvy-like symptoms. Shackleton was suffering the most because of a serious chest complaint that dogged him until his death, but all were on the verge of collapse. Fortunately the weather cleared enough to locate the depot, which was marked by only a single flag as opposed to a series of marker flags as used by experienced polar travellers. Even in Franz Josef Land Jackson, Armitage and Koettlitz had marked their depots with multiple flags and cairns. The members of the southern party should have been well aware of this crucial safety procedure.

The return to the ship now had to be accomplished without delay. Shackleton was struggling, the dogs had been killed, skis had been abandoned, and all three were in a dreadful condition. The constant physical stress of hauling the loaded sledges caused further strain on the already acrimonious relationship between Scott and Shackleton. Wilson continued as the go-between, a role he would later perform on the fatal second Scott-led expedition. As the conditions worsened Scott wrote: 'We regret that we threw away our ski.'[6] Fortunately, one pair had been retained, which Shackleton used to help him as he struggled forward, undoubtedly saving his life. By the time they reached the final depot their food was down to a bare minimum. Because of worsening weather they had to remain tent bound. Shackleton's condition deteriorated. Despite Wilson's worst fears Shackleton did recover and by the time they reached the *Discovery* on 3 February 1903 he was moving as easily as his two companions. It had been a close-run experience, and many of the problems had been brought on by poor preparation. Not a single dog survived the journey, a result of Scott's lack of knowledge and their combined inability to use and feed them properly.

Bernacchi wrote many years later in his book praising Captain L. E. G. Oates who died with Scott on the disastrous second attempt on the South Pole:

> No expedition should go out with less than 100 to 200 dogs. A dog team without a load may do as much as 40 to 50 miles a day. With loads averaging 100lb per dog, a team probably would cover 20 miles a day and even that could not be expected every day. One of the weaknesses of British explorers has been their failure to utilize dogs to their full extent. The unreasonable prejudice against them has led to suffering and hunger, heroic deeds and death. Man-hauling of sledges already has been obsolete for two or three decades. There is no necessity not even any valid excuse for it. Dog traction, ski and fresh meat are the essentials; these make polar travel as safe as possible, besides reducing its toil and hardship.[7]

This statement covers the three essential elements that Nansen, Armitage, Koettlitz and Bernacchi had attempted to convey to Scott but without success. He continued to believe – even in the face of overwhelming evidence – that he knew best. This attitude continued on his second expedition to the Antarctic, despite experiencing the problems first-hand during the *Discovery* expedition.

This initial journey to the south, combined with Shackleton's physical condition, would soon lead to another controversy, culminating in Shackleton being sent home on the relief ship the *Morning*, which had arrived in their absence.

1. Albert B. Armitage – *Two Years in the Antarctic*, page 125.

2. Roland Huntford – *Scott and Amundsen*, Chapter II.

3. R. F. Scott – *The Voyage of the Discovery*, first published 1905, Vol. I, Chapter II.

4. *Ibid.*, Chapter XII.

5. *Ibid.*, Chapter XII.

6. R. F. Scott – *The Voyage of the Discovery*, first published 1905, Vol. II, Chapter XIV.

7. L. C. Bernacchi – *A Very Gallant Gentleman*, published 1933, page 226.

25

Shackleton's departure

The relief ship the *Morning*, under the command of Captain William Colbeck, had followed the trail of letters placed by the *Discovery* and located the ship within McMurdo Sound. Here the *Discovery* was locked into ice five miles deep with little hope of release. Colbeck was an experienced seaman from the merchant fleet with previous Antarctic experience, having been selected as navigating officer and magnetic observer for the Southern Cross expedition led by the Norwegian Carsten Borchgrevink. It was a British-financed expedition and the first to over-winter on the Antarctic continent. As mentioned, Louis Bernacchi was also a member of that expedition.

On 3 November, in Scott's absence, Koettlitz accompanied by Skelton and Hare made a short journey to Erebus Bay to ascertain if there was an Emperor penguin rookery there or close by. After a thorough examination of the Erebus Glacier snout they camped adjacent to the larger Razorback Island, and ascended to a height of 150 feet to get a good all-round view but no Emperors were to be found. After an uneventful journey they returned to the ship in the evening of 5 November.

This was a prelude to the main sledge journey made by Koettlitz in support of Armitage during which they explored in the direction of, and ascended, the Western Mountains. The objective was to find a route onto the Antarctic ice cap itself and explore as far as possible inland within the restrictions placed by safety, food and the physical condition of the men. The overall party consisted of 21 men; Armitage led the main group of 11 men, including Skelton and Wild. Koettlitz's party consisted of another eight men in support. This journey became one of outstanding endurance, with first-class leadership shown by Armitage. Both groups were led by experienced polar explorers. This largest and most experienced sledge party by far departed the *Discovery* on 29 November 1902, the main group carrying rations to sustain them for up to two months. Koettlitz was due to return after approximately three weeks having supported the main party.

It became an exceptional journey and resulted in Armitage being the first man to ascend to, and discover, the great Antarctic polar plateau. They crossed the outlet of the Koettlitz Glacier, ascending via great crevasses, mountains and the Ferrar Glacier, eventually reaching a height of nearly 9,000 feet on the plateau itself. By 3 January 1903, Armitage had decided that with his supply lines extended it would be wise to turn back towards the *Discovery* before the party was affected by serious injury or illness.

Due to sound advice from Koettlitz, regarding killing seals en-route to cache food for the return journey, the men remained generally fit although tainted slightly by scurvy. On 10 December Dr Koettlitz made a medical examination of the main group. They were to press on once again with Armitage before Koettlitz departed on his own return journey. He pronounced them fit to proceed but warned Armitage against overtaxing them, on account of the scurvy. Armitage was concerned but determined to push on as far as they could without endangering the lives of the men. The sledges were re-packed. Armitage sought the advice of Koettlitz as to the best route of descent to the Ferrar Glacier. Ferrar spent time geologising, while Koettlitz held Armitage on the end of a rope as he examined the route from the cliff edge. They agreed that a better route might be found southward of their current position, a decision which delayed the eventual ascent to the plateau. The joint party dined together at 'Separation Camp' and following a hearty three cheers by all, they went their separate ways, Armitage to further discovery, Koettlitz returning to the ship.

The return journey was not wasted, with both Koettlitz and Ferrar making geological assessments and gathering rock samples en-route. They discovered that the further inland they were, the more the composition of the rocks was granite, often split and broken by the wind and extreme weather. The lower or outer hills consisted of quartzite with basalt ridges running through them. The journey, although very foggy at times, was made without incident and they all returned safely to the ship on 18 December, ending a successful three-week sledge journey over difficult, unexplored territory.

Western sledge journey: Camp at 3000 ft

Western sledge journey: Main glacier

Western Mountains: Koettlitz return party at luncheon camp

Camp showing total Western sledge party

Lieutenant Armitage returned with his companions on 18 January after making the most impressive journey of the expedition to date. He had ascended the most difficult of mountain ranges and glaciers, discovering new land – the great polar plateau itself, a discovery with which he is often not credited. The following year Scott himself made the same journey using Armitage's knowledge, although having found an easier access route to the plateau. He travelled further inland than Armitage and can therefore claim to have made the furthest journey onto this great expanse of snow and ice. But it was Armitage and Koettlitz who pioneered the initial exploration.

Having returned in good health from the western support party Koettlitz was keen to carry out further sledge journeys, both for scientific reasons and to improve his knowledge of the area. He had already made a successful sledge journey to the Brown and Black Islands, as mentioned. Between 29 December and 8 January he made a second journey to this region, accompanied by Ferrar and Hodgson, a truly scientific team that hoped to uncover further information concerning the age and composition of the islands. Their equipment was cobbled together in the form of a rough sledging unit, as the bulk of the equipment was still on the march with Armitage and Scott. Koettlitz was confident of success, especially as Ferrar had gained useful sledging experience during the western journey.

Koettlitz's sledging notes record that on leaving the ship they headed directly for the centre of Black Island in order to avoid the treacherous rough ice as much as they could. En-route they nevertheless encountered much wet and rough ice caused by the recent thaw, but by 31 December they had reached the island. They continued along the northern shore of Black Island, and across the channel to within three miles of Brown Island. Here the sledges could be pulled no further, so they walked through deep ice debris and water-filled channels until they reached Brown Island. They immediately ascended Brown Island to a height of 2,750 feet and discovered it consisted of a volcanic cone with crater. The island was formed of lava and volcanic ash which had weathered to a reddish brown colour interspersed with blocks of granite. From this elevated position they had a clear view of the area towards and beyond Mount Discovery.

Koettlitz confirmed that the impressive glacier at the back of Mount Discovery, which became known as the Koettlitz Glacier, passed away in a long tongue along the shore of the mainland towards the north. A long deep bay existed between Brown Island and the mainland, with Mount Discovery and the plateau of the mountain at its head. The channel between Brown Island and Mount Discovery was choked with lines of heaped-up morainic material and debris and appeared impassable. Geological samples were taken and marine specimens discovered amongst the rock. Koettlitz described the distant scene appearing as 'A tumultuous frozen sea with high crested waves curling towards us'.[1]

After completing their scientific examinations the three men headed back to the ship, arriving without incident on 8 January 1903. It was another short but successful journey led by Dr Koettlitz. Scott himself conceded that the journeys led by Koettlitz had resulted in an important and interesting discovery: that the ice on which they had first landed marked nothing less than the end of the Great Ice Barrier.

Koettlitz was to make only one more journey of any substance before being effectively confined to the ship and its immediate surroundings, Scott having stated that the senior and most experienced surgeon must be present on the ship. A similar situation was to befall Lieutenant Armitage following his return from leading the western party onto the polar plateau.

The final sledge journey of any importance made by Koettlitz was in the company of Hartley Ferrar, the official expedition geologist. The two geologists headed for Minna Bluff, a piece of land that jutted out from Mount Discovery into the Ross Ice Barrier. It was an area familiar to Koettlitz following his trips to Brown and Black Islands. They set out on 14 January but the journey was beset by bad weather. The objective was to ascend The Bluff to examine its geology and the pressure ridges as the ice passed the point of The Bluff.

By 20 January they had still not reached their goal and due to the extreme weather were forced to make camp for several days. By the 23rd they were within walking distance of The Bluff. Although confined to their tent for many hours both men managed to walk to a shoulder of The Bluff. They ascended to a height of 300 feet where there was a fair view in all directions, but the extreme weather hampered their progress. After collecting some geological specimens Koettlitz decided that the weather was worsening and so they returned to camp.

The two scientists were not equipped for an extended stay away from the ship and it was decided to return to base. In a raging blizzard, and using a sail lashed to the sledge, they made good progress, arriving back at the *Discovery* on 26 January 1903. It was another short but successful sledge journey led by Koettlitz. They had identified new routes for the following season and added to the geographical knowledge of the region. His experience in polar travel had resulted in safe and successful journeys. In particular, his experience provided great support to Armitage during their trip to the Western Mountains. On this

Koettlitz sledge journey to The Bluff

final short journey he had also experimented with different forms of sledging food in an attempt to beat the scurvy menace. Armitage commented on his return: 'how very fit the doctor looked'.[2]

In total Koettlitz carried out 81 days of sledge travel. Although he wished for more it was not to be. Writing to his mother, Koettlitz said: 'Some of the time (sledging) was spent in low temperatures, the temperature once, when we got up for breakfast reached –56 degrees or 88 degrees of frost. Notwithstanding it being so cold I am glad to say it did not trouble me very much.'[3]

Many years later he was often asked in South Africa how a man so tall and thin could withstand such extreme conditions. His response was always similar: that he was an experienced, fit and well-prepared traveller. He was aware of the dangers of such conditions and tackled them in a professional manner. This experience should have been exploited to its full on the National Antarctic Expedition.

The *Discovery* was still stuck fast in the ice and there was no hope of her departing with the *Morning*. Another winter in Antarctica was unavoidable. Stores were being transferred from the *Morning* as fast as was practicable; Colbeck was concerned about his ship also being beset. Scott and his two companions from the southern journey, Wilson and Shackleton, were taking a long time to recover from their exertions. Wilson and Scott had taken to their beds for days at a time and Shackleton still suffered from his chest complaint but was up and about before the other two. It was clear that they had all been badly affected by scurvy, with

Scott and Wilson in particular having very swollen gums, legs and ankles. All three men were extremely tired.

Scott made his first visit to the *Morning* on 18 February, 15 days after his return from the south, and described it as an awful grind. He had already decided that with the *Discovery* obviously beset for another year, the size of his expedition must be reduced. The combination of men from the Royal Navy and the Merchant Navy had never been much of a success and he was keen to remove the bulk of the merchant men. This included Lieutenant Shackleton. He had asked for volunteers to return and was surprised and pleased that eight names were put forward which almost matched his own list.

The removal of Shackleton was glossed over in a single paragraph by Scott in *The Voyage of the Discovery*. His true reasons for the dismissal were deep and personal and Koettlitz became a main player in the drama that continued in one form or another until the deaths of both Scott and Shackleton. As established earlier, Shackleton and Koettlitz had been on good terms prior to the departure of the *Discovery*. Following the return of the *Discovery* to England they discussed at length the planning of the subsequent journey south made by Shackleton (the *Nimrod* expedition).

The events leading to Shackleton's removal have been recorded in great detail by Roland Huntford in *Scott and Amundsen* and were commented on by Armitage in his writings, in particular in a letter from Armitage to H. R. Mill in 1922. Armitage wrote of his discussions with Scott on the *Discovery*: 'I then went to Scott, and asked him why he was sending him (Shackleton) back. I told him there was no necessity from a health point of view, so after much beating about the bush he (Scott) said, "If he doesn't go back sick he will go back in disgrace."'[4]

Armitage had discussed Shackleton's state of health with Koettlitz. It was obvious that Wilson was in a far worse condition, being confined to his bed for weeks. Scott put Koettlitz in a very awkward, if not impossible, position. He demanded to know if Lieutenant Shackleton was in a fit state to undertake any duty demanded of an executive officer upon the expedition. Koettlitz responded: 'Mr Shackleton's breakdown during the southern journey was undoubtedly in Dr Wilson's opinion due in great part to scurvy taint. I certainly agree with him, he is practically recovered from it, but, referring to your memorandum as to the duties of an executive officer, I cannot say that he would be fit to undergo hardships and exposure in this climate.'

The truth was, of course, that Shackleton had recovered more quickly than both Scott and Wilson, and that none of them would have passed the test set down by the captain at that time. Scott had not forgotten Shackleton's challenge to him on the southern journey and his very presence on the ship now challenged his authority, not only with the merchant seamen but with the Royal Navy members as well. Shackleton's strong personality and leadership skills made him a popular officer in both the wardroom and mess deck and he had to be removed.

It was unfortunate that Koettlitz happened to be the final judge of Shackleton's departure. Koettlitz wrote in a letter home: 'One member of our ward room mess is returning also, much to the regret of us all. He broke down in health while out sledging with the skipper and Wilson upon the long journey southward.'[5] Shackleton's departure would be felt by all apart from the captain, whose power and authority would now be less threatened.

Shackleton was cheered on his way as he left the *Discovery* to board the *Morning*. Only two merchant men remained and one officer. Armitage could not be removed due to the employment conditions in his contract, although Scott indicated that perhaps he should return home for personal and family reasons. The stubborn Dr Koettlitz also had his stay confirmed by contract and despite his many doubts and regrets in relation to the expedition he would stay to the bitter end.

Following the return of the *Morning* to Lyttelton, New Zealand, a very interesting article appeared in *The Morning Post* concerning the departure of Shackleton and the others from the expedition:

> It is worthy of note that the naval members of the crew of the *Discovery* have all apparently volunteered to remain for such further time as the vessel may be detained in the ice, those members of the crew who have returned on the *Morning* being whaling men who, presumably, found the unaccustomed naval discipline maintained on board the *Discovery* somewhat irksome.[6]

This is a classic example of the establishment working to deflect any criticism from Markham and Scott and to show that the naval man was superior. The use of the term 'whaling men' was not relevant and a slur that would continue to be used until a certain fortuitous encounter with whalers the following year.

1. Koettlitz National Antarctic Expedition sledging notes – Koettlitz family archives.

2. A. B. Armitage – *Two Years in the Antarctic*, page 196.

3. Letter from Koettlitz to his mother in England dated 21 February 1903, *Discovery* Winter Quarters – Koettlitz family archives.

4. Letter from A. B. Armitage to H. R. Mill dated 24 May 1922. SPRI archive and also Roland Huntford – *Scott and Amundsen*.

5. Letter from Koettlitz to his mother in England dated 21 February 1903 – Koettlitz family archives.

6. *Morning Post* article, 31 March 1903, 'Captain Scott's Plans' – Don Aldridge papers.

26

The mystery of colour photography

In addition to his other skills Koettlitz was an experienced photographer. He had made use of the camera on his previous expeditions to Franz Josef Land, East Africa and the Amazon. Many of his photographs were contained in the reports of these expeditions.

On the *Discovery* the official expedition photographer was Lieutenant Reginald Skelton, the engineer officer on the ship. During the journeys to and from Antarctica and the time spent on land Skelton took a large number of excellent black and white photographs, often assisted by other expedition members.

Skelton was an admirer of Koettlitz's skills in various ways, in particular when it came to skiing and polar survival. He noted in his diary on 22 March 1902:

> Armitage is supposed to be our authority on sledging, personally I would sooner take Koettlitz's advice on the matter – as I think the former has very bigoted opinions – notably one, that ski are no good for hauling sledges. He has always driven dogs or ponies. There is no doubt that old Koettlitz is alright about sledging, he can do his work with the best and seems to have jolly good stamina.

The first colour photographs ever taken on the Antarctic continent were captured by Dr Reginald Koettlitz which is not widely known. He had a personal camera and plates and between February 1902 and November 1903 took a series of colour photographs, totalling 58 images. The first was of Mount Erebus and Erebus Bay, while the final plate was of the midnight sun showing over the horizon. A full list of his colour photographs, with locations and descriptions, is published here for the first time (see Appendices).

Once again Koettlitz was ahead of his time. It was to be many years before the next colour photographs were taken on the continent. As with many issues relating to Koettlitz, there is a perplexing mystery in relation to this: neither the plates nor the photographs were used in the expedition reports, and together with Koettlitz's expedition journal have never been located. The collections, journals, drawings, photographs, scientific data and logs were the property of the Royal Geographical Society and Royal Society. These organisations would have disposed of them as they saw fit at the time.

No books, narratives or other publications were permitted until six months after the publication of the official expedition reports. Presumably the Koettlitz material would have been submitted under these conditions. However, since that time they have not been located, either in London or Dover, despite extensive research for this book and especially by A. G. E. Jones, the polar historian.

It is recorded on file that Captain Scott gave an instruction that no prints were to be made from the colour plates.[1] They would have made a wonderful addition to Dr Wilson's superb sketches.

The images from the first colour photography to take place on Antarctica should have been a crucial element in the expedition reports, but it seems they have been lost to history. They included photographs taken on the first journey to the Western Mountains, the ascending of Brown Island, the discovery of the huge Koettlitz Glacier and the return of Wilson and Shackleton from the southern journey, all depicting major historic events in polar history. There was no such mystery surrounding the large numbers of black and white photographs taken by others.

There is a possibility the images were subsequently returned to Koettlitz. It is also possible that this valuable historic material was lost amongst the other artefacts presented to Dover Museum by the Koettlitz family following damage to the family museum during the Second World War.

---

1. SPRI photographic collections and note made with regard to Koettlitz colour negatives and A. G. E. Jones research – Koettlitz family archives.

27

The second winter and surgery

The second winter spent in Antarctica continued in a similar vein to the first with one notable exception. The concert parties, theatrical performances and other such activities so prevalent in the first winter were significantly absent. Hopefully, the ship's activities were now concentrated on planning the next sledging season, in an effort to avoid the unprofessional, mistakes made in the first season. Or perhaps the leader and his close associates were by this point devoid of ideas for keeping the men active and busy. Once again improving the men's skiing skills was not a high priority. Hockey became the favourite sporting pastime.

The *Discovery* remained firmly imprisoned by the polar ice. At least with the supplies brought by the *Morning*, together with the seals and birds being killed for consumption on a regular basis, there would be no sign of scurvy. An added bonus to the improved diet would be the fitness of the men for the next season's man-hauling across the polar wastes.

Pondering on these matters Scott wrote about the attitudes of those on board:

> It is certainly a great matter for congratulation that we are rid of the undesirable members of our community. Although they were far too small a minority to cause active trouble, there was always the knowledge that they were on board, mixing freely with others, ready to fan the flame of discontent and exaggerate the smallest grievance.[1]

Whether he was referring directly to Lieutenant Shackleton is not recorded.

Midwinter's day passed with some excellent food, including turtle soup from a whole turtle brought from New Zealand, tinned halibut, roast beef with artichokes and devilled wing of skua, all washed down with the last of the champagne. Even a warship's wardroom in Portsmouth Harbour would not have dined in finer fashion. Dinner was followed by dancing, with Royds at the piano.

Around this time Koettlitz was interviewed for the *South Polar Times* in his so-called 'inner sanctum', a cabin filled with laboratory instruments, books and collections made not only on this expedition but on his previous expeditions to Franz Josef Land and Africa. By now he was thoroughly disillusioned with certain members of the expedition, its aims and objectives and his own role within it. He had suffered the silly games and high jinks throughout the winter and been the butt of stupid pranks, cartoons and comment, but still he gave an interview which might add to the merriment of some at his expense. He had by now already formed the opinion that he would be excluded from the final scientific reports and papers on return to England.

He is described by the interviewer as a tall, emaciated gentleman of a tough, healthy, leathery appearance with hair slightly, but not unbecomingly, awry. As always Koettlitz could only partake in serious debate, and after discussing and explaining in detail his duties and receiving little positive response from the interviewer he commented: 'I am afraid you either display an extraordinary amount of misapprehension or you are most deplorably ignorant'.[2] A classic Koettlitz response, of the sort which did not endear him to some of his colleagues.

But he did manage to include in the interview his experiences in Franz Josef Land, Africa and Brazil, and his friendship with Dr Nansen.

The sun returned on 3 September. An improvement in the weather and summer's return meant a start could be made to the second sledging season. Clothing, sledges, foodstuffs and other equipment had been worked on throughout the winter. A sledging plan had been prepared by Scott that did not include Koettlitz. There were to be no journeys of significance made by Armitage either. The first sledge journey was led by Royds and headed for the Cape Crozier penguin rookery on 7 September.

Scott was reassured by Koettlitz that there was no sign of scurvy following the winter's inactivity.

The main sledging effort was to be made by Scott to the Western Mountains following the route pioneered by Armitage and Koettlitz the previous season. Between September and November other sledge teams spread out from the *Discovery* base in various directions. This included another journey to Cape Crozier by Wilson to further examine the Emperor penguin rookery visited previously by Royds. Armitage was permitted a short, two-week journey to the Koettlitz Glacier late in November. There was no attempt to better the furthest south that had been made by Scott, Shackleton and Wilson the previous season.

It seemed that Scott was determined to achieve both firsts: the furthest south and the furthest west onto the plateau. Up to this time the most pioneering and professional journey had been led by Armitage with Koettlitz in support, up the Ferrar Glacier into the Western Mountains and onto the plateau itself. For the captain to achieve both goals he had to beat Armitage's record. Koettlitz remained restricted to his laboratory, carrying out geological and scientific surveys in the area around the *Discovery*.

But Koettlitz's professional ambition could not be denied and during the summer he carried out the first surgical operation on a patient on the Antarctic continent. He had had to treat broken limbs, twisted joints and other minor ailments throughout their stay, but had not used his full array of surgical instruments until Lieutenant Royds developed a large cyst on his cheek. Although starting small, it continued to grow until it reached a size where he was advised to have it surgically removed.

Armitage who had had direct experience of Koettlitz's skills whilst in Franz Josef Land, vouched for the doctor's skill as a surgeon. Koettlitz was keen to keep his ability finely honed and was eager to operate. Armitage describes in detail, and with some glee, the operation:

> Koettlitz was nothing loth to perform the operation, and made his preparations before the eyes of the patient. The operation was to take place on the wardroom table. He brought out

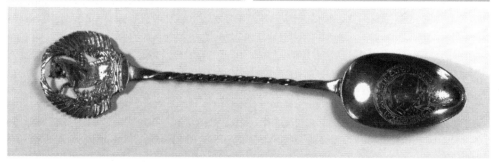

Koettlitz Discovery *matchbox & spoon with Koettlitz crest and penguin on expedition crest*

many knives and explained their various uses, trays of carbolic, in which were placed small pincers and scissors, their uses being also fully entered into.[3]

The operation was to be performed before an admiring crowd made up of all those left on the ship, some of whom were to assist. Armitage continued:

> Incidentally, too, he displayed before his victim's admiring eyes many other surgical instruments and appliances, and told us of the marvellous deeds that could be performed with them. Then he brought out, with all due solemnity a sterilizer, some lint, gauze, cotton wool and bandages while Royds looked on.
>
> Bernacchi next rolled up his sleeves, ready to play the part of nurse, and I grasped a phial of patented freezing mixture wherewith to spray the cheek of our First Lieutenant. Koettlitz leading the team was in his element. Royds was told to lie full length on the operating table, the wardroom table, and the operation commenced. As soon as Koettlitz thought the time had come, he attempted to make an incision in Royds cheek, but the knife would not cut the frozen skin, so we paused a little and made reassuring remarks to the patient.
>
> Again the knife was pressed against the frozen cheek, and this time we were rewarded by a small flow of blood, and an emphatic 'Yes' on answer to our queries as to whether it hurt or not. The spray once more came into play, and hit the patient's eye and the nurse (Bernacchi) mopped away with a piece of lint, mostly in the wrong place, but practice made perfect. The cyst was removed, the cheek stitched up, and all that remains to tell of this first operation on the southern polar continent is a small scar on Royds' cheek. A notable first for any surgeon.

Dr Koettlitz was an accomplished surgeon who had had many years of practice, not only on Franz Josef Land but also in and around the mines of County Durham. Royds was not to forget this incident, together with the skills and friendship of Koettlitz as a polar traveller and companion. Following Koettlitz's death in South Africa, Royds was active in raising funds to erect his memorial in Cradock, South Africa.

Whilst Koettlitz remained within his laboratory and the wardroom, engaged with his bacteriological research, occasionally wandering in the near vicinity of the *Discovery*, Scott and his companions man-hauled approximately 240 lbs per man up the Ferrar Glacier towards the polar plateau. It was hugely exhausting work, sometimes ten hours a day. When weather had forced a period tent bound, Scott drove the men even harder. There is no doubting Scott's strength and dogged determination to succeed but not all men can maintain the same commitment. Skelton urged the captain to ease this drive to beat the record achieved by Armitage before some of the men collapsed due to the altitude and the constant toil. Towards the end of November Skelton turned back for the *Discovery*, leaving Scott with Petty Officer Evans and Leading Stoker Lashly, both men of strength and fitness, to forge ahead. Scott admired their great strength and excellent condition.

By 1 December, after another two weeks of extreme hardship, bad weather and struggling to survive in the inadequate clothing, food and fuel were running low. They would be dangerously exposed on the return journey, especially if they became tent bound for any length of time. In fact, it was almost a repeat of Scott's first long journey made with Shackleton and Wilson. However, the leader's luck held this time too. They returned to the ship on 24 December, with the skis in perfect condition due to their lack of use. Scott had

Sawing ice

Explosion of 16lbs of gun cotton in an attempt to break the ice

beaten Armitage's record to the west with his two hardened Royal Naval colleagues. They had travelled over 700 miles, man-hauling all the way, under very difficult conditions. Each journey pushed them to breaking point. The southern polar regions are the most unforgiving in the world if not treated with respect.

On Scott's return only four men were found on the ship, including Koettlitz. Attention was to be turned once more to freeing *Discovery* from its icy grip. In the interim Armitage, following Scott's orders, had erected a camp approximately ten miles to the north of the *Discovery* with the intention of sawing and using explosive to try to break up the ice. Koettlitz photographed the early attempts to break the ice using guncotton and to test the sawing mechanism. After a few small charges a 16 lb charge of guncotton produced a minimal effect. Moving the heavy sawing beams was a task in itself.

Progress in another area had been made by Seaman James Dell, described by Sir Clements Markham as a 'smart but ill conditioned little fellow'.[4] Dell had worked the young dogs into an efficient sledging team. He had made suitable harnesses for the dogs and spent time training them. They now proved their worth in dragging the heavy spars to the sawing locations, beating the man-hauling team by a substantial time and distance. If only such skill could have been utilised during the earlier sledge journeys.

On his return, and following a period of recovery, Scott journeyed to the 'sawing camp' to inspect Armitage's work. The very large tented structure was split into two compartments, one for the officers and one for the men. There were good cooking facilities. On Scott's arrival 30 men were engaged in the very heavy work of sawing the ice. But they were still ten miles from open water and the chances of sawing the way clear were, at best, remote. The ice was over six feet thick and after a further 12 days sawing only two parallel cuts of 150 yards each had been achieved – and even those began to freeze over. By 3 January 1904 Scott admitted that 'our sawing efforts have been an experience, but I'm afraid nothing more'.[5] It had been a useless exercise from the start.

Armitage was following Scott's orders in creating the sawing camp but even Skelton said the sawing was 'the most fearful waste of time one can possibly think of. One would think Armitage was entirely devoid of common sense, but he was just carrying out orders'.[6]

On 5 January, whilst Scott and the others pondered on what to do next in the effort to free the *Discovery*, two ships were spotted in the distance. Scott wrote he had seen them whilst out camping with Wilson but it would appear others had also seen the vessels. They turned out to be the *Morning* and the very powerful Dundee whaler the *Terra Nova* under the command of Captain Harry McKay, one of the most experienced ice masters and navigators in the British whaling fleet. His crew were hardened Dundee whalers, used to weathering the extremes of Arctic sailing. If the *Discovery* was to be freed it would be by the *Terra Nova*.

The orders the ships had brought from London were short but concise: 'If the *Discovery* cannot be got out of the ice, you will abandon her and bring your people back in the relief ships, as My Lords cannot under any existing circumstances consent to the further employment of officers and men of the Royal Navy in the Antarctic Regions'.[7]

By allowing the *Discovery* to be iced in for two seasons, the expedition – and Scott in particular – had caused a major upheaval in London between the Royal Geographical Society, Royal Society, the Naval Board and the government. Sir Clements Markham's many enemies

Captive Emperor penguin – weight 65lbs

Emperor Penguins in region of Discovery *base*

had turned on him revelling in the opportunity. The Admiralty had taken over control of the relief operation, despite the protestations from an outraged Clements Markham. Even Lieutenant Shackleton had been retained as an advisor to the relief committee, although he refused an offer to travel as Chief Officer on the relief expedition – an initiative that would no doubt have prompted an interesting reaction from Scott. At some considerable expense to the Admiralty, the *Terra Nova* had been towed by Royal Navy cruisers as far as the Arabian Gulf, in order to make her rendezvous with the *Morning*. They knew it was unlikely that the *Morning* would be able to release Scott's ship itself and that the *Terra Nova* would be essential to this task.

---

1. R. F. Scott – *The Voyage of the Discovery*, first published 1905, Vol. II.

2. *South Polar Times*, 1st edition – Koettlitz family archives.

3. A. B. Armitage – *Two Years in the Antarctic*, Chapter XV, page 247; Louis Bernacchi – *Saga of the Discovery*, page 51.

4. Sir Clements Markham RGS – *Antarctic Obsession*, page 92.

5. R. F. Scott – *The Voyage of the Discovery*, first published 1905, Chapter XVIII.

6. Don Aldridge – *The Rescue of Captain Scott*, page 88. Taken from Skelton diary entry 17 December 1903.

7. Don Aldridge – *The Rescue of Captain Scott*, quoted on page 91.

28

The release of the Discovery

On the *Morning*'s previous visit to the *Discovery* only five miles of ice separated the two ships; now Colbeck found that 20 miles separated the relief ships from the ice-bound vessel. It would not be a fast release; and time was not on their side. The vast breadth of Captain McKay's experience would be required. Matters were not improved by the gloom that had settled upon Scott. The orders from the Admiralty had shocked him, as he realised that the release of the ship was not guaranteed. Having to abandon the ship would be the ultimate failure, with potentially serious consequences on his return to London. McKay intended to butt the ice with his powerful ship, something the *Morning* was incapable of doing. McKay was confident that by using this method, together with explosives, the *Discovery* could be reached. There was no time to lose. Scott was not impressed by the prospect of being saved by a so-called 'common' whaling captain from Dundee. In the following weeks he showed little interest in assisting the efforts of the *Terra Nova* and the underpowered *Morning*.

He commented little in *The Voyage of the Discovery* about the methods being used by McKay to break up the ice, apart from stating that, in his view, 'using the Terra Nova to butt the ice would not work'.[1] If he had paid more attention he would have seen it *was* working: day by day McKay's methods were making inroads into the ice that was at times seven feet deep. It was increasingly evident that the transporting of the scientific specimens and other material that had been going on between the *Discovery* and the relief ships might not have been necessary. Equally, the stores that had been transferred from the *Terra Nova* to the *Discovery* could have stayed on the relief ship.

McKay would have preferred more inclement weather to assist the ice breaking up – it would enhance his butting and explosive techniques – but the seas and air remained resolutely calm. Towards the end of January Scott was still of the opinion that the *Discovery* could not be freed, but others had been paying more attention to the efforts of the *Terra Nova*. Skelton and Royds, who had been liaising closely with McKay, thought the ice was breaking up by at least 100 yards a day. Royds had taken a crash course in the use of explosives from McKay and was making good use of this knowledge closer to the *Discovery*, with encouraging results. They were confident that the continual use of the explosives was making an impact on the ice. Gradually larger cracks began to appear.

Scott was still not convinced that all this effort was of any use – he thought that only nature, linked with an act of divine intervention, would be able to free the *Discovery*. A giant swell might be the answer.

Despite encouraging reports from his officers, on 27 January he wrote: 'I fear, I much fear, that things are going badly for us'.[2] Then, the following day as he lay in his bunk, Scott was astonished to hear the ship creaking. On rising he found it was actually moving. Despite ascending Hut Point and witnessing movement in the ice he still could not see this as a hopeful sign of release. On 29 January he still wrote that he was sceptical of reports of the ice breaking up before the approaching relief ships. On 30 January, accompanied by Koettlitz, he saw from Hut Point that the ice was beginning to break away and the relief ships were clearly making progress. This continued by extensive use of the explosives and on 4 February Scott visited Captain McKay for the first time in weeks and noted, 'McKay is excellent company for a depressed state of mind'.[3] McKay was confident and following this visit, Scott vigorously promoted the use of explosives close to the Discovery and could now see and understand, at last, the effect of such use.

It had taken approximately six weeks for him to acknowledge the effectiveness of the explosive but Scott was still of the opinion that a heavenly swell was the only true answer to his predicament. He thought that abandoning the ship was still a distinct possibility and had drawn up the orders to do so. By 12 February providence had intervened with a large swell which lifted his gloom, but by the following day his depression had returned as no good news arrived from the relief ships. Just 24 hours later the strong wind was back and whilst they were taking dinner a shout was heard: 'the ships are coming sir'. They all raced to Hut Point and sure enough there was the Terra Nova followed by the Morning butting her way towards the Discovery, the ice breaking before them. By late in the evening of 14 February 1904 the two ships were moored close to the Discovery with the crews able to shake each other by the hand.

The debate continues to this day. Was it the 'hand of God' providing the great swell that released the Discovery or the even more powerful hand of Captain McKay in the Terra Nova, supported by his extensive use of explosives? Don Aldridge, in his extensively researched book The Rescue of Captain Scott, explains in great detail the release of the ship, showing clearly it was the Terra Nova supported by the Morning that saved the Discovery. There was greater movement of the sea as the ice was broken, created by the actions of the Terra Nova over the past 40 days.

This is supported by Koettlitz, who described the scene in a letter to his brother written from Port Ross, Auckland Island on 21 March 1904:

You will see, by the above address, that the good ship Discovery is once more afloat and is released from her imprisonment in the ice from the time the relief ships arrived. The two of them, when we first saw them, surprised us exceedingly – which was on the 3rd or 5th of January, until the 14th of last month, some forty days, was a period of suspense for during that time some 22 geographical miles of from 7 to 9 feet thick ice has had to be got rid of, for that amount separated us from the open water. That this actually did shift you now know, but you should have been with us to realize what intense excitement reigned when the last three miles suddenly, within the same number of hours, broke away and the two relief ships at last anchored to the floe, in Discovery Winter Harbour close to our still imprisoned ship. Two days waiting, with the help of judiciously placed big charges of gun cotton here and there soon released us, now the three ships were afloat in company.

Discovery *with relief ships* Terra Nova *and* Morning *approaching release*

Discovery *trapped in ice*

Discovery *from the east*

Relief ships approaching the Discovery

When Aldridge wrote his book he was not aware of the Koettlitz letters, which supported his view that it was indeed 40 days of butting the ice and using explosive guncotton that released the *Discovery* from its Antarctic grip. Koettlitz has confirmed any doubt that it was the *Terra Nova* and Captain McKay that saved the *Discovery* and, ultimately, the reputation of its leader.

There was to be one more very serious incident before the ship was finally free from the coast at McMurdo Sound. The weather had deteriorated once more, forcing the *Terra Nova* to head for open water, interrupting a dinner of seal and penguin (delicacies now regularly on the menu) which was being hosted by Scott.

Eventually the *Discovery* had raised enough steam to move away from the ice under her own power, but then she immediately struck the bottom. There she remained for almost 12 hours being bumped and ground on the sea bed. It was a severe test of the ship's construction but she survived.

Koettlitz wrote: 'The ship lay helplessly bumping and grinding horribly on the bottom, with seas breaking over us, we were fearing the worse'.[4] The shipyard in Dundee, despite all the previous criticism in particular relating to the speed problems on the journey south, had succeeded in constructing a ship of immense strength. Scott, though, preferred to thank the forces of nature, blaming the strong southerly wind which reduced the water level for running the ship aground and crediting the wind's reduction for the water's return and the re-floating of the ship. It is surprising that the shoal in question had not been identified during the years *Discovery* had been there.

Scott took coal from both relief ships, leaving the *Morning* dangerously low in fuel and ballast. With that, all three left for their arranged rendezvous at Port Ross, Auckland Island. En-route the team on the *Discovery* observed that land masses and a number of islands that had previously been recorded did not in fact exist, but exploration on the journey was restricted by the limited amount of coal. On 14 March the *Discovery* arrived at Port Ross, being joined over the following days by first the *Terra Nova* and then the *Morning*. The latter's crew had experienced a particularly hair-raising journey, with Captain Colbeck considering the ship virtually unseaworthy due to its un-ballasted condition. Scott agreed that it was only the splendid seamanship of Colbeck and his crew that saved the ship. The great coal debate was to rage for many years and is covered in detail by Don Aldridge in *The Rescue of Captain Scott*.

The ships remained at the Auckland Islands for approximately two weeks for repair and preparation for their arrival in Lyttelton. This was to prove a momentous reception for Scott and the men of the *Discovery*. They were entertained royally by New Zealand – so much so, in fact, that the *Discovery* and the *Morning* did not leave for the return journey to England until 8 June.

The captain and men of the *Terra Nova* had not been so involved in the round of social activities and had departed two weeks earlier. The hardened whalers from Dundee were not keen to socialise; members of the Lyttelton and Christchurch establishment and a number of the Royal Naval officers found their company tiresome. However, it was the whalers responsible for the *Discovery*'s rescue who really deserved praise.

For Koettlitz it became a time of reflection on what had been achieved by the expedition and by himself in particular. Koettlitz detested the social snobbery that was taking place in

Lyttelton, having already endured almost three years of unjust taunting and criticism from certain members of the expedition. Although he was a member of the Masonic Lodge and Savage Club together with Scott and others on the *Discovery*, he found the kind of snobbery encountered on their return most distasteful and was determined to extricate himself.

At the first opportunity, having fulfilled his share of public speaking engagements and official dinners, he made haste to the North Island in company with Royds to examine what else New Zealand had to offer. His tour of the North Island lasted for 22 days and in this time he visited and studied the volcanic region of Rotorua. He found the area of great fascination and wrote in detail to his sister, Mabel, of the wonders of the hot springs, boiling water and magnificent geysers, commenting that 'His Satanic Majesty could not be far off here!'[5]

It was a short, relaxing period away from the sensationalism of the *Discovery*'s return and the sometimes unpleasant experiences with his messmates. He had written to his brother whilst in Port Ross, Auckland Island that he found their companionship very trying at times:

> They are a very different class of man to any I have associated with before, and a class not altogether to my taste except now and then, the reason being that everything is a joke with them, life is a joke, everything one says, and every argument or topic of conversation is turned into an absurdity.[6]

Koettlitz found this very wearying and was in no doubt that it had greatly impeded his scientific work. A trip which should have been one of scientific and medical discovery had been compromised by others within the wardroom. He was of the opinion that the 'well to do classes, who know nothing of poverty and have no knowledge of the working classes',[7] also have no application for professional scientific study, which in his opinion should have been the main thrust of Scott's expedition.

Once the expedition was over Koettlitz was determined to distance himself from this 'class'. His opinions were well known to his fellow travellers and this would ultimately lead to his virtual exclusion from the preparation of the final expedition reports. He confided to both his brother and Dr Nansen that he was not at all satisfied with the work he had been able to carry out in Antarctica. He felt he would have fared much better if he had travelled with William Speirs Bruce on the *Scotia* expedition.

The work he had managed to complete had been continually ridiculed and belittled from the captain downwards. The other expedition members did not understand or appreciate the importance of his many hours spent examining specimens in his laboratory and even more hours peering through his microscope. The opportunities to gather botanical specimens were very limited on Antarctica compared with the Arctic regions, with moss being the highest form of vegetation found. Activity relating to his other responsibility, phytoplankton and oceanographic study, was limited due to the lack of time allowed by the captain for deep sea trawling and the gathering of specimens, with the *Discovery* being unsuitable for this type of work. Even his discovery of the new peridinium, named '*Peridinium Scottanium*', was eventually passed over as being of no consequence.

His first love, geology, had been under the control of Ferrar and although Koettlitz assisted in the gathering of specimens and was mentioned in the final report, his contribution was limited. In the letter to his brother written in Port Ross he described Hodgson the biologist as a 'Cad and a Bounder';[8] who often led the tormenting behaviour to which Koettlitz was subjected.

The *Discovery*, overhauled and refitted, returned to England by the most direct route with a short stop in Punta Arenas and the Falkland Islands. Koettlitz was surprised by the size and prosperity of Punta Arenas, inhabited by Chileans with a number of German and English settlers. He recorded that he was very disappointed not to encounter ethnic Fuegians. He was also surprised by the scale of the Falkland Islands and how desolate the majority of the islands were – largely windswept, undulating and rocky with a form of tussock grass covering the surface. He could not comprehend how people could live in such a place, the islands being dreary in the extreme.

Whilst in the North Atlantic Ocean he penned another letter to Nansen, in which his assessment of the expedition was at its most critical:

> Personally, with regard to this (*Discovery*) expedition, I am far from satisfied. Though very good, as well as a considerable amount of work has been done by everyone, the spirit under which it has been done has, in large part, been a frivolous and happy-go-lucky one. These naval and other officers look upon everything that happens and that they do as a 'bit of fun', as sport, and they do it in sporting style. There is no backbone in it, and much of it is carelessly done. There is also too much of the official tradition in it, and too much 'red-tape'. Never the less work has been done.[9]

Koettlitz thought the atmosphere in the wardroom immature and the behaviour of his companions amateurish and unprofessional. Even the caricatures of Koettlitz in the *South Polar Times* by Wilson and Barne were unkind and would have added to his discontent with the party.

He observed that despite Captain Scott's bouts of temper and irritability everybody remained loyal to him. Koettlitz had endured three years of frustration and occasional humiliation but still had the courage to comment on his loyalty to Scott who had been responsible for much of the expedition's unsatisfactory nature. Scott never understood or recognised Koettlitz's scientific and medical skill or knowledge.

Despite the drawbacks he encountered, Koettlitz's papers and the studies he undertook are carefully recorded, in particular those relating to the plankton and bacteria of Antarctica. His collections register 540 items in the main collection and 288 marine items. His recordings of the measurements and medical samples taken from the expedition members are catalogued in great detail. Regrettably, none of his work was used in the final scientific reports, including his ground-breaking colour photography. Koettlitz had been almost entirely excluded from them, relegated to a footnote in history despite his crucial role and the scientific research he had carried out.

The difference of opinion between Scott and Nansen concerning Koettlitz is remarkable, one (Scott) failing to see any merit and the other considering him a valued scientist worthy of respect. As historian Roland Huntford sums up: 'It takes a first-rate man to recognize a first-rate man.'[10]

---

1. R. F. Scott – *The Voyage of the Discovery*, first published 1905, Vol. II, Chapter XIX.

2. *Ibid.*, Chapter XIX.

3. *Ibid.*, Chapter XIX.

4. Letter from Koettlitz to his brother in England dated 21 March 1904, *Discovery*, Port Ross, Auckland Island – Koettlitz family archives.

5. Letter from Koettlitz to his sister Mabel in England dated 17 May 1904 – Koettlitz family archives.

6. Letter from Koettlitz to his brother in England dated 21 March 1904, *Discovery*, Port Ross, Auckland Island – Koettlitz family archives.

7. *Ibid.*

8. *Ibid.*

9. Letter from Koettlitz to Fridtjof Nansen dated 29 August 1904, *Discovery*, North Atlantic – Koettlitz family archives. Original in Norwegian National Library.

10. Roland Huntford quote used by this author.

29

Final days in England

With the return of the *Discovery* to Portsmouth Harbour a series of social and ceremonial engagements began, continuing unabated from Portsmouth to London for some considerable time. Sir Clements Markham was first to board the ship to congratulate his protégé and no doubt brief him on the political fall-out between the two societies and government that had taken place in his absence. Scott had been made a Member of the Victorian Order on departure, and on his return was promoted from Commander to Captain. A new polar medal authorised by the King was to be presented to selected members of the expedition, including Koettlitz.

From Portsmouth the *Discovery* sailed up the Thames and berthed in the East India Docks in the Port of London. At a grand luncheon, which included the Press, held in a shed at the dockside, Sir Clements Markham, Chairman of the Royal Geographical Society presided, but Sir William Huggins, President of the Royal Society, was significantly absent. Leading London scientific figures were present together with the officers and scientists of the *Discovery*.

Markham's first announcement, to hearty cheering all round, was that Captain Scott had been invited to Balmoral by the King and that he should take Dr Wilson's superb sketches and Engineer-Lieutenant Skelton's photographs for royal examination. The first colour photographs from the Antarctic continent taken by Dr Reginald Koettlitz were not included.

Koettlitz was mentioned at a subsequent dinner at the RGS when Scott described how he went daily to a thermometer on the ice floe to prove the temperature was 20 degrees lower than on the ship. Sadly, all this produced was laughter from the audience. In proposing the toast, Markham described Scott and his officers as 'like knights of old'[1] meeting and overcoming great perils in unknown lands. Remaining loyal to the end, Koettlitz, responding on behalf of the scientists, said how supportive Scott had been to their endeavours and how they all looked upon his promotion as an endorsement of the work by all aboard the *Discovery*.

There were further engagements at the Savage Club where a dinner had been held before departure and other London establishments. Koettlitz was impatient to break away from the endless round of social gatherings. He had by now realised that he would not be asked to take an active role in preparing the scientific reports and was anxious to obtain a doctor's practice without delay. Even a report to the *British Medical Journal* in July 1905, entitled 'The Medical Aspects of the *Discovery*'s Voyage to the Antarctic', was presented by Edward A. Wilson, Koettlitz's deputy on the ship. Koettlitz felt keenly the snubbing inherent in his exclusion from involvement in the scientific reports of the expedition. It was later commented in South Africa that this moment accounted for his sad demeanour for the rest of his life. He had been away from his new wife for over three years and did not have independent means to support her and his household. An appointment in medicine had to be found with haste.

In his home town of Dover Dr Koettlitz had not been forgotten; on the contrary, he was greatly admired. He had previously given a lecture at Dover College to rapturous applause following his return from Franz Josef Land and his meeting with Nansen. On Wednesday 11 January 1905, a civic reception was held in Dover Town Hall, an outstanding building that was perfect for the event. Koettlitz had obtained authority to give a lecture from Markham and Scott. Such presentations were generally not made until Scott would have completed his own account of the expedition.

The illustrated lecture, entitled 'Furthest South', was given before a packed town hall. It was reported in the local Dover and Kent press that Koettlitz held the audience spellbound for over two and a half hours with many interruptions for hearty applause.

More importantly, he showed the first ever colour slides taken by himself during the expedition. The new three-colour process perfected by Koettlitz was shown for the first and only time in public. The audience much admired the splendid colour reproduction and found it hard to believe the pictures were the result of a photographic process. To add further realism a local man was dressed in Koettlitz's polar clothing and withstood the two and a half hours without complaint. Koettlitz paid due deference to Captain Scott and acknowledged his furthest south journey made with Wilson and Shackleton and his subsequent journey in the footsteps of Armitage and himself. At the end he confirmed that it was the butting and explosive work of the *Terra Nova* and the *Morning* that eventually released the *Discovery* from her icy trap. It was a splendid occasion and for Koettlitz probably the height of acclaim for his endeavours on the expedition.

In the meantime, Shackleton had not forgotten Koettlitz and invited him to join an expedition he was currently planning to the Antarctic. The objective was to be the first to make the South Pole, thus eclipsing the previous efforts of Scott. He had not forgotten his dismissal from the National Antarctic Expedition and being blamed for Scott not achieving a greater distance south during the southern journey with Wilson. Koettlitz had already decided not to go south again so soon but threw his energies into assisting Shackleton's planning.

In a bitter letter written in July 1913 to Professor Nansen from South Africa Koettlitz wrote about this planning with Shackleton:

> Shackleton had originally planned his expedition in conjunction with me and we had almost decided to go as leaders jointly, but then the plans hung fire. I could not wait, hoped that by coming out here I should be able to make some money quickly and thus missed my chance of further work. Shackleton, when I was out of sight, forgot me, so that, when the wherewithal in money was forthcoming, he decided to go alone and ignored my existence and has done so ever since, though he did not forget my plans.[2]

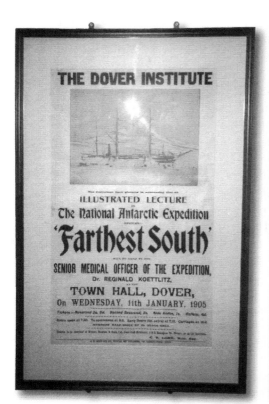

Left: Koettlitz lecture poster, Dover Town Hall
Right: Collection of rare birds from New Zealand and Franz Josef Land (Koettlitz Collection)

The expedition Koettlitz is referring to is the Shackleton-led *Nimrod* expedition in which Shackleton turned back from the South Pole only 97 miles short. Shackleton realised that even if he and his companions made the South Pole, which they undoubtedly could have done, they would die on the return. There is no mention of Koettlitz with regard to the *Nimrod* expedition, but its outstanding achievements were in part due to his contribution in its planning.

Koettlitz had spent almost ten exhausting years travelling the globe as a member of expeditions. His brother had taken over his practice at Butterknowle, County Durham, and his search for a general practitioner's position led him to South Africa. He had endured two expedition leaders, Jackson on Franz Josef Land, who was an uncontrollable tyrant and the other, Scott on Antarctica, who in his view, was an incompetent and devious amateur. His exclusion from involvement in the *Discovery* expedition reports was the final insult.

His wife Louise had lost their only child at birth and they agreed to move overseas. Koettlitz was impatient to replenish the family bank balance and settle down. He had considered British Columbia, Canada, where he had owned a plot of land since 1901, but decided it was too cold in the winter months for someone having endured six years in the polar wastes. New Zealand had been his original choice, following his time spent there on the *Discovery*'s outward journey. But the display by the Christchurch and Lyttelton elite on the return leg had convinced him it must be South Africa. Koettlitz had enjoyed their reception in Cape Town whilst en-route to New Zealand, and his knowledge of the German language might also be an advantage.

He saw a general practice in the Somerset East District advertised and was soon appointed. This is now the Eastern Cape Region of South Africa. The practice was on a farm at Grobbelaars Kraal, Darlington – a remote location which is now at the bottom of Lake Mentz, an artificially enlarged lake constructed to improve irrigation in the region. Koettlitz took over the practice from Dr D. B. Stoney.

---

1.   Royal Geographical Society's Dinner, Criterion Restaurant, September 1904.

2.   Letter from Koettlitz to Fridtjof Nansen dated 8 July 1913, South Africa – Koettlitz family archive. Original in Norwegian National Library.

30

The rural doctor and farmer

Koettlitz arrived in South Africa, then known as Cape Colony, in their autumn of 1905. His authority to practise as a doctor and pharmacist is recorded in the Medical & Pharmacy Register, dated 22 June 1905. He had left England before the presentation of the RGS *Discovery* expedition King's medals; these were later forwarded to him at Grobbelaars Kraal. His home farm and practice were located near the confluence of the Sundays and Riet rivers. At this time Darlington was nothing more than a frontier outpost. It consisted of a hotel, a postal agency, a London Missionary Society school and a Congressional Chapel, all serviced by a small number of retail outlets and local farms. It held a mixture of English and Afrikaans-speaking patients to whom Dr Koettlitz administered care.

It was a remote location even by South African rural community standards. He travelled to see his patients by horse, or by pony and trap. For his wife it must have been a lonely existence compared with Dover or London, especially having lost their only child before leaving England. It showed her great commitment to her husband. Even in this new environment she maintained high standards of dress and composure.

Grobbelaars Kraal ostriches (Note sock on head)

Marie Louise Koettlitz at Grobbelaars Kraal, South Africa

When posed the question by a youthful Don Craib, later Professor Craib, as to why he had chosen such a remote, isolated and sparsely populated practice in which to retire Koettlitz stressed his need for 'a long rest somewhere in the sun'.[1] Koettlitz lived and worked from Grobbelaars Kraal for nearly ten years. He was highly regarded for the painstaking and thorough care he provided for his patients, although he maintained a low profile outside his work. He had transferred to the local Masonic Lodge in the area and been appointed a Justice of the Peace, but his most extravagant leisure activities revolved around a game of chess. Perhaps it reminded him of his regular truimphs over Scott on board the *Discovery*. He would be happy to travel considerable distances for the chance to play a worthy opponent.

He transformed the Kraal into a fertile oasis. He kept ostriches, poultry and angora goats and was a keen gardener, no doubt relishing the contrast with man-hauling over the frozen wastes of the polar regions. Koettlitz had hoped to sell the ostrich feathers but as soon as his ostriches were ready to produce their plumes the fashion for them collapsed, leaving a business without demand. This financial venture, like his Amazon investment and other potential ventures, was not a success.

Koettlitz was well thought of within the Cape, where he was an active member of the community. In addition to being a Justice of the Peace he was a member of the Legislative Assembly, secretary of the school board and District Surgeon, with regular opportunities to practise his skills. But it became increasingly clear that Koettlitz was not going to raise enough money to satisfy one ambition which still remained: to mount one final journey to the southern polar region.

During his time in South Africa he maintained his correspondence with Nansen and other contacts in London within the RGS and Royal Society. In one remarkable letter in February 1911 to an old friend, Dr D. H. Mill, Koettlitz wrote of his plans. The letter showed how Koettlitz was still at the forefront of ideas regarding polar travel. After initial pleasantries he wrote:

> I wish I could find someone with money who would finance an expedition to the south, such as briefly this – take ships and go south of here or as nearly so as possible, land at the first available place with properly adapted motor vehicles, say six.
> These would of course have to be properly thought out and tried in Norway, before it was decided that they were practicable and all other requisites, with small huts.
> Leave a party on the coast (seen the ship home or rather back to a civilized part, till it returns to fetch us).
> And then, with another party and by means of the motor vehicles with a hut in sections and plenty of stores and instruments motor to the pole. There set up the hut and spend if possible a year there taking regular observations the whole time.
> I think that, when properly thought out and [with] properly tried motor vehicles, the transport to the pole would be of not much difficulty, given reasonable luck and for a party to live there and take meteorological observations for over six months, would without doubt be a most valuable contribution to meteorological as well as other science.

(The letter goes on to discuss Shackleton's expedition and Scott's proposed second attempt on the pole.)

This is an amazing proposition, way ahead of any other scientific thinking at the time as regards transiting the Antarctic continent. Koettlitz was utterly frustrated by the scientific approach on the *Discovery*. In the letter he is emphatic that this was to be a scientific expedition with no pole-bagging or glory-seeking. He had discussed the use of motor vehicles with Shackleton but it is doubtful that the technology was available at the time to produce such a sturdy and reliable means of transport. Scott later tried using motor vehicles on his *Terra Nova* expedition with little success. Possibly their failure was due to the lack of intensive testing in severe conditions prior to departure.

Koettlitz had by this time realised that his decision to move to South Africa had not been financially productive, and was anxious to break out from his role as a rural GP in the Cape Colony. Sadly he was to remain a frustrated polar scientist until his death. His grand vision with the motorised plan outlined to Mill was not to become a reality for many decades to come.

He wrote to Nansen of his frustration: 'I came out to South Africa in the hope of making a little money somewhat quicker than I had done, or had the chance of doing at home; but I am sorry to say that my hope has not been realized and I remain the poor man I have always been.'[2]

This was followed by a series of letters concerning Roald Amundsen's achievement in reaching the South Pole, in doing so eclipsing Captain Scott's attempts. By now the death of Scott and his comrades had been much discussed throughout the world. The final sections of Scott's journal, similar to *The Voyage of the Discovery*, depict their glorious sacrifice and death in the true manner of English heroes and had been widely broadcast. However Amundsen has in certain circles never been given appropriate levels of credit for his outstanding journey, achieved using his professional skill and his understanding of polar survival techniques. By his more extreme critics Amundsen has even been held responsible for the death of Scott and his companions. Remarkably even Koettlitz put this argument to Nansen, Amundsen's mentor. It was an extreme route to take, foolish even, but Koettlitz remained loyal to Scott to the end. His letters to Nansen were becoming less constructive although he still wrote fondly of their time together geologising on Franz Josef Land.

Koettlitz reasoned that on finding they had been beaten to the pole, Petty Officer Evans in particular was greatly affected and from that moment there began a rapid spiral in his mental and physical condition. The others, being mentally stronger, handled the situation better but the rapid decline of Evans slowed their progress to such an extent that disaster became inevitable. It was not Scott or the other men who were worst affected but 'this strong, very strong man physically but not mentally that first broke down and caused the primary and most fatal delay!'[3]

He agreed with Nansen that scurvy was probably a factor and that mistakes made on the *Discovery* expedition had been repeated on this second expedition. Koettlitz considered Amundsen should not have kept his plans secret until the last moment, when he (Amundsen) was aware that Scott was heading south. In effect, he thought Amundsen had trespassed on Scott's territory.

In an effort to avoid entirely derailing his friendship with Nansen, Koettlitz did concede that he sympathised with and understood Amundsen's reasons and greatly admired his achievement. He penned: '[Do not] take these criticisms in bad part. You know how absolutely I trust you to be, in scientific and just thought, par excellence, honest and upright.' Koettlitz's judgement may have been biased by his patriotism and prior relationship with Scott. He was anxious to point out that his comments were not influenced by the environment in which he was now living, as he was surrounded by a Dutch population with whom he was on good terms.

In closing, Koettlitz wrote: 'Scott's and his men's deaths were magnificent. The most ideal, if one may so express oneself, manner of dying that one can think of. But, Scott's is enhanced in magnificence by the few, well chosen, simple, yet touching messages he sent home; written too in a calm, brave, fine spirit.'[4]

Koettlitz was well aware of Scott's fine prose, as he had himself suffered from its biting tone at times. But in the circumstances in which he found himself, he remained loyal to the man who had effectively scuppered his polar-related scientific studies.

Although Koettlitz achieved far greater scientific results from his three other expeditions, he will always be associated with the National Antarctic Expedition, with the *Discovery* and Captain Robert F. Scott. The question often asked, in particular in South Africa, is whether Koettlitz in any way could have prevented the death of Scott and his companions on their return from their unsuccessful bid to be the first to the South Pole.

As established in this book, Scott had a determined reluctance to take advice from experienced polar travellers. Both Koettlitz and Armitage were largely overlooked on the first Antarctic expedition. Koettlitz was at the time the leading expert on scurvy prevention – scurvy should not have appeared in either of Scott's expeditions, yet it manifested itself during both and was probably a factor in his death. Koettlitz was an expert in the use of skis and related polar survival techniques. Yet Scott would not accept his advice, insisting instead on man-hauling and spending valuable training time playing football and hockey and encouraging stage-plays amongst the men.

Koettlitz had experience of using dogs and ponies to assist the hauling of sledges, even making custom harnesses for the dogs on the Jackson-Harmsworth Expedition. He was the creator of the pyramid tent used on the *Discovery* expedition. Yet when sledge journeys commenced the men had no idea how to erect the tents, especially in severe weather conditions. The same applied to the lighting and use of the Primus stove, essential for heating food on the march.

Scott had all this information on his first Antarctic expedition but did not utilise it even on his return with the *Terra Nova*. It was a seeming inability to communicate that led to crucial lessons being continually neglected.

Both Scott and Markham described Koettlitz as 'a good natured duffer but short of common sense'.[5] Both men made serious errors during the planning and execution of the National Antarctic Expedition, and many were repeated during the *Terra Nova* expedition, to calamitous cost.

Some might consider this 'good natured duffer's' advice should have been heeded as he was one of only two men on the *Discovery* who possessed such knowledge.

---

1.   Comment by Don Craib included in Sam Bergman article in Adler Museum Bulletin, South Africa, November 1979.

2.   Letter from Koettlitz to Fridtjof Nansen dated 21 April 1913 – Koettlitz family archives.

3.   Letter from Koettlitz to Fridtjof Nansen dated 8 July 1913 – Koettlitz family archives and Norwegian National Library.

4.   *Ibid.*

5.   Sir Clements Markham RGS – *Antarctic Obsession*, page 83; R. F. Scott – *The Voyage of the Discovery*, first published 1905.

31

Death of an explorer

The effort of supporting his ailing wife and performing the duties of a doctor in such a location were beginning to take their toll.

With the failure of his ostrich and angora goat farm Koettlitz was compelled to concentrate on practising medicine and surgery but needed to find a more lucrative but less demanding practice. In June 1915 he purchased the practice of Dr J. Mckinnon, who was away on active army service, and they moved to Somerset East, a town as charming now as it was then. The change provided not only a welcome boost to his income but an opportunity for his wife to widen her social activities, which had been virtually non-existent in Grobbelaars Kraal. Mrs Rina Delport, writing in 1978, remembered Mrs Koettlitz creating the most beautifully coloured paper dolls for the local children from magazines she received from France.

Unfortunately Marie's health continued to deteriorate. The constant pressure of caring for his wife and attending assiduously to his Somerset East patients was affecting his own health. An elderly local lady, Mrs Sita Palmer, was to write later:

> He was a remarkable man and all who remember him speak of his excellence as a doctor and his devotion to both his wife and his patients. He was particularly sweet and attentive to children.

In January 1916, after only six months in the relative comfort of Somerset East, Koettlitz developed dysentery and weakened markedly. His wife's heart condition also worsened. The sudden deterioration of them both was dramatic. They had only recently placed orders for new clothing and other goods with suppliers back in England, confirmed by a series of telegrams between the post offices in Somerset East and Cradock.

On 5 January 1916 Koettlitz received a telegram from Dr Bremer in Cradock Hospital asking if he could obtain and use the ambulance train to transport his wife to Cradock Hospital for urgent treatment that very day. The plan was that Koettlitz would accompany her. However, Koettlitz was in a very poor condition himself, so Nursing Sister Tomkin was sent by train from Port Elizabeth to Somerset East to escort them both on the ambulance train to the Queen's Central Hospital, Cradock, for emergency treatment. They were attended by Dr Bremer. The local Freemasons had been assisting in the process and they were also met by Mr C. F. Freeman-Lake, the leader of the Cradock Lodge.

Telegrams sent from Cradock as the Koettlitz' health declined

POST OFFICE TELEGRAPHS.
POSTKANTOOR TELEGRAAFDIENST.
UNION OF SOUTH AFRICA.   UNIE VAN ZUID-AFRIKA.

Handed in at / Ingeleverd te Cradock

From / Van Freeman Lake   To / Aan Stegman

Somerset East

Mrs Koetlitz passed peacefully
away wire immediate instruction

POST OFFICE TELEGRAPHS.
POSTKANTOOR TELEGRAAFDIENST.
UNION OF SOUTH AFRICA.   UNIE VAN ZUID-AFRIKA.

Handed in at / Ingeleverd te Cradock

From / Van Freeman Lake   To / Aan Stegman

Somerset East

Koetlitz died last night
burying together this morning

Telegram relating to the Koettlitz deaths

Both Koettlitz and his wife deteriorated at an alarming rate and on 10 January 1916 the polar explorer, surgeon, geologist and botanist and his wife died within two hours of each other, Marie Koettlitz of heart disease and Dr Reginald Koettlitz of acute dysentery.

Koettlitz, a man who had survived the extremes of two polar expeditions, trekking through North East Africa and the Amazon, discovering unexplored regions had succumbed to a common African ailment. Koettlitz was 55 years of age, his wife a year younger.

When news of his death reached Somerset East all flags in the town were flown at half-mast in recognition of his life and commitment to the community which he had served with such distinction.

His last wish was made to his fellow Freemason, Mr Freeman-Lake: that he and his wife would be carried to their last resting place by Freemasons only. The following day this wish was respected. The Freemasons gathered in Cradock Anglican Church and, after what was described as a very sad service, they were carried to Cradock cemetery by local Freemasons, where they were buried close to British soldiers killed in the Boer wars a ghostly link to the England which he always regretted leaving.

News of the death of Dr Reginald Koettlitz spread around the world, with obituaries appearing in *The Lancet*, national and local newspapers in New York, New Zealand and Australia, and articles written in *The Times* and the RGS obituary pages.

For many years the bodies of Dr and Mrs Koettlitz lay in an unmarked grave. Apart from recognition in Dover, Koettlitz had been largely forgotten in England. In the Cape Colony he was still regarded with affection and admiration but there was no memorial to this explorer from the heroic period of polar exploration.

In 1922 the Rev. C. W. Wallace, Rural Dean of Cradock, started a process to correct what he regarded as an important historical oversight. He commenced a campaign locally amongst the Freemasons and local citizens which soon widened into Europe, to raise a memorial at the Koettlitz family grave.

In England the initiative was organised by Koettlitz's old *Discovery* colleague Captain Charles Royds, a man who had always thought Koettlitz should have received more recognition for his contributions to polar exploration. He saw the opportunity to restore some balance at last and contacted Professor Nansen in Norway. Nansen willingly made a donation and then corresponded with other polar contacts and past colleagues of Koettlitz in and around London. In a fitting letter to Dr H. R. Mill, who had supported Koettlitz throughout his life, Royds wrote:

> It would be a very right and desirable thing to place some memorial in the local church and on his grave to a man who was a sterling, modest, upright and loyal character, and who also had devoted so much of his life to the advancement of science and exploration without seeking notoriety or reward.

Dr Koettlitz could not have wished for a more fitting epitaph from such a man as Royds, supported by his friends, confidants and one of the greatest explorers and geologists of the time, Professor Fridtjof Nansen.

Nansen replied to Royds' letter saying:

> It is regrettable that so little has been done in memory of our friend Dr Koettlitz and I am glad you gave me the opportunity to contribute my little share towards his memorial. I am

The Koettlitz Memorial in Cradock

sorry it could not be more, he was a very good man indeed and a fine character and it is always a pleasure to think of the time when we were together on Franz Josef Land.

This tribute from Nansen is a powerful validation of Koettlitz's achievements and a reminder that he had contributed so much more than just being a successful rural doctor. It is a true reflection of the standing of the man and the esteem in which he was held by those he greatly respected.

In England there is no memorial to Dr Reginald Koettlitz but an imposing reminder of him remains in Dover Museum, Kent. Here you can still find the huge polar bear he brought back from Franz Josef Land, accompanied by the poster advertising his *Discovery* lecture and the wood-wormed skis he used on Antarctica. Not much else survives due to errors and accidents in the storage of the materials over the decades. Of particular note are the missing Koettlitz *Discovery* expedition journals which to this day have never materialised. Koettlitz was a dedicated compiler of expedition journals. If these journals reappear, they will without doubt endorse his outstanding polar contributions.

However, the overwhelming evidence in support of Dr. Reginald Koettlitz's remarkable achievements, may, at last, bring recognition beyond the towns of Dover, England, Somerset East and Cradock, South Africa, for Scott's forgotten surgeon.

Appendices

Jackson-Harmsworth Expedition to Franz Josef Land 1894-1897

Expedition members and polar interlocutors

Mr Alfred Harmsworth, later Lord Northcliffe – Newspaper magnate and main financier of expedition

The Misses Dawson and Lambton – Expedition supporters/financiers

Arthur Montefiore – Expedition secretary and Royal Geographical Society

Frederick George Jackson – Expedition leader

Albert Borlese Armitage – Second in command, meteorological and magnetic observations

Dr Reginald Koettlitz – Expedition surgeon and geologist

Josiah F. Child – Mineralogist, returned to England after year two

Harry Fisher – Botanist and zoologist

H. A. H. Dunsford – Assistant, returned to England after year two

John W. Heyward – Cook and handyman

K. Blomkvist – Ex-member of *Windward*'s crew, ski-runner and climber

S. Burgess – Assistant, returned to England after year two

William Speirs Bruce – Replaced Fisher as zoologist and botanist in final year (leader of *Scotia* expedition to the Antarctic 1902–1904)

David W. Wilton – Ski-runner replaced Blomkvist in final year (later member of *Scotia* expedition); HM Consul in Archangel

Captains Schlosshauer (original journey) and Brown (two relief journeys) – Captains of the S.Y. *Windward*

John Crowther – *Windward*'s ice master

Dr Fridtjof Nansen – Leader of the *Fram* Norwegian polar expedition

Lieutenant F. H. Johansen – Member of the *Fram* expedition

[The above two met, probably saved, by members of the Jackson-Harmsworth Expedition on their return from their attempt on the North Pole]

Benjamin Leigh-Smith – Leader of *Eira* expedition

William Henry Neale – Surgeon of *Eira* expedition

Julius Payer – Austrian army officer and discoverer of Franz Josef Land

Dr Almroth Wright – London doctor/surgeon and writer on scurvy

Mr E. T. Newton and Mr J. J. H. Teall – Royal Geographical Society

Herbert Weld Blundell Expedition to North East Africa 1898-1899

Expedition members and relevant interlocutors

Herbert Weld Blundell – Expedition leader

Lord Lovat – Expedition member and nephew of Weld Blundell

Mr Harwood – Expedition member and taxidermist

Dr Reginald Koettlitz – Expedition surgeon, geologist, anthropologist and field manager

Unidentified camp valet – Acting as camp major-domo

Captain J. L. Harrington – UK political representative in Addis Ababa

Mr M. McKelvey – British/Irish soldier captured at battle of Magdala, interpreter, used by the British Agency

Ras Makonnen – Governor of Harar

King Menelik – Ruler in Abyssinia

Colonel Lewis – Decorated British army soldier, army commander in Sennaar

Colonel Maxwell – British army commander in Khartoum and Omdurman garrisons

Mr R. T. Ormond – Scottish Meteorological Society

National Antarctic Expedition
1901~1904

Expedition members and interlocutors

Sir Clements Markham – Royal Geographical Society (RGS) and Managing Owner!

Admiral Sir Leopold McClintock – RGS and Royal Navy (RN)

Sir Archibald Geikie – Royal Society

Professor J. W. Gregory – British Museum and initial Head of the Scientific Staff

Dr Scott Keltie – RGS

Dr H. R. Mill – RGS and expert in oceanography and meteorology

George Murray – Fellow of the Royal Society and Chief of Scientific Staff until South Africa

Professor Edward B. Poulton – Royal Society, zoologist

The *Discovery* – relevant ship's officers, men and scientific staff

Robert Falcon Scott – Commander RN and expedition leader

Albert B. Armitage – Navigator Royal Naval Reserve (RNR) and second in command

Charles W. R. Royds – First Lieutenant RN

Michael Barne – Second Lieutenant RN

Ernest Shackleton – Sub-Lieutenant RNR

Reginald Skelton – Lieutenant engineer and photographer RN

Dr Reginald Koettlitz – Expedition senior surgeon and botanist/bacteriologist

Edward Wilson – Assistant surgeon, Zoologist and expedition artist

Frederick E. Dailey – Carpenter RN

William Lashly – Stoker RN

Arthur I. Quartley – Stoker RN

Frank Plumley – Stoker RN

Edgar Evans – Petty Officer RN

William Macfarlane – Petty Officer RN

Charles T. Bonner – Seaman RN

James W. Dell – Seaman RN

Frank Wild – Seaman RN

Thomas Crean – Seaman RN

George T. Vince – Seaman RN

Charles R. Ford – Steward

Scientists

Louis C. Bernacchi – Physicist

Thomas V. Hodgson – Biologist

Hartley T. Ferrar – Geologist

Relief ships

Captain Harry McKay – *Terra Nova*

Captain William Colbeck – the *Morning*

First colour photographs of the Antarctic continent by Dr Reginald Koettlitz 1902-1904

It has not previously been acknowledged that Koettlitz was an accomplished photographer. He took this extensive list of colour photographs, given here for the first time. These include notable events in Antarctic polar history (e.g. the first ascent to the Western Mountains led by Armitage, the return of Wilson and Shackleton following their 'furthest south' with Scott, and the first ascent of Brown Island by Koettlitz), as well as the Antarctic midnight sun.

1902

February 1902 – Mt Erebus & Erebus Bay with open water – Turtle Rock

19 October 1902 – Ice Cliff off Cape Armitage

22 October 1902 – Ice effects in hummocky pressure ridges Pram Point

22 October 1902 – Sunset Photo (2nd day before midnight sun)

22 October 1902 – Ice effects in broken hummock

23 October 1902 – Sunset over Black Island (negative spoilt)

24 October 1902 – First midnight sun. Black Island & Bluff Range

26 October 1902 – Mt Erebus distant – Observation Hill is near

1 November 1902 – Ice face with overhanging curtains. Snowdrift Cape Armitage

13 November 1902 – -ditto- – shore close to danger slope

13 November 1902 – -ditto- -ditto-

15 November 1902 – Ship & Mt Discovery from near summit Harbour Hill

15 November 1902 – Mt Erebus (smoking) -ditto-

16 November 1902 – Mt Erebus -ditto-

16 November 1902 – Mt Erebus 16 miles away from floe in McMurdo Straight

22 November 1902 – Light shining through a line of Hummocked ridges

22 November 1902 – Seals, Cow & Calf. Pram Point

24 November 1902 – Western Mountains from ship – Hodgson shelter – sasturgi

25 November 1902 – North portion Western Mountains & clouds

25 November 1902 – Western Mountains from summit Crater Hill – clouds

27 November 1902 – Mt Erebus – Observation Hill in foreground

27 November 1902 – Western Mountains

3 December 1902 – Quartzite Hill slope & Western sledge journey

4 December 1902 – Portion Western Mountains

5 December 1902 – Western Mountains, camp in foreground

5 December 1902 – White & Yellow – Quartzite Hill

6 December 1902 – Western Mountains

9 December 1902 – Western Glacier

9 December 1902 – Rocks & ice cascade, south side of glacier

10 December 1902 – The glacier from top of Descent pass

10 December 1902 – Cathedral Rocks -ditto-

11 December 1902 – Yellow & pink Quartzite Hill

11 December 1902 – Mt Erebus & Terror in far distance

26 December 1902 – Ship Mt Discovery, Brown island, Table Mt from ski slopes

26 December 1902 – Ship, Hut point, Western Mountains

27 December 1902 – Mt Erebus from summit Observation Hill

27 December 1902 – Mt Terror -ditto-

30 December 1902 – Ponds, frozen – Sledge journey to Brown Island

31 December 1902 – The old ice, ponds etc sledge journey to Brown Island

1903

4 January 1903 – Canal like pond rivers, Eskers etc & sledge journey to Brown Island

5 January 1903 – Glacier behind Mt Discovery from top of Brown Island

8 January 1903 – Mt Erebus from top of Brown Island

18 January 1903 – The Bluff (my ---). Sledge journey to Bluff

23 January 1903 – Ice river amongst Eskers etc sledge journey to Bluff

26 January 1903 – Camp, Mt Erebus, sledge journey to Bluff

3 February 1903 – Ship dressed to welcome return of Southern party

3 February 1903 – Wilson & Shackleton just returned from Southern trip

5 February 1903 – Observation Hill, Mt Erebus etc

5 March 1903 – Mt Erebus, Castle Rocks etc

20 March 1903 – Western Mountains from ship – sunrise

30 March 1903 – Hummock pressure ridges Pram point

30 March 1903 – -ditto-

16 April 1903 – Sunset in mountains

19 April 1903 – Observation Hill. Rose tint sunset light

21 April 1903 – Mt Discovery

23 April 1903 – Western Mountains

21 October 1903 – Midnight sun just below horizon

November 1903 – Western Mountains (1 plate spoiled)

Index